Home
for the
Holidays

Mom—

WE BOTH THOUGHT OF YOU WHEN WE SAW THIS—

LOVE & ENJOY

BOB + HELEN S

Home
for the
Holidays

Festive Baking with
Whole Grains

Ken Haedrich

Bantam Books
New York • Toronto • London • Sydney • Auckland

HOME FOR THE HOLIDAYS

PUBLISHING HISTORY

Bantam hardcover edition / November 1992
Bantam trade paperback edition / October 1994

All rights reserved.
Copyright © 1992 by Ken Haedrich.
Book design by Barbara Cohen Aronica.
Cover art copyright © 1994 by Kristin Hurlin.
Library of Congress Catalog Card Number 92-17152.

ISBN 0-553-37413-3

Published simultaneously in the United States and Canada

*Bantam Books are published by Bantam Books, a division of Bantam Doubleday
Dell Publishing Group, Inc. Its trademark, consisting of the words "Bantam
Books" and the portrayal of a rooster, is Registered in U.S. Patent and Trademark
Office and in other countries. Marca Registrada. Bantam Books, 1540 Broadway,
New York, New York 10036.*

PRINTED IN THE UNITED STATES OF AMERICA

FFG   0 9 8 7 6 5 4 3 2 1

This book is dedicated to my children,
Ben, Tess, Ali, and Sam.
Our holidays — and our kitchen — just wouldn't be the same
without you.
Merry Christmas,
Pop

Acknowledgments

I feel incredibly lucky to have worked on this book with a great team of Bantam editors, including Coleen O'Shea, Fran McCullough, and Becky Cabaza. Thanks to all of you.

My agent, Meg Ruley, deserves anything she wants from Santa, for her sage counsel and for putting up with my occasional rantings.

Chris Benton, my linguistic drill sergeant, once again whipped my raw manuscript into fighting shape.

Barbara Cohen Aronica is the gifted designer of these pages and my previous book; thank you so much.

I wish to thank the many bookstore owners and staff I've worked with over the past few years on special promotions, whose advice I have sought and found quite useful, and the numerous food writers who have been so generous to me in articles and reviews.

A *special* thanks to our garland fairy, Sandy Dunfey, for her help with the cover. And to Mark Homan for his incredible patience (once again) and skill with the cover photo.

Happy holidays to my parents, brothers, and sisters; may we always remember fondly the holiday seasons of our younger days.

And love to my wife, Karen, and our kids — Ben, Tess, Ali, and Sam — for bringing so much joy into my life.

Contents

Contents

Contents

xi

Contents

xii

A Season of Joyous Baking

Here at the foot of Stinson Mountain, when the blush of ocher and red streaks the wooded New Hampshire hillsides, my family and I begin to feel the first twinges of excitement for the holiday baking season. The holidays themselves may still be weeks away, but the crisp mountain air and changing seasons ignite a little baking spark in us. Fueled by the arrival of fall apples, pears, cranberries, and squashes, we soon settle into a happy baking routine that becomes a central focus of our holiday season.

This is a book of holiday baking recipes, a sort of open file of family favorites we hope will help to ignite the baking spark in you. The accent is on whole grains — for health reasons, sure. But more important because whole grains add an element of flavor and texture — *character* — that you can't get using white flour alone. My intention here is not to sell you on whole grains, however; they'll sell themselves once you try them. I hope simply to see you through the holiday baking season in good taste by giving you answers to many of the questions home cooks face during this busy time of year: What shall I put in the Thanksgiving breadbasket? Or on the Christmas breakfast table? Or serve at my annual New Year's Eve party? By focusing on specific aspects of the holiday season, I hope you'll be able to come up with quick and delicious solutions to all of your holiday baking needs.

A holiday baking book, like any cookbook, is bound to reflect the personal biases of the author, and this one is no exception. As you'll see right away, I don't care for fancy or complicated recipes, possibly because I'm a self-taught baker. It also has a lot to do with the fact that I am a father of four who works at home; there just isn't

time for elaborate pieces of architecture in my baking repertoire. But that may come as something of a relief. So, these aren't fancy recipes.

Above all, these recipes reflect my belief that good baking is a natural extension of the season. Good holiday baking accepts certain limitations and capitalizes on them. Many recipes here use the winter staples — apples, pears, bananas, coconut, and dried fruits. In the absence of summer's fresh berries, peaches, and the like, there's chocolate and spice and lots of nuts to make the season bright. There are breads made with holiday leftovers and puddings made with leftover holiday breads. There are squash desserts, hearty whole grain Christmas cookies, and plenty of rich, cheesy tarts to chase away the winter chill.

If you are an experienced baker, you'll probably be able to sift right through these pages, pull out something good, and go for it. On the other hand, if you have limited holiday baking experience, here are a few words to the wise.

First and foremost — and I still make this mistake after two decades of home baking — don't bite off more than you can chew. At that point baking can become a real chore, no matter how much you enjoy it. How many times have I drawn up a list of 20, 30, or 40 family members and friends, thinking I would send two dozen cookies to each of them, only to scale my plans way back to more sane proportions? Be realistic about the amount of time you can devote to your holiday baking. Better to have one beautiful home-made roll in your Thanksgiving breadbasket than to get over-whelmed trying to bake three or four kinds.

When you do figure out your time, *double your estimate if you plan to involve your kids.* Kids love to bake, especially cookies, and there's no better way to cultivate family spirit than with a big holiday bake-off. Encourage them to join in, but don't pressure them. Don't criticize their efforts or try to be too helpful unless they ask for help. Be patient and keep your sense of humor. This is the voice of experience speaking: I've managed, despite my best intentions, to sabotage these family baking days on a number of occasions. But I'm getting the knack of it. Give the kids some pretty little bags to put their cookies in, one for each of their good friends, and some stickers to decorate them with. (And if your kids are three or five years old, like my two youngest, don't expect the cookies to reach their intended recipients.)

Everyone I talk to seems to get crazy at this time of year. The

pressures of the holidays, the shopping, the commercialization of Christmas — all of it seems to erode our goodwill toward our fellow man and sap our spirits. I don't have all the solutions to this problem, but I have found that creating a private, sane little nook of family baking during this season is an excellent way to shore up our resistance to the craziness. Baking puts us in touch with our family and our capacity for creative work. It turns gift giving into an individual expression instead of a credit card blitz. And it reminds us, just like our moms used to say, that the simple things in life are some of the best things. Amen, and pass the cinnamon.

Happy holidays!

KEN HAEDRICH

The
Thanksgiving
Breadbasket

At our house the Thanksgiving breadbasket deserves as much attention as the rest of The Big Meal itself. Too often, in the general commotion of Thanksgiving, the breads get overlooked, and you end up grabbing something convenient from the supermarket shelf. But that's not necessary, and with a little planning anybody can have fresh homemade rolls or a special bread at the Thanksgiving table with minimal fuss and bother.

Back when I was cooking full-time, feeding 40 ravenous kids and adults at the group home where I worked, I always loved to do a bang-up job with the Thanksgiving breadbaskets. And deciding which breads to include was always a challenge, because everybody had individual favorites and I had mine. It usually boiled down to one biscuit, one soft roll, and one steamed bread, but even then I felt I could have done more. We would take big wicker baskets, line them with pretty cloths, and arrange all three kinds of bread in each one — the biscuits and rolls still steaming hot — then pull up the sides of the cloths to keep the breads warm while they waited on the table.

Since I've had my own kids, and Thanksgiving has become a more intimate and relaxed affair, I'm happy to bake one roll or biscuit, and if I get to the steamed bread the day before — so we have it on Thanksgiving — that's great. I don't want the breadbasket to upstage the rest of the meal, but I don't want it to be any slouch either.

If you're a bit intimidated about incorporating yeasted rolls or bread into your Thanksgiving Day cooking, take a look at your options. First, if you haven't made yeasted breads before, or you're a bit rusty, it would help to practice a week or several days ahead. That way you won't be lost on Thanksgiving; old techniques will come back to you; you'll limber up your kneading arm and get used to the bread-making rhythm.

If you decide that there just isn't time to bake bread on Thanksgiving, you can always either freeze the dough and bake it on Thanksgiving or freeze the baked rolls. I much prefer the baked rolls system: you just wrap the cooled rolls in foil, maybe six to a package, slip them into plastic bags, seal, and freeze. To warm the rolls, put the foil packages in a 400° oven for about 10 minutes or until heated through.

If you don't mind fussing with freezing dough, punch the risen dough down and refrigerate for one hour. Punch it down again, slip the dough into a double plastic bag, seal, and freeze. The day before Thanksgiving, transfer the dough to the fridge. The next morning, give the dough a brief but vigorous kneading to warm it up, then transfer the dough to a lightly oiled bowl. Let the dough double in a warm, draft-free spot, then shape and bake as usual.

The whole grain rolls in this section are tasty and healthy but not at all heavy; there'll be plenty of room left for the turkey and mashed potatoes. And there are still more options: a light mixed-grain buttermilk biscuit, which is a good alternative to fiddling with yeast. And finally, there are several other quick breads and steamed breads that can round out your Thanksgiving bread-basket or be the star attraction.

Whole Wheat Parker House Rolls

MAKES ABOUT 36 ROLLS

This is a whole wheat adaptation of the soft dinner rolls made famous by Boston's Parker House hotel. I've had those a number of times, and they are quite good; so are these, and I hope Parker House forgives me for taking liberties with the recipe.

When I first started making yeast breads, this was the only Thanksgiving roll I would bake because it was so popular — so light and soft, nobody could believe it was a whole wheat roll. It was also one of the breads that won the heart of my wife, Karen, when we first met in New Hampshire many years ago.

These rolls love butter, so have plenty of softened unsalted butter ready to go.

> 1/2 cup lukewarm water
> 1 1/4-ounce package (about 1 tablespoon) active dry yeast
> 2 cups lukewarm milk
> 1/4 cup honey
> 3 cups whole wheat flour
> 2 teaspoons salt
> 1 large egg at room temperature, lightly beaten
> 5 tablespoons unsalted butter, melted and cooled slightly
> 2 1/2 cups (approximately) unbleached flour
> 1/4 cup unsalted butter, melted, for brushing the rolls

Pour the lukewarm water into a small bowl and stir in the yeast. Set aside for 5 minutes. While the yeast dissolves, pour the lukewarm milk into a large mixing bowl and stir in the honey. Stir in the dissolved yeast and then the whole wheat flour, beating well with a wooden spoon for 2 minutes. Cover this sponge with plastic wrap and set aside in a warm, draft-free spot for 15 minutes.

After 15 minutes, stir the salt, egg, and 5 tablespoons melted butter into the sponge. Using a wooden spoon, beat in enough of the unbleached flour, about 1/2 cup at a time, to make a soft, kneadable dough, stirring well after each addition. Turn it out onto a floured surface and knead for 8 minutes, using as much of the remaining unbleached flour as necessary to keep the dough from sticking; after 8 minutes of kneading, the dough should be smooth and elastic. Place the dough in an oiled bowl, turning it to coat the entire surface. Cover the dough with plastic wrap and set it aside in a warm, draft-

4

free spot until it is doubled in bulk, about an hour. Lightly butter a large baking sheet.

Once the dough has doubled, punch it down and turn it out onto a lightly floured surface. Knead the dough for 1 minute, cover with plastic wrap, and let rest for 10 minutes.

Roll the dough a little more than 1/2 inch thick on a lightly floured surface. Using a 2 1/4- or 2 1/2-inch-diameter biscuit cutter (or a glass), cut the dough into circles, keeping the cuts as close together as possible. Leave the circles where they are, pick up all the scraps, and knead them into a ball. Cover with plastic wrap and set aside.

Brush the surface of each circle with a bit of melted butter. Working with one circle at a time, make a fairly deep indentation across the diameter using a pencil or chopstick. Fold the circle in half—using the indentation as the hinge—so the buttered halves meet; you now have what looks like a big pair of lips. Put the lips on the sheet flat side down. Repeat for the remaining circles, placing the lips so they barely touch. As you lay each one down—all pointing in the same direction—give the entire surface a light brushing of butter. When you start a second row, the edges should barely touch the first row. Reroll and cut the scraps and place them on the sheet. Cover the rolls loosely with plastic wrap and set aside in a warm, draft-free spot. Preheat the oven to 375°; the rolls should rise fairly quickly, in about 30 minutes.

When the rolls have doubled in bulk, bake them for 25 minutes. As soon as they come out, brush the rolls with more of the melted butter. Serve hot or slide them onto a rack to cool.

FREEZING: These rolls freeze well. Just break the cooled rolls into several large blocks and wrap in foil. Slip the foil packages into plastic bags and freeze. Reheat the rolls—right in the foil—for about 10 to 15 minutes in a 400° oven.

Maple Mustard–Filled Cornmeal Rolls

MAKES 20 ROLLS

The beauty of some rolls, like Parker House, is their plainness and simplicity. Others, like these sweet and tangy rolls, like to stand up and be noticed. Turkeys, ducks, hams, roasts — the holidays, for many people, are a big meat season, and this is the roll to go with almost anything that ends up on the carving platter. These are best eaten fresh, hot from the oven, but if you would rather make them ahead, they'll freeze nicely; wrap about 6 together in pieces of aluminum foil as soon as they have cooled, slip the packages into plastic bags, and seal. They can go right from the freezer in their foil packages into a 400° oven for about 10 minutes, perhaps a little longer, until heated through.

> 1 3/4 cups lukewarm water
> 1 tablespoon blackstrap molasses
> 1 1/4-ounce package (about 1 tablespoon) active dry yeast
> 1/2 cup yellow cornmeal, preferably stone-ground
> 1/2 cup whole wheat flour
> 3 1/2 cups (approximately) unbleached flour
> 2 teaspoons salt
> 2 tablespoons unsalted butter, softened
> 1 cup (3 ounces) grated Cheddar cheese

FILLING

> 2 tablespoons unsalted butter
> 2 tablespoons pure maple syrup
> 2 tablespoons Dijon mustard
> freshly ground black pepper to taste

Mix the lukewarm water and molasses in a large bowl and stir in the yeast. Set aside for 5 minutes, then beat in the cornmeal, whole wheat flour, and 1 cup of the unbleached flour. With a wooden spoon, beat well for 1 minute, then cover this sponge with plastic wrap and set aside in a warm, draft-free spot for 15 minutes.

After 15 minutes, stir in the salt and softened butter, then begin mixing in the remaining unbleached flour about 1/2 cup at a time, stirring well after each addition. When you have a cohesive, kneadable dough, turn it out onto a lightly floured surface and knead for 7 minutes, using sprinkles of flour to keep the dough from sticking. Place the dough in a lightly oiled bowl and turn it to coat the entire

surface. Cover with plastic wrap and set aside in a warm, draft-free spot until doubled in bulk, about 1 to 1 1/2 hours.

While the dough is rising, prepare the filling: melt the 2 tablespoons butter in a small saucepan and whisk in the maple syrup and mustard. Bring to a boil, then immediately remove from the heat.

When the dough is fully risen, sprinkle half of the Cheddar cheese over the top, then punch it down. Turn the dough out onto a lightly floured surface and knead in the remaining cheese. Let the dough rest, covered with plastic wrap, on a floured surface for 10 minutes. Butter a 12- by 18-inch jelly roll pan or 20 large muffin cups.

Roll the dough into a rectangle approximately 20 inches long by 12 inches wide. Spread the maple-mustard mixture over the rolled-out dough up to the short sides and to within 1 inch of each long edge; I find it is easiest just to use my hands to spread it. Dust the surface with black pepper.

Starting at the long edge closest to you, begin rolling the dough up as you would a carpet, keeping it snug but not overly tight. Using a pastry brush or finger dipped in water, lightly moisten the other long edge just before you get to it, then pinch the dough there to seal the log.

Using a sharp, serrated knife, saw the dough in half, then cut each half in half. Cut each quarter-section into 5 equal slices, then lay them on the sheet swirl side up, almost touching, or in the muffin tins. On the jelly roll pan, you'll probably get 4 rows of 5.

Cover the rolls loosely with lightly oiled plastic wrap and set aside in a warm, draft-free spot until doubled in bulk, usually 30 to 40 minutes; about 15 minutes before they reach this point, preheat the oven to 350°. When doubled, bake the rolls for about 35 minutes until lightly browned. Cut them apart and transfer the rolls to a cooling rack. If you want to keep them soft, rather than have a chewy, harder crust, brush them with a little melted butter when they first come out of the oven.

Sesame Twists

MAKES 14 ROLLS

*Sesame twist sounds like some sort of sixties dance, doesn't it? But
actually it's a jaunty little holiday roll that will add an abundance of good
taste to your Thanksgiving breadbasket. The twisting is done with a super-
simple sleight of hand: you just poke a hole in a ball of dough and twist.
This combination of about half whole wheat and half unbleached flour
makes a light but still grainy roll. I specify water for the liquid, but milk
will give you an even more tender, soft roll. (If you do use milk, still use
1/4 cup of water to dissolve the yeast in, deducting that from the total
amount of liquid.) The sesame flavor is underscored with the addition of
toasted sesame seeds to the dough; to accent it further, add a tablespoon of
light sesame oil to the dough if you happen to have it on hand.*

> **2 cups lukewarm water or milk (see above paragraph)**
> **1 tablespoon honey**
> **1 1/4-ounce package (about 1 tablespoon) active dry yeast**
> **2 cups whole wheat flour**
> **1/2 cup sesame seeds**
> **1 1/2 teaspoons salt**
> **3 tablespoons unsalted butter, softened, or 2 tablespoons unsalted
>   butter plus 1 tablespoon light sesame oil**
> **2 1/2 cups (approximately) unbleached flour**
> **egg wash: 1 large egg beaten with 1 tablespoon milk**

Pour the lukewarm water into a large mixing bowl and stir in the
honey, then the yeast; set aside for 5 minutes. After the yeast has
dissolved, stir in the whole wheat flour, then cover this sponge with
plastic wrap and set aside for 15 minutes.

While the sponge is resting, toast the seeds: heat a medium-size
skillet and add the seeds; a nonstick skillet works nicely because you
can "stir" the seeds by simply picking up the pan and jerking the
handle forward as if you were flipping an egg in midair. Otherwise,
stir almost continuously for about 6 minutes, until the seeds darken
by several shades. Immediately transfer the seeds to a small bowl.
Lightly butter 2 large baking sheets.

After 15 minutes, stir the salt, softened butter, and 1/4 cup of
the seeds into the sponge. Add the unbleached flour 1/2 cup at a
time, beating well after each addition. When you have a soft, kneadable dough, turn the dough out and knead on a lightly floured

surface for 7 minutes, using just enough flour to keep the dough from sticking. Place the dough in a lightly oiled bowl, turning to coat the entire surface. Cover the bowl with plastic wrap and set aside in a warm, draft-free spot until doubled in bulk; it should take less than an hour.

Once the dough has doubled, turn it out onto a lightly floured surface and knead briefly. Using a dough scraper, divide the dough in half, cover one half with plastic wrap, and divide the other half into 7 more or less equal-size pieces. Shape each of the pieces into a ball, cover with plastic wrap, and let rest for 5 minutes.

Using a floured thumb, poke a hole right through the center of each dough ball. Slip this doughnut over your index finger and twirl it to open the hole up a couple of inches. Holding opposite sides of the doughnut in both hands, give one side a half (180°) turn; now you have your pretty twist. Place it on the sheet and repeat for the remaining balls of dough, leaving as much space between them as you can. Cover loosely with lightly oiled plastic wrap. Divide and shape the other half of the dough, placing the rolls on the second sheet; cover. Place the rolls in a warm, draft-free spot until nearly doubled in bulk, about 30 minutes. About 15 minutes before you think they'll be fully doubled, preheat the oven to 400°.

Just before baking, brush the rolls gently and sparingly with the egg wash. As you brush each one, sprinkle it with some of the remaining seeds. Bake the rolls for 20 to 25 minutes, until nicely browned. Serve right away or let cool on a rack. To reheat, wrap the rolls in foil and place in a 400° oven for 10 minutes.

F R E E Z I N G : These rolls freeze beautifully. Just wrap the fully cooled rolls in foil, 3 or 4 together, and slip them into a plastic bag and freeze. When you want to serve them, heat — still in the foil — for 15 minutes in a 400° oven.

N O T E : To make sesame knots, pull opposite ends of the twist down and pinch together underneath — a simple procedure.

The Thanksgiving Breadbasket

A Thanksgiving Grace for All Year Round

Before every meal, we join hands and say this simple prayer of thanks for the things we care for most . . .

We are thankful for our happy hearts
For rain and sunny weather,
We are thankful for the foods we eat
And that we are together.

Squash Quick Bread with Cider Raisins

MAKES 2 LOAVES, ABOUT
10 SERVINGS EACH

Here's a bright addition to any Thanksgiving breadbasket, a golden-hued loaf packed with toasted walnuts and cider-spiked raisins. The top of the loaf is covered with walnuts too and sprinkled with a little sugar before baking; that makes the top crunchy and semicrisp, giving it a contrast of textures you often miss with quick breads. I like to toast up some extra nuts and sprinkle them in the bottom of the pan before I pour in the batter; it's a nice touch, especially for nut lovers.

> 3/4 cup apple cider
> 1 cup raisins
> 3 cups cubed peeled butternut or other winter squash (1 small squash will do)
> 1 1/2 cups whole wheat flour
> 1 1/4 cups unbleached flour
> 1/4 cup yellow cornmeal, preferably stone-ground
> 1 tablespoon baking powder
> 1 teaspoon salt
> 1 teaspoon ground nutmeg, preferably freshly grated
> 1 teaspoon ground cinnamon
> 2 large eggs
> 1/2 cup flavorless vegetable oil
> 1 cup packed light brown sugar
> 1 cup (about 1/4 pound) chopped walnuts, preferably toasted (see page 111 for toasting instructions)
> 1 teaspoon white granulated sugar

Bring the cider to a boil in a small saucepan and reduce by about half; it doesn't have to be exact. Add the raisins, cover, and remove from the heat. Set aside.

Put the squash cubes in a large saucepan and cover with about a quart of lightly salted water. Bring to a boil, cover, and reduce the heat to a low boil. Cook for about 20 minutes, until the squash is fork-tender. Drain briefly, then puree the squash in a blender, in a food processor, or with a food mill. Measure out 1 cup, reserving the rest for another use; this puree adds nice body to soups. Butter and lightly flour 2 4- by 8-inch loaf pans — preferably not dark ones — and preheat the oven to 350°.

Sift the flours, cornmeal, baking powder, salt, and spices into a bowl; include any pieces of bran left in the sifter. In another bowl, lightly beat the eggs. Beat in the squash puree, oil, and brown sugar.

Stir the dry ingredients into the liquid mixture in several stages. Fold in the raisins — and any unabsorbed cider — and 2/3 cup of the walnuts.

Divide the batter evenly between the loaf pans and smooth it out with a fork. Sprinkle the nuts over both loaves, gently embedding them with your hand, then sprinkle about 1/2 teaspoon sugar over each loaf. Bake the loaves for 50 to 55 minutes, until a tester inserted in the center of the loaf comes out clean. Cool in the pan for 15 minutes. Put a piece of wax paper on your cooling rack, then turn the loaves out and place on the wax paper right side up. Cool the loaves thoroughly — if you aren't going to eat them right away; this bread is great warm — then immediately wrap them in plastic and overwrap in foil or a plastic bag. Store in the fridge for up to 4 days.

The
Thanksgiving
Breadbasket

Steamed Winter Squash and Date Nut Bread

MAKES 1 ROUND LOAF,
ABOUT 8 TO 10 SERVINGS

Steamed breads are a labor of love, harking back to the days when most everything was cooked in a pot and ovens were either few and far between or quite unreliable. Why steam at all? Aside from the novelty of it, I've never had a quick bread as moist, or one that stayed as moist, as a steamed bread. And since I heat with wood, using the woodstove to steam breads is energy-efficient, though a burner set on low does an equally fine job. In neither case are you tied to the stove, because the cooking is unattended for the most part.

Here's a steamed bread that uses winter squash puree; it reminds me of the harvest moon, big and round, colored a radiant shade of orange. It really stands out in the Thanksgiving breadbasket and throughout the late harvest season. I love it in thick slices, smeared with cream cheese and honey. Dates and walnuts are my embellishments of choice, though you might prefer another combination, like raisins and pecans. Chopped dried apricots are also pretty. Wrapped tightly in plastic, this keeps for up to a week in the refrigerator.

2 cups cubed peeled butternut or other winter squash
2 tablespoons unsalted butter, melted
1/2 cup honey
finely grated zest of 1 orange
1/2 cup yellow cornmeal, preferably stone-ground
1/2 cup whole wheat flour
1/2 cup unbleached flour
1 1/2 teaspoons baking powder
3/4 teaspoon salt
1/2 teaspoon ground cinnamon
1/2 cup chopped pitted dates
1/3 cup (almost 2 ounces) chopped walnuts

In a medium-size saucepan, cover the squash with about a quart of lightly salted water. Bring to a boil, cover, and reduce to an active simmer. Cook the squash until very tender, about 15 to 20 minutes; drain and cool slightly. Puree the squash in a food processor, in a blender, or with a food mill, then scrape into a large mixing bowl. Stir the melted butter, honey, and orange zest into the puree.

While that's cooling, butter the insides of a 1-pound coffee can, including the lid; set aside. Put about 3 1/2 inches of water in a large, tall covered pot; ideally, it should be tall enough to accommodate the coffee can, sitting on a trivet, with the lid on, but if need be, you can cover the pot with a foil tent. Put a trivet in the center of the pot, cover, and bring to a boil. If you don't have a trivet, use a couple of old wooden chopsticks or butter knives, on the flat, to get the can off the bottom of the pot.

As the water heats, combine the cornmeal, flours, baking powder, salt, and cinnamon in a large bowl, tossing with your hands to mix. Make a well in the dry ingredients and stir in the liquids just until blended. Fold in the dates and walnuts. Spoon the batter into the prepared can and put on the lid. Press a double layer of foil over the top and secure it with heavy twine.

When the water comes to a boil, reduce the heat to a simmer. Place the can on the trivet; the water should come about halfway up the sides. Cover the pot and steam the bread for about 2 hours, until the top is springy and a cake tester inserted in the center emerges clean. Remove the lid and cool on a rack for 5 minutes. Invert the can and let the bread slide out. Cool on a rack for at least 15 minutes before slicing with a serrated knife. Cool thoroughly, wrapping leftovers securely in plastic.

N O T E : Because this bread comes out of the can with a slightly damp exterior, you may want to dry it out slightly by putting it on a lightly buttered baking sheet in a 350° oven for 5 minutes.

Three-Grain Biscuits

MAKES 12 TO 16 BISCUITS

*I don't usually serve biscuits alone for Thanksgiving, but I think it's a
perfectly fine idea. This is not a heavy biscuit, which is one of the main
reasons I think it works well in the context of an already sumptuous feast.
The oats and sour cream give the biscuit a soft, creamy interior almost like
a dinner roll. But you still get that nice exterior biscuit crunch, accented
by the cornmeal. These bake fast enough that you could put them in even
as everyone is gathering around the table. By the time the plates are piled
up, they will be done.*

> 1 1/3 cups unbleached flour
> 1/3 cup yellow cornmeal, preferably stone-ground
> 1/3 cup rolled oats (*not* instant)
> 1 teaspoon baking powder
> 1 teaspoon baking soda
> 1/2 teaspoon salt
> 1/4 cup cold unsalted butter, cut into 1/4-inch pieces
> 1/2 cup sour cream
> 1/2 cup milk

Lightly butter a large baking sheet — preferably a dark one — and
preheat the oven to 450°. Combine the flour, cornmeal, oats, baking
powder, baking soda, and salt in a mixing bowl. Add the butter and
rub or cut it in until the mixture resembles a coarse meal. Blend the
sour cream and milk in a separate bowl, make a well in the dry
ingredients, then add the liquid to the well all at once. Stir the dough
until it is evenly mixed.

Sprinkle the dough, your hands, and a work surface with a little
flour, then turn the dough out and knead it gently for 20 or 30
seconds; use a little more flour, if necessary, to keep it from sticking.
Pat the dough out to a thickness of about 3/4 inch. Cut the dough,
using a 2-inch or 2 1/4-inch round cutter; keep the cuts close
together. Place the biscuits on the buttered sheet, then bake for 13 to
14 minutes, until browned and crusty. Serve at once.

14

Breakfast Baking:
Treats to Make
the Season Bright

Somewhere in each of us, I think there's a soft spot for breakfast. And by breakfast I don't mean the sort of quick fuel-up that's come to be accepted as the norm: a bowl of cold cereal and a slug of instant coffee on the run. I'm talking about the good old-fashioned, sit-down family-style breakfasts we either once knew or at least aspire to in our hectic lives. I'm talking about freshly ground and brewed coffee, creamy scrambled eggs, and homemade coffee cakes that perfume the entire house and draw the bleary-eyed to the kitchen like a magnet. That's what I mean by breakfast.

I've always considered holiday breakfasts a special opportunity to nurture family ties. It's a perfect time to huddle up with the family, talk about the exciting events — like Christmas tree hunting — in the days and weeks ahead, and watch the holiday spirit work its special magic on the kids.

I like to get up at 5:00 on a cold December morning — honest — and start mixing up a yeasted coffee cake. I might go for a morning ski while the dough is rising, or I might just turn on the Christmas tree lights and kick back

with a good book and a cup of tea. It never seems like a chore, my early morning baking, because I like the time alone and we all love breakfasting together on the fruits of my endeavors.

I'm flexible about breakfast most of the year, but during the holidays I always like to serve something freshly baked. And my absolute favorite is yeasted coffee cake. Yeasted coffee cakes are generally built around a sweet dough, teamed up with fruits, nuts, spices, or a custard. Sometimes the filling is rolled up inside the dough, and other times the dough is simply pressed into a pan and a topping is poured over it. Then there are times when the dough is cut into separate pieces to make breakfast buns (see Cider-Glazed Sticky Buns, page 40). None of these are difficult to make, and the sensory pleasures of working with sweet vanilla-scented doughs, fruits, and spices abound.

Naturally there are days when you'll want something really fast, perhaps a special muffin or a quick coffee cake or a savory main dish breakfast; they're all here in abundance too.

*Breakfast
Baking*

Jam Muffins with Crumb Topping

MAKES 10 MUFFINS

Here is a moist whole grain muffin that my kids like: there's a surprise of fruit preserves in the center. The jam gets pushed into the top of the batter, and the top is then covered with a little crumb topping; as they bake, the preserves settle in, causing a little crater or cave — "cave muffins," my son Ben calls them. Any of your favorite preserves will do. Don't stir up the jam before you use it; that will thin it out, and it may leak into the muffin cups instead of staying in the muffins.

TOPPING

    3 tablespoons unbleached flour
    2 tablespoons packed light brown sugar
    1 tablespoon cold unsalted butter, cut in half

BATTER

    1 1/2 cups whole wheat flour
    1/3 cup unbleached flour
    1/3 cup yellow cornmeal, preferably stone-ground
    1 teaspoon baking soda
    1/2 teaspoon salt
    1 large egg
    1/3 cup packed light brown sugar
    1/4 cup unsalted butter, melted
    1/2 cup milk
    1/2 cup sour cream
    1/3 cup (approximately) fruit preserves

In a small bowl, mix the flour and brown sugar for the topping. Add the cold butter and rub it into the dry mixture until everything is uniformly moistened by the butter. Place the bowl in the freezer. Preheat the oven to 400° and butter 10 muffin cups.

Make the batter by combining the flours, cornmeal, baking soda, and salt in a bowl. In a separate bowl, beat the egg lightly, then whisk in the brown sugar, melted butter, milk, and sour cream. Make a well in the dry mixture, add the liquid, and stir just to blend. Divide the batter evenly among 10 muffin cups. Spoon about 1 1/2 teaspoons of preserves over the center of each muffin and push it into the batter just a little bit. Sprinkle a little of the crumb topping over each one and bake for 20 minutes. Cool in the pan for 3 or 4 minutes, then transfer to a cloth-lined basket and serve at once.

Maple Walnut Muffins with Maple Cream Sauce

MAKES 12 MUFFINS

Christmas is a very maple time of year for us. We tend to overlook the dramatic price jumps of the past few years and use it with a free hand in all kinds of baking. These maple oat muffins are quite good enough to stand alone, but I sometimes like to get carried away and drizzle the warm muffins with the accompanying maple cream sauce. The sauce can be used as a glaze to top the muffins or served at the table over split muffins. We almost always serve applesauce with these muffins, and sometimes plain yogurt too.

> 1 1/2 cups whole wheat flour
> 1/2 cup unbleached flour
> 2 1/2 teaspoons baking powder
> 1 teaspoon ground cinnamon
> 3/4 teaspoon salt
> 1 large egg
> 1 1/4 cups milk
> 2/3 cup pure maple syrup
> 3 tablespoons unsalted butter, melted
> 1 cup (about 1/4 pound) finely chopped walnuts

MAPLE CREAM SAUCE
> 1/3 cup pure maple syrup
> 1/4 cup heavy cream

Preheat the oven to 400° and butter 12 muffin cups. In a large mixing bowl, mix the flours, baking powder, cinnamon, and salt. Set aside. In a separate bowl, whisk the egg. Blend in the milk, 2/3 cup maple syrup, and melted butter. Make a well in the dry mixture and add the liquids. Blend the batter with a few strokes, adding the nuts on the last stroke or two. Divide the batter evenly among the muffin cups. Bake for 20 minutes. Let the muffins cool in the pan on a rack while you make the sauce.

Combine the maple syrup and cream in a small nonreactive saucepan. Bring to a boil over medium heat, then boil for 2 minutes. If you're using the sauce to glaze the top of the muffins, spoon it directly over them as they sit in the pan. Otherwise, bring the saucepan to the table and spoon the sauce over the split muffins.

Pumpkin Spice Muffins

MAKES 12 MUFFINS

Most of our pumpkins — and much of our produce, in fact — comes from our friend Chris Owens. Chris grows several acres of pumpkins every year, and we often swap him pies or cookies or something else baked for our share of sugar pie pumpkins, as well as the bigger ones the kids love to carve up and decorate. (Chris, his kids, and friends carve several hundred pumpkins right before Halloween; he lights and displays all of them along the road where he lives and sells produce; it's quite a spectacle.)

We try to keep some pumpkins after Halloween, so we can enjoy these muffins at Thanksgiving. They're sweet, spicy, bright orange, and they taste very pumpkiny. Baking a sugar pie pumpkin is no more difficult than baking a potato, but if you can't get your hands on one, canned pumpkin will do. Bear in mind that the pumpkin must be baked ahead, either the night before or a couple of hours before you plan to serve these.

1 small sugar pie pumpkin (about 2 pounds) *or* 1 cup
    canned pumpkin
1 large egg, lightly beaten
3/4 cup packed light brown sugar
1/3 cup orange juice, fresh or prepared frozen
finely grated zest of 1 lemon
1/4 cup unsalted butter, melted
1 tablespoon unsulfured molasses
1 cup unbleached flour
3/4 cup whole wheat flour
1/3 cup yellow cornmeal, preferably stone-ground
2 1/2 teaspoons baking powder
3/4 teaspoon salt
1/2 teaspoon ground cinnamon
1/4 teaspoon ground nutmeg, preferably freshly grated
1/4 teaspoon ground cloves
1/4 cup milk
1/2 cup raisins, chopped dates, or chopped walnuts

Preheat the oven to 450°. Pierce the pumpkin in several places with a fork and place it on a small baking dish; a pie pan is perfect. Bake the pumpkin for about 1 hour or until a sharp knife easily punctures the flesh. Remove and cool. When cool enough to handle, cut the pumpkin in half, scoop out and discard the seeds, then scoop out

the flesh. You'll need 1 cup. (What flesh you don't need can be spooned into plastic containers and frozen for later use.)

Preheat the oven to 400° and butter 12 muffin cups.

Puree 1 cup of the flesh with a food mill, in a blender, or in a food processor. Blend it in a bowl with the egg, brown sugar, orange juice, lemon zest, melted butter, and molasses. In a separate bowl, mix the flours, cornmeal, baking powder, salt, and spices. Make a well in the dry mixture, add the liquid mixture, and stir a few times. Add the milk and continue to stir until the batter is uniform. Fold in the dried fruit or nuts.

Spoon the batter into the muffin tins; for slightly larger muffins, use only 11 of the cups. Bake for 22 minutes. Cool the muffins in the cups for 2 minutes, then turn them out and serve right away.

Christmas Day Breakfast

Cooking is my way of dealing with post-Christmas stress, the widespread syndrome that begins with kids playing trampoline on your body at 5:00 Christmas morning ("Can we open our presents now? Can we?"). Once I have stoked the stoves, shepherded tons of wrapping paper into garbage bags, and slipped on my new socks or slippers, I'm ready to think about making breakfast.

Don't try to break much new gastronomic ground on Christmas morning; you aren't running a restaurant, so be content to serve the kinds of things you're comfortable making and you know your family will enjoy. In other words, if you haven't ever worked with yeast, Christmas Day is no time to learn. Stick with muffins, biscuits, and eggs or something simple and reliable. And blessed is the cook who has stashed a stollen or another coffee cake in the freezer for a carefree Christmas breakfast.

If you want to suffuse your Christmas breakfast table with an aura of holiday cheer, put the extra effort into special little touches like pretty table linen and candles. Get the family involved. Bring out your biggest basket and have the kids make up a free-form centerpiece of fresh fruit, unshelled nuts, evergreen boughs, and dried flowers. Have one or more of the kids set the table; another can be your assistant cook or server. Everybody should pitch in.

Breakfast should be by consensus. We always discuss ahead what we want to serve for Christmas morning, then make sure we have the necessary ingredients on hand. We like to start with something savory — like hash and eggs — then take a break. At some point I'll start a dough for sticky buns or a special coffee cake, and we'll have that midmorning with freshly squeezed orange juice and coffee. We like to make plenty so there's a little something to offer friends when they drop by later in the day.

Remember that a relaxing, wholesome breakfast can help set the tone for a pleasant Christmas Day; think it through ahead, prepare, and you can't go wrong.

Lemon Poppy Seed Muffins

MAKES 12 MUFFINS

We make these at all times of year, but I like them most around Christmas, when I'm really in the poppy seed spirit. They're superb with just butter, but they're best of all with Lemon Curd (see page 217). My son Ben eats these muffins like there's no tomorrow; one time he ate five at one sitting — and lived to tell about it.

    1/3 cup poppy seeds
    1 1/4 cups milk
    1/4 cup cold unsalted butter
    1/2 cup packed light brown sugar
    finely grated zest of 1 lemon
    1 large egg, lightly beaten
    1 1/4 cups whole wheat flour
    1 cup unbleached flour
    2 teaspoons baking powder
    1 teaspoon ground cinnamon
    1/2 teaspoon salt
    sugar to sprinkle on top

Put the poppy seeds and milk in a small saucepan and bring almost to a boil. Pour the mixture into a bowl and add the cold butter, brown sugar, and lemon zest. Cool the liquid for 5 more minutes, then stir in the egg. Preheat the oven to 375° and butter 12 muffin cups.

In a large bowl, mix the flours, baking powder, cinnamon, and salt. Make a well in the dry ingredients and stir in the liquid just until evenly blended. Divide the batter evenly among the muffin cups, filling each about two-thirds full, and sprinkle a generous pinch of sugar over each one. Bake for 20 minutes, until lightly browned on top. Serve at once.

23

Lemon Cream Scones

MAKES 8 SERVINGS

Golden brown outside and in, these crusty wedge-shaped scones are a lovely start to any holiday breakfast. They are rich enough to eat alone, but you can curry favor with your fellow breakfasters by serving them with a little crock of Lemon Curd (page 217) on the side. And for the absolute quintessential lemon breakfast, serve these as the base for the Lemon Gratin Shortcake (recipe follows).

>1 1/3 cups unbleached flour
>1/3 cup whole wheat flour
>1/3 cup sugar
>1 teaspoon baking soda
>1/2 teaspoon salt
>1/2 teaspoon ground ginger
>1/4 teaspoon ground cinnamon
>finely grated zest of 1 lemon
>6 tablespoons cold unsalted butter, cut into 1/4-inch pieces
>1/2 cup heavy cream
>1/4 cup milk
>1 tablespoon fresh lemon juice
>1 teaspoon lemon extract
>a little extra cream and sugar to glaze the top

Preheat the oven to 400° and lightly butter a large, heavy baking sheet; a dark one is good.

In a large mixing bowl, mix together the flours, sugar, baking soda, salt, ginger, cinnamon, and lemon zest. Add the butter and cut it in with a pastry blender until the mixture resembles fine crumbs. Make a well in the center of the dry ingredients and add the cream, milk, lemon juice, and lemon extract. Stir the liquids first, then stir them into the dry ingredients until the dough coheres. Knead the dough once in the bowl, then place it in the center of the baking sheet. Dust the dough lightly with flour, then use your hand to flatten it into a 10-inch circle.

Using a sharp knife, cut the dough into 8 sections, as you would cut a pie; the cuts can go all the way through. Brush the top of the dough with cream, then sprinkle it with several large pinches of sugar. Bake for 25 minutes, until golden brown. Cut the wedges apart at the existing score marks, then transfer them to a cloth-lined basket and serve at once.

Protecting Your Bakeware from Rust

Anybody who likes to bake eventually discovers, the hard way, that bakeware is prone to rusting: Leave a drop of water in one of your tin pie or bread pans and the next time you go to use it, you find a quarter-size rust spot. Not only are rust spots unsightly, but the rust can spread and adversely affect a pan's ability to bake evenly.

Even if I towel-dry my bakeware, I now go one step further and let it air-dry in a warm spot. I keep a rack on top of my woodstove just for this purpose. On it I place all my bread, pie, and loaf pans for about 15 minutes before I put them back on the shelf. Lacking a woodstove, any warm, dry spot will do. If you have a gas oven where the pilot is always on, just plopping your pan into the oven will do the trick.

I find this to be a particularly effective way of drying any pan with a crease because water can hide there from a towel. It's especially good for cookie cutters, which take forever to dry by hand. I just shake the cookie cutters dry, put them in a wicker basket, and hang them over the woodstove.

Lemon Gratin Shortcake

MAKES UP TO 8 SERVINGS

This is the ultimate holiday breakfast: a crusty lemon cake (actually a scone), topped with fruit, then blanketed with lemon curd lightened with whipped cream. The top layer is dusted with brown sugar, then the whole thing is run under the broiler to caramelize the sugar and make the top crusty. The finished dish offers an incredible range of textures and flavors: the soft fruit, softer lemon curd, crunchy top, and crusty bottom.

You can use all sorts of fruits here. Fresh winter raspberries are costly, but they're a good choice. Strawberries, halved or quartered, are also often available in the winter marketplace; look for other berries as well. Soft, ripe, juicy pears — peeled and thinly sliced — are another favorite of mine. I have even used home-frozen blueberries (thawed) with good results, but I've been less than thrilled with store-bought frozen fruit. Unless you are an early riser and very ambitious, start this the day before by making the lemon curd and mixing it with the whipped cream so it has time to chill. If you are serving the shortcakes for brunch, however, you could prepare this in one morning without getting into a panic. Slackers can substitute sliced pound cake for the scones.

> 1 recipe Lemon Curd (page 217)
> 3/4 cup whipping cream
> 1/3 cup confectioners' sugar
> 1 recipe Lemon Cream Scones (preceding recipe)
> 3 to 4 cups fruit of your choice (see above paragraph)
> 1/2 cup (approximately) packed light brown sugar

Prepare the lemon curd as directed. While you are waiting for it to cool, whip the cream until fairly stiff. Add the confectioners' sugar and continue to beat until stiff. Whisk in the lemon curd, about half at a time, until evenly blended. Cover and refrigerate for at least 2 hours before using.

When you are ready to proceed, get out 8 ovenproof dishes. Split each scone in half and lay the halves next to one another, soft centers facing up, on the individual dishes. Cover the scones with 1/3 to 1/2 cup berries or sliced pears. Spoon about 1/3 cup of the lightened lemon curd over the fruit, covering all but the outer edge of the fruit, then sprinkle about 1 tablespoon brown sugar over the top. Run each dish under the broiler for 2 to 4 minutes, just until the top is golden brown and caramelized; watch it closely so it doesn't burn. Serve at once.

N O T E : If you don't have 8 ovenproof dishes, you can put the shortcakes on a baking sheet. If you get the curd too close to the edge, it will tend to ooze over just a little, but that's no big deal.

Almond Shortcake with Pears and Lavender Cream

MAKES 6 SERVINGS

*At our house, we think fruit shortcake is much too good to limit it to the
summer months. So we've gotten into the habit of winter shortcakes that
add a celebratory note to our holiday breakfasts. Here is one we especially
like made with thinly sliced, honeyed pears served with lavender cream on
an almond shortcake. The touch of lavender—and I do mean touch, since
you need a mere drop of lavender oil—is a soft, fragrant reminder of
summer. And of course this is just about the perfect breakfast—or
dessert—to serve an herb gardener friend. These shortcakes are also
tremendous topped with poached figs (page 221) and mascarpone or coffee
ice cream and chocolate sauce. If you're fresh out of lavender oil, simply
flavor the cream with several drops of pure almond extract, to taste.*

> 1/2 cup (2 ounces) shelled almonds
> 1 cup unbleached flour
> 3/4 cup whole wheat flour
> 1/4 cup sugar
> 2 teaspoons baking soda
> 1/4 teaspoon salt
> 6 tablespoons cold unsalted butter, cut into 1/4-inch pieces
> 1 large egg, lightly beaten
> 3/4 cup milk
> milk and sugar to sprinkle on top (optional)
> 4 large ripe pears, peeled, cored, and sliced
> 2 tablespoons honey
> juice of 1/2 lemon

LAVENDER CREAM

> 1 cup heavy cream
> 3 tablespoons confectioners' sugar
> 1 drop lavender oil (available at health food stores)

Preheat the oven to 350°. Spread the almonds on a baking sheet and
place in the oven for 8 minutes. Tilt them out onto a plate and cool.
Once they're cooled, grind them to a coarse meal in a food processor
or a blender; if you are using the latter, stop the machine periodically
to fluff up the nuts so they don't compact under the blades. Preheat
the oven to 425°.

Mix the nuts, flours, sugar, baking soda, and salt in a medium-
size bowl. Add the butter and cut it in until it is broken into very fine

pieces, as if you were making a piecrust. Blend the egg and milk in a separate bowl, make a well in the dry ingredients, and stir in the liquid all at once; it will probably seem a little damp. Let the dough sit for 5 minutes while you lightly butter a large baking sheet.

Divide the dough in half, in the bowl, just for a reference, knowing you need to get 3 shortcakes from each half. Form the shortcakes by scooping up one sixth of the dough into your floured hands. Carefully ball up the dough, then drop the ball onto the sheet from about 4 inches up, to flatten it a little. Repeat for the remaining dough, leaving about 3 inches between the balls. If you want very crusty shortcakes, brush them with a little milk and sprinkle each one with a big pinch of sugar. Bake for 20 minutes, then transfer the shortcakes to a rack to cool.

While the shortcakes are cooling, toss the pears with the honey and lemon juice. Cover and set aside.

To make the lavender cream, beat the cream with an electric mixer until it is well on its way to thickening. Beat in the sugar, then stop the mixer — because you don't want to bungle this part — and very carefully add the drop of lavender oil; it helps to pour the drop into the cap first, or use a dropper if you have one. Continue beating until the cream has thickened. Cover and refrigerate until serving time.

To serve, cut the shortcake in half and pile the sliced pears and their juice on the bottom half. Top with lavender cream and then the other half of the shortcake.

NOTE: This recipe makes 6 pretty big biscuits, good if you like big biscuits. However, you can easily stretch it to serve 8. Just make 8 biscuits, use an extra pear or two, and use 1 1/2 cups of heavy cream, with an extra tablespoon of sugar to sweeten it.

Cranberry Scones

MAKES 8 SERVINGS

*These scones are as simple to make as biscuits or muffins. They're dark
and just a little sweet, with a firm, grainy texture. The cranberries give
them a tart edge, but you can also add a few raisins to balance out the
tartness. Serve them with butter and honey on the side. Serve alone, with
egg dishes — in place of biscuits — or with a winter fruit salad.*

> 1 1/2 cups whole wheat flour
> 1/2 cup unbleached flour
> 1/4 cup sugar
> 2 teaspoons baking powder
> 1/2 teaspoon salt
> 1/4 teaspoon ground cardamom
> 1/4 teaspoon ground nutmeg, preferably freshly grated
> 5 tablespoons cold unsalted butter, cut into 1/4-inch pieces
> 1/3 cup heavy cream
> 1/3 cup plus 1 tablespoon milk
> grated zest of 1 lemon
> 3/4 cup fresh cranberries
> 1 tablespoon heavy cream for the glaze
> sugar for the glaze (optional)

Preheat the oven to 425° and lightly butter a large baking sheet,
preferably a dark, heavy one. In a large bowl, combine the flours,
sugar, baking powder, salt, and spices. Add the butter and cut it in
with a pastry blender until the butter is broken into very small
pieces.

Make a well in the center of the dry ingredients and add the 1/3
cup cream, milk, and lemon zest. Stir several strokes, add the
cranberries, and continue to stir until the dough coheres. Form the
dough into a ball and place it in the center of the baking sheet. Pat it
into a disk 9 inches in diameter. Using a long-bladed knife, score the
dough deeply — almost all the way through — into 8 wedges, as you
would cut a pie. Brush the entire surface with the tablespoon of
cream; if you want a sweet, crunchy surface, sprinkle the top with
several big pinches of sugar too. Bake the scones for 25 minutes.
Slide the entire circle onto a cutting board, then cut the scones apart
at the score marks. Serve hot.

Apple Raisin Pandowdy

MAKES ABOUT 8 SERVINGS

I have frankly never been able to figure out exactly what a pandowdy is; I have seen pandowdies with pastry crusts, biscuit doughs, with the fruit on top instead of the bottom. At the risk of adding even more confusion, here's my variation of pandowdy, this one topped with a yeasted pastry crust. I like it for breakfast, especially at this time of year, when the apples are fresh and hearty breakfasts are the order of the day. The filling couldn't be simpler — apples, lemon, sugar, and spice. It has no thickening, and it doesn't need one because there's no bottom crust to worry about. The juices tend to migrate upward into the breadlike pastry crust, bathing it lightly. For breakfast, this is great served with plain or lemon yogurt; for a filling dessert, add vanilla ice cream.

1 recipe Wheaten Yeasted Pastry (page 245)

FILLING

5 large tart apples, peeled, cored, and very thinly sliced

1 cup raisins *or* 1/2 cup raisins and 1/2 cup chopped pitted dates

juice of 1 lemon

2/3 cup packed light brown sugar

1 teaspoon ground cinnamon

1/4 teaspoon ground cloves

GLAZE

2 tablespoons milk or cream

1 or 2 teaspoons sugar

Chill the prepared pastry. Generously butter a 10-inch deep-dish pie pan, preferably a pretty ceramic or glass one instead of metal. Preheat the oven to 375°.

Combine and mix all of the filling ingredients in a large bowl, then turn them into the buttered dish. On a sheet of lightly floured wax paper, roll the pastry into a 12-inch circle. Lay the pastry on top of the apples and tuck the overhang down in the pan. Brush the surface of the pastry with the milk or cream and sprinkle the sugar on top.

Bake the pandowdy on the bottom rack of the oven for approximately 40 minutes, until the apple slices are tender. Cool on a rack for 5 minutes before serving.

Blueberry and Toasted Almond Coffee Cake

MAKES 8 TO 10 SERVINGS

I love almond anything, and I must go through 10 or 15 pounds of these nuts between November and January. This sensationally good coffee cake is filled with a toasted and ground almond mixture and blueberry preserves. The toasted almond filling is a lazy cook's answer to homemade almond paste, because you don't have to blanch the almonds or make a sugar syrup. Because the almonds are toasted, it doesn't taste too much like the traditional almond paste, but it sure tastes good. The blueberry preserves are spooned over the almond filling, giving a moist, fruity element to the coffee cake. This coffee cake is excellent warm, but it can also be made several hours ahead if you like; don't reheat it, though, or the pastry will dry out.

> 1 recipe Wheaten Yeasted Pastry (page 245), shaped into a
> rectangle and chilled

FILLING

> 1 1/4 cups (about 5 ounces) toasted almonds (see page 111
> for toasting instructions)
> 1/3 cup packed light brown sugar
> 2 tablespoons orange juice, fresh or prepared frozen
> 1 tablespoon unsalted butter at room temperature
> 1/4 cup (about 2 whole crackers) fine graham cracker crumbs
> 3/4 cup blueberry preserves

GLAZE

> egg wash: 1 large egg beaten with 1 tablespoon milk
> 1/3 cup confectioners' sugar
> 1 teaspoon milk

Prepare and chill the pastry as directed, being sure to shape it into a rectangle instead of a circle. While it chills, make the almond filling: Put the almonds and brown sugar into a food processor and process until the mixture resembles a fine meal. With the machine running, add the orange juice in a stream, then the butter. Stop the machine as soon as the butter is incorporated. Scrape the mixture into a bowl, add the graham cracker crumbs, and work them in with your fingers. Cover and refrigerate. Preheat the oven to 350° and get out a large cookie sheet.

After the dough has chilled for at least 30 minutes, roll it into a 10- by 14-inch rectangle on a sheet of lightly floured wax paper.

Invert the pastry into the center of the cookie sheet and peel off the paper. Put the sheet in the refrigerator for 5 minutes to firm the dough.

Mentally divide the dough into thirds, lengthwise; it helps to lightly score the dough so you have a visual reference. Spread the almond mixture evenly on the center third of the pastry, keeping it 1 1/2 inches in from each end. Spoon the blueberry preserves evenly over the almond mixture.

Using a dough scraper, cut the 2 flanking thirds into 1 1/2-inch-wide strips, right up to the filling; keep the cuts on each side directly opposite one another. Using a sharp knife, cut the center third on each score mark down to the intersection of the first strip; do this on each end and you will be able to remove the four corner sections of dough. Discard them. Take the resulting two end flaps of dough attached to the center section and lay them up over the filling.

Starting at one end, pull the strips up and over the filling, laying them down on the filling at a 45-degree angle to the edge. Alternate from one side to the other, weaving a latticelike top. Tuck the last 2 strips under the end of the coffee cake. Put the coffee cake back in the refrigerator for 5 minutes.

After 5 minutes, brush the surface of the coffee cake sparingly with the egg wash. Bake for 35 minutes. Slide the cake onto a rack to cool. While the cake is still warm, make the glaze by whisking together the confectioners' sugar and milk. Drizzle it over the cake, lengthwise, with a fork or whisk. Serve warm. If you aren't serving the cake warm, don't glaze it until you're ready to serve it. Wrap the cake loosely in foil until then.

Dried Cherry and Almond Coffee Cake

MAKES 10 TO 12 SERVINGS

Nuts and dried cherries are two items I use without restraint during the holidays, here combined in a fabulous coffee cake made with yeasted pastry. This looks gorgeous when you slip it out of the pan, the rustic bronze-colored crust surrounding a golden almond filling. It is best served warm, about 30 minutes out of the oven, though it rewarms nicely too; just cover with foil and place in a 350° oven for 10 to 15 minutes. For a pretty presentation, serve on a large tray, surrounded with nuts in their shells.

1 recipe Wheaten Yeasted Pastry (page 245)

FILLING

3/4 cup dried sour cherries
1 1/4 cups (5 ounces) shelled almonds
1 tablespoon unbleached flour
1 teaspoon baking powder
1/4 teaspoon salt
1/2 cup (1/4 pound) unsalted butter, softened
1/2 cup packed light brown sugar
2 large eggs at room temperature
1 teaspoon vanilla extract
finely grated zest of 1 lemon

Prepare and chill the pastry as directed. I prefer to bake this in a 10-inch tart pan or flan ring with 1 1/2-inch-high sides. Lacking that, a 10-inch springform pan will do. In any case, lightly butter the pan (and the baking sheet, if you're using a flan ring). On a lightly floured sheet of wax paper, roll the pastry into a 13-inch circle; it will go a little over the edges, but don't worry. Invert the pastry over the pan, peel off the paper, and gently tuck the pastry into the pan as you would a pie shell. If there's any overhanging dough, simply fold it over and press it into the side to beef it up; the dough should be even with the top of the pan or, in the case of a springform pan, about halfway up. Cover the pastry with plastic wrap and refrigerate. Preheat the oven to 350°.

If your cherries are on the dry side, put them in a steamer basket and then in a small saucepan and steam them for 5 minutes, then set them aside to cool. Using a food processor or blender, pulverize the almonds to a fine, even consistency; in a blender, this is best accomplished at low speed, stopping occasionally to fluff the nuts up with the handle of a wooden spoon. Put the nuts in a small mixing bowl. Mix the flour, baking powder, and salt and add to the nuts.

Using an electric mixer, beat the butter in a medium-size mixing bowl until creamy. Beat in the brown sugar and then the eggs, one at a time, followed by the vanilla extract and lemon zest. Stir the nut mixture into the creamed ingredients until evenly blended, then fold in the cherries.

Spread the filling evenly in the pastry shell, then bake for 35 minutes. Cool on a rack for 10 minutes, then remove the sides of the pan and cool for about 20 more minutes before serving. If not serving right away, wrap snugly in foil and refrigerate for up to 3 days.

*Breakfast
Baking*

'Twas the Night Before Christmas . . .

When the sun sets on Christmas Eve, we begin preparing for our annual tradition of singing to the neighbors. The neighbors we sing to, however, don't live in nearby houses. They're the furred and feathered neighbors who live in our yard and the surrounding woods. This is our way of saying thanks for their company: to squirrels who chase one another up and down the ash trees outside the living room window; to the plucky little chickadees who brave the cold in search of food.

It's a funny little custom, but the kids come to it quite easily and with remarkable enthusiasm. What I'm constantly reminded of as I see them cramming big bags with cranberries, popcorn, and cookies they've baked — treats we'll take down to our singing spot and scatter about — is how young children experience such a close and trusting connection with the natural world. As adults, we tend to lose that connection. But even to glimpse it in the eyes of a child is a gift worth cherishing.

Our singing spot is a patch of frozen stream about 50 feet from the back door. If we've had a recent snowfall — which is often the case — the older kids will shovel a path earlier in the day so the younger ones don't get bogged down in snowdrifts. They'll clear an area large enough for our family and a few friends to stand in a close circle, border it with luminaria, and hang peanut butter–stuffed pinecones from nearby boughs.

Our friends and their children arrive after dinner. The kids exchange bags of cookies they've baked with their friends. We snack on cookies, cake, hot spiced cider, and cocoa.

When the excitement becomes too much, we bundle them up in mittens and scarves and line the kids up at the back door. Each one is given an apple, bored out at the top and fitted with a candle. When the candles have all been lit (and blown out half a dozen times) we march in slow procession, flickering, swaggering, and bobbing up and down to a soft chorus of "Silent Night."

Standing in a circle, we sing most of the favorites — some sweet and soothing, some rowdy. And then, in the distance, we hear the first jingle of Santa's sleigh bells. That's our cue to break into our favorite song of the evening (to the tune of "Row, Row, Row Your Boat"), wildly swinging our bracelet bells:

> Ring, ring, ring the bells,
> Ring them loud and clear,
> To tell all the animals in the woods
> That Christmastime is near.

When the song ends, we scatter our bags of animal treats in all directions. Exchanging quick, chilly good-byes with our friends, we scamper inside and light the candles on the Christmas tree, sing a few more tunes, and cram shoulder to shoulder on the sofa to read " 'Twas the Night Before Christmas." Then we blow out the candles and go off to bed early; tomorrow's the Big Day, and we'll be up bright and early, opening presents and watching our animal friends enjoy theirs.

Coconut Custard Coffee Cake

MAKES 8 TO 10 SERVINGS

This is a very simple, rich, and creamy coffee cake flavored with candied ginger and lemon. There's absolutely no fussing with the topping — nothing to peel or slice — and the yeasted pastry crust takes only minutes to throw together. The pastry can be made the night before if you want to make this a really quick operation on some otherwise hectic morning — Christmas or New Year's, for instance.

1 recipe Wheaten Yeasted Pastry (page 245)

TOPPING

1 cup sour cream

1/4 pound cream cheese, at room temperature

1/2 cup sugar

1 large egg

1 large egg yolk

2 teaspoons fresh lemon juice

finely grated zest of 1 lemon

2 teaspoons minced candied ginger

1/2 teaspoon vanilla extract

1/2 cup unsweetened shredded coconut (available at health food stores) or sweetened flaked coconut

Chill the prepared pastry. Preheat the oven to 350° and butter an 8-by 12-inch baking dish.

On a lightly floured surface, roll the dough into a rectangle measuring 10 by 14 inches. Line the pan with the pastry, tucking it gently into the bottom creases so the pastry does not tear. Fold any overhanging dough over or just push it down, so the dough comes about halfway up the sides. Let the dough sit at room temperature while you prepare the topping.

In a large bowl, beat the sour cream, cream cheese, and sugar with an electric mixer until soft and fluffy. Beat in the egg, egg yolk, lemon juice, lemon zest, candied ginger, and vanilla. Stir in the coconut. Scrape the topping over the pastry, then bake for 35 minutes. When done, the topping will have puffed up and set (it won't be wobbly), though it should not brown. Cool the coffee cake in the pan on a rack for at least 10 minutes before serving. This cake is best eaten the same day.

Sweet Potato Sugar Cake

MAKES 12 GENEROUS SERVINGS

This is a take on the well-known Moravian sugar cake, a traditional Christmas indulgence of those Protestants who came from Moravia and Bohemia to settle in Pennsylvania in the 1700s. The very soft yeasted dough is patted into a buttered baking dish, dimpled with your fingers, then covered with brown sugar, cinnamon, and butter — the holy trinity of holiday baking — and baked to crusty ecstasy. In this version I have replaced the traditional potato with sweet potato, which gives the cake an attractive tawny hue; rather than cook the potato as instructed, you can replace it with 1 cup of leftover mashed or candied sweet potatoes, then puree it with the milk as described. It's a good way to use up any leftover sweet potatoes from Thanksgiving, though I can assure you there won't be any of this left over.

1 1/2 cups (1 large) diced peeled sweet potato in 1/2-inch cubes
1/2 cup milk
1/4 cup lukewarm water
1 1/4-ounce package (about 1 tablespoon) active dry yeast
1/4 cup honey
1 cup whole wheat flour
1/2 teaspoon salt
2 large egg yolks
1/4 cup unsalted butter, melted and cooled
2 1/2 cups (approximately) unbleached flour

TOPPING

3/4 cup packed light brown sugar
1 teaspoon ground cinnamon
1 tablespoon milk
6 tablespoons unsalted butter, melted

Put the sweet potatoes into a saucepan with about 1 quart of lightly salted water and bring to a boil. Boil for about 15 to 20 minutes, until the potatoes are very tender. Drain. Transfer the potatoes to a blender or food processor, add the milk, and puree. Pour the puree into a large mixing bowl. (If you are using leftover sweet potatoes, measure out 1 cup and puree them with the milk; use very warm milk if the potatoes are cold.)

Measure the lukewarm water in a glass measuring cup and stir in the yeast. Set aside for 5 minutes, then stir the dissolved yeast into the pureed potatoes along with the honey and whole wheat flour. Beat vigorously with a wooden spoon for 1 minute, then cover this sponge and set aside in a warm, draft-free spot for 15 minutes.

After 15 minutes, beat the salt, egg yolks, and 1/4 cup melted butter into the sponge. Stir in enough unbleached flour, 1/2 cup at a time, to make a soft, kneadable dough. Turn the dough out and knead—somewhat gently, because this is a soft dough—for 10 minutes, using enough of the remaining flour to keep the dough from sticking. Put the dough in a lightly oiled bowl, turning to coat the entire surface. Cover with plastic wrap and set the dough aside in a warm, draft-free spot until doubled in bulk, about 1 hour. Butter a 9- by 13-inch baking dish and set it aside.

When the dough has doubled, rap the bowl gently on the counter to deflate the dough, but don't punch it down. Dump the dough into the center of the buttered dish, cover loosely with plastic wrap, and let sit for 5 minutes. After 5 minutes, flour the top of the dough lightly and pat the dough out evenly into the pan. Cover loosely once more and set aside in a warm spot for 15 minutes.

While that rises, make the topping by rubbing together the brown sugar and cinnamon. After the dough has risen for 15 minutes, preheat the oven to 350°. Gently brush the surface of the dough with the milk and sprinkle the brown sugar mixture evenly on top. Using floured fingers, gently poke shallow indentations all over the surface about halfway through the dough; what I do is poke with 2 fingers, making 3 long rows with them. Spoon the melted butter over the dough and into the indentations, then let the dough rise in a warm spot, uncovered, for 15 more minutes.

Bake for 35 minutes; the top will become dark brown and crusty. Cool in the pan on a rack for 5 minutes, then slice and serve. Leftovers can be wrapped in foil and reheated in a 400° oven for 10 minutes.

Cider-Glazed Sticky Buns

MAKES 12 LARGE BUNS

We love sticky buns so much that we like to see what sorts of seasonal variations we can come up with; this is one harvest version that became an instant hit, something you might like to serve during Thanksgiving week to kick off the big baking season. The soft oatmeal sweet dough is filled with cinnamon, chopped apple, and raisins, then glazed with an apple cider reduction. It doesn't take long to reduce the cider — less than 15 minutes, usually — and it can be accomplished painlessly while the dough rises, filling your kitchen with a lovely aroma. Whatever pot you use to reduce the cider, I recommend first pouring 2/3 cup of water into the bottom of it so you get an idea what that volume of liquid looks like in the pot; the memory of that will be a handy reference to tell you when the cider is reduced enough.

1/2 cup rolled oats (*not* instant)
1/3 cup packed light brown sugar
3 tablespoons cold unsalted butter, cut into 1/4-inch pieces
1 cup hot milk
1/4 cup lukewarm water
1 1/4-ounce package (about 1 tablespoon) active dry yeast
2 teaspoons salt
1 large egg at room temperature, lightly beaten
2 teaspoons vanilla extract
1/2 cup whole wheat flour
3 1/2 cups (approximately) unbleached flour
2 tablespoons unsalted butter, melted
1 tablespoon ground cinnamon
1 cup raisins
1 cup finely chopped peeled apple

CIDER GLAZE

1 quart fresh preservative-free cider
1/4 cup unsalted butter, cut into small pieces
1/2 cup packed light brown sugar

Put the oats, 1/3 cup brown sugar, and cold butter into a large mixing bowl and pour the hot milk over them. As that mixture cools, pour the lukewarm water into a measuring cup and stir in the yeast; set aside. When the milk has cooled to about body temperature, stir in the dissolved yeast, salt, egg, and vanilla. Stir in the whole wheat flour, then enough of the unbleached flour, about 1/2 cup at a time, to make a soft, kneadable dough, beating well after each addition. Turn it out onto a floured surface and knead for about 8 minutes, using as much of the remaining flour as necessary to keep the dough from sticking. Place the dough in a lightly oiled bowl, turning to coat the entire surface. Cover with plastic wrap and place in a warm, draft-free spot until doubled in bulk, about 1 to 1 1/2 hours. Butter a 9- by 13-inch baking pan; I use glass.

While the dough rises, reduce the cider: Pour it into a large pot and bring to a boil over high heat. Boil vigorously until the liquid is reduced to a little more than 1/2 cup but not more than 2/3 cup; you can quickly pour it into a measuring cup to find out where you stand. When you have the right measurement, strain it — I just line a strainer with a paper towel — and pour it back into the pot. Add the 1/4 cup butter and 1/2 cup brown sugar and heat gently just until the butter melts. Scrape this glaze into the buttered pan.

When the dough has doubled, punch it down and knead briefly; cover with plastic wrap and let the dough rest for 5 minutes. Roll the dough into a 12- by 15-inch rectangle and brush the surface with the melted butter. Sprinkle evenly with the cinnamon, then cover with the raisins and apple. Starting on the long side, roll the dough up like a rug, keeping it snug but not overly tight.

Using a sharp, serrated knife, score the dough at the center, then at the center of each half; these are reference marks. Saw each quarter-section into 3 even slices and place the slices, swirl side up, in the pan, making 3 rows of 4. Press each one down slightly to expand it. Cover the rolls loosely with plastic wrap and place in a warm, draft-free spot until doubled in bulk, about 30 to 40 minutes. About 15 minutes before they reach this point, preheat the oven to 350°.

When the rolls have doubled, bake for 40 minutes, until the tops are golden brown. As soon as they are done, lightly oil a large baking sheet and place it over the hot rolls, then invert them onto the sheet. Lift off the pan, cool for 5 to 10 minutes, and serve hot.

Cornmeal Sticky Buns with
Maple Hazelnut Glaze

MAKES 12 LARGE BUNS

Here's another great sticky bun we like with steaming mugs of hazelnut coffee: soft cornmeal-crunchy buns with a sweet coating of maple syrup, toasted hazelnuts, and coffee. Don't be deterred by the large recipe if you don't need 12 big buns, because you can always freeze any leftovers in aluminum foil, then reheat them in a 400° oven for 10 minutes.

DOUGH

>1/4 cup lukewarm water
>
>1 1/4-ounce package (about 1 tablespoon) active dry yeast
>
>1 cup lukewarm milk
>
>1/4 cup unsalted butter, cut into 1/4-inch pieces
>
>1/3 cup packed light brown sugar
>
>1 large egg plus 1 large egg yolk, lightly beaten
>
>2 teaspoons vanilla extract
>
>2 teaspoons salt
>
>1/2 cup yellow cornmeal
>
>4 to 4 1/2 cups unbleached flour

GLAZE AND FILLING

>1/3 cup maple syrup
>
>6 tablespoons unsalted butter
>
>2/3 cup packed light brown sugar
>
>1 tablespoon fine pulverized coffee beans (I use a coffee mill)
>
>1 cup (about 1/4 pound) toasted chopped hazelnuts (see page 111 for toasting instructions)
>
>1 teaspoon ground cinnamon

Pour the lukewarm water into a small bowl and sprinkle on the yeast. Stir with a fork, then set aside for 5 minutes. Put the lukewarm milk, 1/4 cup butter, 1/3 cup brown sugar, egg, egg yolk, vanilla, and salt in a large bowl. Stir in the dissolved yeast and cornmeal. Stir in enough of the unbleached flour, 1 cup at a time, to make a soft, kneadable dough, beating well after each addition.

    Turn the dough out onto a floured surface and knead for about 7 minutes, using as much flour as needed on your hands and the work surface to keep the dough from sticking. Place the dough in a buttered bowl, turning it to coat the entire surface. Cover the bowl

with plastic wrap, then set it aside in a warm, draft-free spot until doubled in bulk, 1 to 1 1/2 hours.

While the dough rises, butter a 9- by 13-inch baking dish; I use glass. To make the glaze, combine the maple syrup, 1/4 cup of the butter, 1/3 cup of the brown sugar, and the coffee in a small saucepan. Bring to a boil, boil for a few seconds, stirring, then pour the glaze into the buttered pan and tilt it to coat the entire surface. Sprinkle the hazelnuts evenly on the glaze and set the pan aside. Melt the remaining 2 tablespoons butter in a small saucepan. Mix the remaining 1/3 cup brown sugar and the cinnamon in a small bowl and set both of these aside.

When the dough has doubled, punch it down and knead briefly on a floured surface. Cover with plastic wrap and let rest for 5 minutes, then roll the dough into a 12- by 15-inch rectangle. Brush the dough with the melted butter and sprinkle it evenly with the brown sugar–cinnamon mixture. Starting at the long edge, roll the dough up like a carpet, keeping it somewhat tight; pinch the seam to seal.

Using a sharp serrated knife, score the dough in the center, then in the center of each half. Cut each of these scored quarter-sections into 3 even slices and lay them in the pan, spiral up; you should have 3 rows of 4, with equal spacing between buns. Cover the pan with plastic wrap and set aside in a warm, draft-free spot until doubled in bulk, 30 to 40 minutes. About 15 minutes before that point, preheat the oven to 350°.

Bake the buns for 35 minutes, until lightly browned. Put a large lightly buttered baking sheet over the pan and invert them; remove the original pan. Let the buns cool for 5 minutes, then serve. Or you may cool them right on the sheet. Store leftovers in aluminum foil.

Mincemeat Coffee Cake

MAKES ABOUT 12 SERVINGS

This oversize yeasted coffee cake is perfect for any big holiday breakfast; if you aren't planning a big spread, just freeze half of the finished cake. The spicy fruit filling is rolled up inside the dough into a log, then cut into sections — though not all the way through — and the sections are pushed slightly to alternate sides, giving the cake a pretty trellised look. The top is finished with confectioners' sugar glaze. Serve with milk, apple cider, or good strong coffee. This will wow them at a holiday potluck or tree-trimming party. This coffee cake keeps exceptionally well (at least several days in the refrigerator), since it's made with a rich, moist whole wheat sour cream dough.

2 1/4-ounce packages (about 2 tablespoons) active dry yeast
1/3 cup lukewarm water
1/2 cup milk
1/4 cup unsalted butter, cut into 1/2-inch pieces
1/2 cup sugar
1/2 cup sour cream
1 large egg, lightly beaten
2 teaspoons vanilla extract
2 cups whole wheat flour
1 1/2 teaspoons salt
1 1/3 cups (approximately) unbleached flour
egg wash: 1 egg beaten with 1 tablespoon milk

FILLING

3 cups Mincemeat (page 220) at room temperature

CONFECTIONERS' SUGAR GLAZE

1/2 cup confectioners' sugar
1 to 1 1/2 tablespoons milk

In a small bowl, stir the yeast into the lukewarm water and set aside. Meanwhile, gently heat the milk in a small saucepan. Put the butter and sugar into a large mixing bowl, pour the hot milk over them, and stir to melt the butter. Stir in the sour cream, egg, vanilla, and whole wheat flour, beating the batter vigorously with a wooden spoon for 1 minute. Cover this sponge with plastic wrap and set aside in a warm, draft-free spot for 15 minutes.

After 15 minutes, stir the salt into the sponge. Stir in enough of the unbleached flour, about 1/3 cup at a time, to make a soft, kneadable dough. Using floured hands, knead the dough for 8 minutes, using as much of the remaining flour as necessary to keep the dough from sticking. Even after 8 minutes, this dough will have a slight tendency to stick, but resist the temptation to keep adding flour. Place the dough in a lightly oiled bowl, turning to coat the entire surface. Cover with plastic wrap and set the dough aside in a warm, draft-free spot until doubled in bulk, about 1 hour.

Once the dough has doubled, punch it down and knead briefly on a floured surface. Cover the dough with plastic wrap and let it rest for 10 minutes. Flour the work surface, then roll the dough into an approximate 12- by 15-inch rectangle. Butter a large baking sheet, preferably one 18 inches long.

Spread the filling evenly over the dough, right up to the long sides but leaving a 3/4-inch margin on the short ends. Starting at one of the short ends, roll the dough up like a carpet, keeping it snug. When you get to the end, moisten the exposed margin with a wet finger, then finish rolling and pinch the seam to seal the log. Pinch off both of the ends, to seal them as well.

Lift the log onto the baking sheet and center it there, seam down. Using a serrated knife, slice the log on the diagonal about three quarters of the way through the dough; start at your right, about 1 1/2 inches in from the end. Continue slicing the dough like this at 1-inch intervals. As you make each cut, push the sections just slightly to alternate sides, so they look staggered. Stop cutting about 2 inches from the other end. Cover the dough loosely with lightly oiled plastic wrap and set aside in a warm, draft-free spot for about 30 minutes, until the dough is quite swollen. About 15 minutes into this last rising, preheat the oven to 350°.

Right before baking, brush the log sparingly with the egg wash. When the 30 minutes have elapsed, bake the coffee cake for 45 minutes, until the surface is a deep golden brown. Enlist a second set of hands and slide 3 or 4 spatulas under the cake; carefully lift it onto a cooling rack. Cool for about 30 minutes before applying the glaze; the easiest way to do this is just by dipping your whisk into the glaze and letting it drizzle right onto the cake as you move it back and forth lengthwise. Serve the coffee cake warm.

To make the glaze, whisk together the confectioners' sugar and milk in a bowl. Add a bit more of either ingredient to make a thickish though still somewhat loose consistency.

Store leftover cake wrapped in foil. To reheat, place in a 400° oven for 10 minutes.

Cardamom Pear Butter Cake

MAKES 12 SERVINGS

Cardamom and pears really sing together, as this cake so deliciously demonstrates. The texture is close to a pound cake, broken only by soft chunks of pears. It's also a very easy cake to make, something you could throw together for a morning holiday breakfast even while you're nursing your first cup of coffee. It's versatile too; it works equally well as a dessert, lightly dusted with confectioners' sugar. Serve with plenty of fresh coffee or a pot of lemon herb tea.

> 2 large pears (I like Anjou), peeled and cut into small chunks
> 1 tablespoon fresh lemon juice
> 1 cup (1/2 pound) unsalted butter, softened
> 1 cup packed light brown sugar
> 4 large eggs at room temperature
> 1 teaspoon vanilla extract
> finely grated zest of 1 lemon
> 1 1/4 cups unbleached flour
> 1 cup whole wheat flour
> 2 teaspoons ground cardamom
> 1 1/2 teaspoons baking powder
> 1/2 teaspoon salt
> confectioners' sugar for top of cake (optional)

Preheat the oven to 350° and butter a 9- or 10-inch springform pan. In a medium bowl, toss the pears with the lemon juice.

Using an electric mixer, cream the butter and brown sugar in a large bowl until light and soft. Add the eggs one at a time, beating well after each addition. Beat in the vanilla extract and lemon zest.

Sift the flours, cardamom, baking powder, and salt into a separate bowl. Stir the dry ingredients into the creamed mixture in 3 stages, blending thoroughly after each addition. Fold in the reserved pears and any juice they've put off. Scrape the batter into the prepared pan and smooth the top with a fork. Bake for 45 to 55 minutes — the latter, approximately, for the larger pan — until the top is golden brown and a tester inserted in the center of the cake comes out clean.

Cool the cake on a rack in the pan for 10 minutes, then remove the side and cool for another 30 minutes before slicing and serving. If you like, sift confectioners' sugar over the cake right before serving. Cover leftovers with plastic wrap and store in a cool place.

The Littlest Bakers

Though I've been a dad for more than a decade now, I've really
begun to enjoy baking with my kids only in the last few years. Up
until my awakening, baking with the kids was an exercise in self-
restraint, a tension-packed blizzard of flour, *don't-do-that*s, and
cutout cookies enmeshed in some sibling's golden locks.

It finally dawned on me that if you want to bake with kids —
and I really do, especially around the holidays — you must let go
of adult notions of order and cleanliness. You know those
magazine pictures of little kids baking with Grandma or Mom?
No goo running down counters; no flour on faces; Mom looking
like she stepped out of an L. L. Bean catalog. Not at our house.
My kitchen looks like a bomb has dropped on General Mills
when we do our family baking. But now that I accept and expect
that, we all have a lot more fun baking together. Not that I
encourage flour fights, but I can live with the mess if the kids are
pitching in, meeting their own creative needs, and basking in the
self-satisfaction that comes from making one's own food.

Ironically, putting up with a little mess brings an unexpected
result: Once we finish the project at hand, I give each of the kids
his or her own piece of dough, which they'll play with sometimes
for as long as an hour. That gives me plenty of time to finish up
some baking or do the dishes in relative calm. All I do is set up
each of the kids at the kitchen table with a little scrap of dough,
pastry, or whatever — I usually make extra just for this purpose —
and provide a few extras like wax paper, rolling pins, flour, and
cutters — and aprons; everyone wears an apron. They'll roll, beat,
cut, pummel, mold, and stretch for the longest time. They'll
decorate with odds and ends like broken spaghetti (hair), make
raisin eyes and garlic-pressed hair. Sometimes they'll want to
bake their whatevers, throw cinnamon or butter or jelly on them,
and I just go along with it. I don't try to correct or make sense of
their creations; that would only ruin it for them. Even if they've
made a big mess, we can get things looking shipshape in just a
few minutes. Everyone pitches in with the cleanup, and the older
ones wash and dry the things they've used.

Not long ago my youngest — little Sam — brought me one of
the most imaginative pieces of kid baking I've ever seen: two AA
batteries, stuck at 45-degree angles into a hunk of whole wheat
bread dough in a miniature tart pan. He called it his "battery-
operated doughnut."

Wheaten Popovers

MAKES 12 POPOVERS

My dictionary defines a popover as a very light, puffy, hollow muffin. It's right on the first three counts, but there's really almost nothing muffinlike about popovers other than the fact they're sometimes baked in muffin tins and therefore bake up looking like overextended muffins. Popovers are crisp on the outside, for the first few minutes, then they begin to soften as they cool; eat them while they're hot.

Popovers are perfect when you want to add some high drama to a Christmas morning breakfast or New Year's Day breakfast. You can't really get a good popover at a restaurant, and almost nobody makes them — at least I've never been offered one — so they can make quite an impression. These are savory popovers, best eaten with morning egg dishes and potatoes, or for an evening meal featuring a roast or ham, or even soup and salad for that matter.

There are two very important rules for successful popovers. The first is not to peek at them by opening the oven door — at least not until the last 10 minutes — or they are likely to collapse; initially, at least, they have a very fragile structure. The second rule is to make a slash in them 10 minutes before you take them out of the oven. The slash releases the steam; if it builds up inside the shell, steam can make the inside soggy or even make the popovers collapse. So, those are the rules; the truth is that even with these precautions, popovers sometimes deflate. Don't worry too much about it because they will still taste good.

You can increase the amount of whole wheat flour to 1/2 cup if you like, decreasing the unbleached flour to 3/4 cup. But if you add too much whole wheat, you don't get the big rise that makes them so awesome.

> 4 large eggs, lightly beaten
> 1 1/4 cups milk
> 3 tablespoons unsalted butter, melted and cooled
> 1 cup unbleached flour
> 1/4 cup whole wheat flour
> 1/4 teaspoon salt
> 1 teaspoon dried basil (optional)

Preheat the oven to 400° and generously butter 12 muffin cups with no less than a 1/2-cup capacity. (If you have one, you can also use a popover pan, which has narrow, deeper cups.) Also butter the top of the pan, the metal that connects the cups.

Using a whisk, blend the eggs, milk, and butter in a large mixing bowl. Whisk in the flours, salt, and basil just until smooth. Divide the batter evenly among the cups; each should be just about half full. Bake on the lower rack of the oven for 40 minutes; do not open the oven before the time is up. After 40 minutes, slide the shelf out a little. Using a long-bladed knife with a sharp point, make a small puncture on the side of each popover to let the steam escape. Bake for 10 minutes more. Remove the popovers from the oven and gently coax them out of their cups. Serve right away.

Herb Shortcakes

MAKES UP TO 9 SHORTCAKES

These are the savory drop biscuit-cakes I use under the creamed turkey and corn in the next recipe, but they are also excellent alone, for breakfast or dinner. Seasoned with the classic combination of rosemary, sage, and thyme, they taste something like turkey stuffing, and they go wonderfully with egg and potato dishes, soups, salads, and stews.

1 cup unbleached flour
1 cup whole wheat flour
2 teaspoons baking powder
1/2 teaspoon herb salt or regular salt
1 1/2 teaspoons dried sage
1 teaspoon dried rosemary
1/2 teaspoon dried thyme
6 tablespoons cold unsalted butter, cut into 1/4-inch pieces
1 large egg
3/4 cup milk or light cream

Preheat the oven to 425° and lightly butter a large baking sheet, preferably a dark one. In a medium-size bowl, mix the flours, baking powder, salt, and herbs. Add the butter and cut it in with a pastry blender until it is broken into very fine pieces. Beat the egg lightly in a small bowl and stir in the milk or cream; reserve 2 teaspoons of this liquid.

Make a well in the dry ingredients and add the remaining liquid all at once. Stir until uniformly blended in a damp, cohesive mass. Scoop 9 more or less equal-size rounded pieces of dough onto the baking sheet, leaving room between them for expansion. Brush each one with a little of the reserved liquid, then bake for about 17 minutes, until the tops are lightly browned; break one open to see if they are baked through. Transfer the shortcakes to a cloth-lined basket and serve hot. Store leftovers in a sealed plastic bag.

Herb Shortcakes with Creamed Turkey and Corn

MAKES UP TO 9 PORTIONS

This is a great breakfast — or dinner — to serve in the days immediately following Thanksgiving, when the appetite for turkey sandwiches is starting to wane. If you have no chicken or turkey stock on hand, just dissolve a bouillon cube in 1 1/2 cups boiling water.

6 or more Herb Shortcakes (preceding recipe)
1/4 cup unsalted butter
1/3 cup finely chopped onion
5 tablespoons unbleached flour
1 1/2 cups turkey or chicken stock
1 cup milk or light cream
salt and freshly ground pepper to taste
1 teaspoon dried thyme
2 cups cooked turkey in bite-size pieces
1 cup corn, frozen and thawed or leftover cooked
1/2 cup chopped fresh parsley

Prepare the herb shortcakes as directed. As they bake, prepare the creamed turkey: In a medium saucepan, melt the butter over moderate heat. Add the onion and sauté for 3 minutes, stirring often. Add the flour and continue to cook, stirring almost continuously, for 1 minute more. Whisk in the stock and milk or cream.

Simmer the sauce over gentle heat, stirring, until it thickens. Add salt and pepper to taste, then stir in the thyme, turkey, and corn. Simmer a few minutes longer, until the turkey and corn are heated through. Serve over the bottom half of the shortcake, with the other half placed on top but a little off to the side. Sprinkle fresh parsley over the shortcake and serve.

51

Christmas Cookies and Bars

For many people, holiday baking is synonymous with making cookies, and I for one could live quite nicely on that sort of narrow thinking. I love holiday cookies, I eat them by the score, and things have only gotten worse — or should I say better? — since Karen and I have had four little cookie monsters of our own. The six of us can polish off a few dozen holiday cookies and a half gallon of milk in the wink of an eye. It's really a wonder we ever bake enough to give away as gifts, but somehow we manage because we know there's almost nothing nicer than being on the receiving end of a dozen or more homemade holiday cookies.

The beauty of making holiday cookies is the simplicity of it all. From your basic larder of flours, sweeteners, butter, eggs, flavorings, and spices you can make a mind-boggling assortment of cookies and bars. There's none of the intimidation associated with yeasted breads, no rolling of delicate dough (usually). The baking and preparation times are brief, and about the only equipment you need is a mixer, a bowl, and a baking sheet. If you can read, you can make a great holiday cookie, a handmade gift from the heart that will put any paisley tie to shame.

Anybody who has kids knows that they naturally gravitate toward cookie making; around here, it is virtually impossible to reach for the vanilla and butter without a horde of youngsters congregating about the baking table, each invoking the name of a favorite recipe, and demanding, "When do we start?"

We like to encourage our kids' natural desire to bake, especially around the holidays; family baking satisfies their desire to belong, to be a contributing member of the group. There's so much for a child to explore and learn in the simple act of making cookies — measurements, textures, neat tools, interesting sounds and movements, and a lot of other adult stuff that often only occurs above head level. Letting the little ones join in, with carols playing and everyone singing, is the sort of thing that really makes the holidays a special time of year for kids, something they'll remember long after the toys are trashed and the new sneakers are outgrown.

Drop cookies are fun, but I think most kids like cutout cookies best. Cutouts let the kids express their own personal tastes: they get to choose the shapes they want, sometimes only after a bitter dispute over who gets the angel or tyrannosaurus first. The pleasure is compounded, of course, by the fact that you get to eat your favorites after they are baked; and in the case of our two youngest, sometimes even before.

This generous assortment of cookies and bars includes something for everyone. Almost all of them feature whole grain flours, including one made with cornmeal and another with buckwheat flour. We like the nutritional balance of whole grains in our holiday cookies, not to mention the diversity of texture and flavor whole grains add. Once you've tried some of these, we think you'll feel the same way.

Ben's Best Whole Wheat Chocolate Cookies

MAKES ABOUT 36 COOKIES

When he first ate these, my son Ben said they were the best cookies I had ever made; everyone agrees that they are pretty incredible. They're made from all whole wheat flour, but the chocolate disguises that fact if you're trying to slip one by the whole-wheat-wary. The best way to finish these is outlined here, by rolling them in toasted walnuts and confectioners' sugar, which gives them a beautiful mottled surface. At the very least, do coat them with the confectioners' sugar before baking; otherwise you won't get the pretty fissures running through the top, and they'll look rather plain.

> 3/4 cup (6 ounces) unsalted butter, softened
> 1/2 cup honey
> 1/2 cup packed light brown sugar
> 1 large egg at room temperature
> 1 teaspoon vanilla extract
> 1 3/4 cups whole wheat flour
> 1/4 cup unsweetened cocoa powder
> 2 teaspoons baking soda
> 1/2 teaspoon salt
> 2 cups (approximately; about 1/2 pound) toasted walnuts, finely chopped
> confectioners' sugar for rolling the dough balls

In a large mixing bowl, cream the butter, honey, and brown sugar with an electric mixer. After 1 minute, beat in the egg and vanilla. Sift the flour, cocoa powder, baking soda, and salt into a separate bowl. Stir the dry ingredients into the creamed mixture in 3 stages, blending until the dough is smooth and uniform in color. Cover the dough and refrigerate for at least 1 hour. In the meantime, lightly butter 1 or 2 large baking sheets. Preheat the oven to 350° about 15 minutes before you plan to bake the cookies. If you haven't already, finely chop the nuts and place them — and the confectioners' sugar — on separate plates nearby.

Using your hands, form balls of dough about 1 1/4 inches in diameter. Roll the balls first in the walnuts, pressing just hard enough to embed them, then in the sugar to coat heavily. Place the balls about 3 inches apart on the sheets and bake for 15 to 17 minutes. They're done once they have puffed up and then flattened out again. Cool the cookies on the sheets for 1 minute — much longer and they'll stick — then transfer to a rack to finish cooling. Store in an airtight container.

N O T E : As I mentioned, you can skip rolling them in the walnuts and use just the sugar, but the walnut version is well worth the extra step, especially if you're giving them away.

Snow Day Baking

Don't you just love snow days? Even as a typically reserved adult, I still feel a childlike tingle of excitement when I hear a Big One is on the way. When it begins at night, I'm up every hour or so turning on the outside floodlights to check the accumulation. I secretly hope the town plow won't make its first pass for hours yet because I *like* feeling temporarily stranded in our little home, surrounded by oceans of snow. And I love to listen for the kids' reactions when they wake up — "Whoa, would ya look at *that*!!"

Snow days are great baking days. There's excitement in the air — no school! — and a session of family-style baking only makes the day more special. Everybody will want to get in on the act, so think of a good cooperative baking project. Cookies are our favorite, because you can divide up the dough and let everyone go at his or her own pace. Once you've bundled the kids up in snowsuits, scarves, and mittens and sent them off to play, tidy up the kitchen and get out your ingredients. Depending on the number and ages of your children, you may also want to premeasure your ingredients or even make the dough; take it as far as you need to, to make the successive stages work comfortably for you. Then put on the hot chocolate, cue up your favorite Christmas tunes, then call a friend or your parents and let them in on the excitement.

Cardamom Shortbread Cookies

MAKES 50 TO 60 COOKIES

I'm not sure what it is about cardamom that makes it taste so much like it belongs with holiday baking, but maybe — once you've tried these delicate cookies — you can figure it out for yourself. I can, however, tell you how addictive these are; one is never enough, and even three or four will leave you wishing you could have a dozen with a tall glass of milk to chase them down. The texture is great — so short they literally fall apart in your mouth the way a good shortbread should. The flour is all whole wheat, so there's a pleasant, earthy nuttiness to them as well. I like to dust them with confectioners' sugar, but they are still wonderful without it.

> 1 3/4 cups whole wheat flour
> 2/3 cup confectioners' sugar
> 1/2 cup cornstarch
> 2 teaspoons ground cardamom
> 1/4 teaspoon salt
> 1 cup (1/2 pound) unsalted butter at room temperature
> 1 teaspoon vanilla extract
> finely grated zest of 1 lemon
> 1 1/2 cups confectioners' sugar for dusting the cookies (optional)

Sift the flour, 2/3 cup confectioners' sugar, cornstarch, cardamom, and salt into a mixing bowl. In a separate bowl, cream the butter with an electric mixer just until soft, beating in the vanilla and lemon zest before you turn the machine off.

Stir the dry ingredients into the butter in 3 stages, fully incorporating each addition before adding the next. When the dough is evenly blended, knead it 3 or 4 times in the bowl, then divide the dough in half. Tear off 2 sheets of wax paper, each about 16 inches long, and place half of the dough on each. Roll each half of the dough into a fat log and place each log lengthwise on the sheet of wax paper.

Begin to roll the log up in the wax paper, tightening it as you go, squeezing the dough into a log 1 1/4 to 1 1/2 inches in diameter. Roll the paper all the way up, then fold or pinch the ends of the paper to seal. Refrigerate the dough for about 1 hour; it may be refrigerated longer, even for several days, but first slip the dough into a plastic bag.

When you are ready to bake, preheat the oven to 325° and get out 2 large cookie sheets. Unwrap the dough, then use a sharp serrated knife to slice off sections of dough approximately 1/3 inch thick; use a sawing motion, not just downward pressure. Place the cookies on the sheet, leaving just a little space between them; these won't spread. Bake for 20 to 25 minutes, until the bottoms are lightly browned.

Transfer the cookies to a cooling rack. If you are dusting the cookies with the sugar, let them cool for 5 minutes, dredge them through the sugar quickly, and put them back on the rack. Dust them a second time once they've cooled completely. Store in an airtight container, with tissue paper between layers.

About Cardamom

Exotic, sweet, with lemon undertones, for me cardamom says "Happy Holidays." I use it throughout the season, in everything from hot spiced cider to yeasted breads and cookies.

Perhaps the most accurate observation I've read about cardamom comes straight out of the technical bulletin published by the American Spice Trade Association: No other spice comes even close to its particular flavor profile.

Cardamom — *Elettaria cardamomum* — is a member of the ginger family. About 80 percent of the cardamom sold in this country comes from Guatemala and most of the rest from India. Like coffee, cardamom is a mountain-grown crop, thriving at altitudes of 2,500 to 5,000 feet.

And why is it so expensive? Again like coffee, cardamom is a labor-intensive crop — which accounts for its high cost — because the pods do not ripen all at the same time. The plants must be picked four or five times during harvest season. And not just anyone can pick cardamom. It can be difficult to judge ripeness because the color of the outer capsule remains green while the seed pods change from an immature white to a ripe dark brown. Pickers must be skilled enough to judge the more subtle signs of a mature pod.

For flavor purposes, the intensity of cardamom is variable, depending on whether you grind your own cardamom seeds at home, use preground cardamom from seeds only, or buy ground cardamom made from whole pods. My advice is to seek out different types at different sources — health food stores, Middle Eastern or Indian markets (which often sell the best grades), and supermarkets — and draw your own conclusions, experimenting with them in different recipes. If you find one is weaker in flavor, simply add more the next time; if it is particularly strong, you can use less. And if you buy whole pods — the health food store is a good source — and want to grind your own seeds, either use a mortar and pestle or crush the pod between sheets of wax paper with a rolling pin. The incredible aroma makes the effort an absolute joy.

A bonus: Whole cardamom pods last a very long time, at least several holiday seasons.

Peanut Butter Carob Cookies

MAKES ABOUT 5 DOZEN COOKIES

Here's a very uncomplicated, all-whole-wheat cookie our kids like to make entirely on their own and give to their friends as Christmas presents. Ben, our oldest, reads off the ingredients and instructions and acts as general counsel; Tess and Ali roll the dough into balls; and little Sam drives everyone nuts by snitching balls of raw dough from the baking sheets and shoving them into his mouth. Good thing that this makes plenty of cookies. Good as they are for giving, my favorite time for these is straight off the sheet — cooked, that is — while they are still warm and cakey.

- **6 tablespoons unsalted butter, softened**
- **1 cup honey**
- **1/2 cup unflavored vegetable oil**
- **1 cup peanut butter, preferably freshly ground**
- **2 large eggs**
- **1 teaspoon vanilla extract**
- **2 1/2 cups whole wheat flour**
- **1/2 cup carob powder**
- **1 tablespoon ground cinnamon**
- **2 teaspoons baking soda**
- **1/2 teaspoon salt**

Using an electric mixer, cream the butter and honey in a large mixing bowl. Add the oil, peanut butter, eggs, and vanilla and beat until smooth.

Into a separate bowl, sift the flour, carob powder, cinnamon, baking soda, and salt. Stir the dry ingredients into the liquid in 3 stages, until uniformly blended. Cover the dough and let it rest at room temperature for 15 minutes while you preheat the oven to 350°. Get out 1 or 2 baking sheets.

Roll the dough into balls about 1 1/2 inches in diameter and place them on the sheets, leaving about 2 inches between them. Using the tines of a fork, flatten the balls in a crisscross pattern; they should be not quite 1/2 inch thick. Bake for 10 to 12 minutes, until the tops are just slightly resistant to light finger pressure; they should not dimple when you touch them.

Briefly cool the cookies on the sheets, then transfer them to a rack to cool. Store in an airtight container.

61

Buckwheat Walnut Shortbread Cookies

MAKES ABOUT 40 COOKIES

Of all the interesting flours out there, I think buckwheat is probably the least appreciated and the least understood. And after many years of working with buckwheat in all sorts of baking recipes, I'm convinced that it has to be used in moderation to be appreciated; the flavor is just too wild, too assertive on its own. This cookie is a really fine way to experience buckwheat, especially if you and your family have never tried it before. The earthy buckwheat flavor isn't hidden by any means, but it's mellowed by the cocoa, walnuts, and sweetening. I love the look and shape of these cookies: dark, studded with a mosaic of walnuts, with a slightly wrinkled surface. They can be served as is, but if you aren't shipping or packaging them you have the option of drizzling on the chocolate glaze, which increases any cookie's appeal exponentially.

> 1 cup confectioners' sugar
> 3/4 cup buckwheat flour
> 3/4 cup unbleached flour
> 1/2 cup cornstarch
> 1/4 cup unsweetened cocoa powder
> 1/4 teaspoon salt
> 1 cup (1/2 pound) unsalted butter, softened
> 1 teaspoon vanilla extract
> 1 cup (about 1/4 pound) finely chopped walnuts

CHOCOLATE GLAZE (OPTIONAL)

> 2 tablespoons unsalted butter
> 3 ounces semisweet chocolate
> 2 teaspoons water

Into a large bowl, sift the sugar, flours, cornstarch, cocoa, and salt. In a separate bowl, cream the butter with an electric mixer until soft and fluffy. Beat in the vanilla.

Stir the dry ingredients into the butter in 4 stages, stirring until thoroughly blended after each addition. When all the flour has been incorporated, stir in the walnuts; the dough will be stiff, so it may be easier to knead the nuts in. Tear off a piece of wax paper about 18 inches long. While the dough is still in the bowl, shape it into a rough log, then lay it lengthwise in the center of the paper. Using floured hands, pat the dough into a brick about 1 inch high by 2 1/4 inches wide and about 14 inches long. Fold the paper closed on top, pinch and seal off the ends and carefully slide this long brick onto a baking sheet. Refrigerate for at least 1 hour before slicing.

When you are ready to bake the cookies, get out 2 cookie sheets and preheat the oven to 325°. Unwrap the dough and use a sharp serrated knife to cut the brick into slices just a hair thicker than 1/4 inch; use a sawing motion, rather than pushing the knife down through. Lay the slices on the sheets, leaving only about 3/4 inch between them; these swell a little, but they don't really spread. Bake for 20 to 25 minutes, closer to the lesser time if you have a dark sheet, the greater if it is shiny and reflective; the surface should feel firm to the touch.

Cool the cookies on the sheet for several minutes, then transfer them to a rack to finish cooling. When they are completely cooled, store in an airtight container. If you want to glaze them with chocolate, apply it an hour or so before serving. To make the glaze, melt the butter in the top of a double boiler. Add the chocolate and let it melt, then whisk until smooth. Whisk in the water. Put the cookies on a sheet of wax paper and simply drizzle the hot chocolate onto the cookies from a spoon, going this way and that to make crisscrossing lines.

Soft Cornmeal Nut Cookies

MAKES ABOUT 40 COOKIES

This is a soft, simple cookie with a slightly gritty texture from the cornmeal and nuts. The cookies have a tangy lemon and cream cheese bite, with just a hint of cinnamon. Do try to use freshly ground cornmeal from a mill or a health food store, preferably ground on the premises; it makes all the difference in the world. By comparison, the commercial variety is rather bland. For the holidays I like to roll these cookies in sugar before I bake them, which gives the surface a glossy, scaled look. These are best eaten within a few days, which shouldn't present any problem at all.

> 1 cup (1/2 pound) unsalted butter, softened
> 1/4 pound cream cheese, softened
> 1 1/4 cups packed light brown sugar
> 1 large egg
> 1 tablespoon fresh lemon juice
> freshly grated zest of 2 lemons
> 1 teaspoon vanilla extract
> 1 3/4 cups unbleached flour
> 1/2 cup yellow cornmeal, preferably stone-ground
> 1 teaspoon baking soda
> 1 teaspoon ground cinnamon
> 1/2 teaspoon salt
> 2 cups (about 1/2 pound) shelled walnuts, finely chopped
> sugar to roll the cookies in

Using an electric mixer, cream the butter and cream cheese. Beat in the brown sugar, about half at a time, followed by the egg, lemon juice, lemon zest, and vanilla. In a separate bowl, mix the flour, cornmeal, baking soda, cinnamon, and salt. Stir the dry ingredients into the creamed mixture until smooth, then stir in the walnuts. Cover the dough and let sit at room temperature for 15 minutes. Meanwhile, preheat the oven to 350° and lightly butter 2 cookie sheets.

Using floured hands, roll the dough into 1 1/2-inch balls, roll the balls in sugar, and place them on the sheets, leaving about 3 inches between them. If you have extra baking sheets, put a second one below the sheets you are baking on; these cookies seem to come out with a better, lighter texture if the bottom heat isn't too intense.

Bake for about 13 or 14 minutes, until lightly browned and puffy; they may or may not lose their puff, but either way they will be excellent. Cool the cookies for a minute or two on the sheets, then transfer them to a rack to cool. Store the cookies in an airtight container.

Cookies for Santa

Our kids, and I imagine all kids, love to leave cookies for Santa Claus. They love to think of the jolly fat guy kicking back in Pop's big easy chair, taking a deserved break, slugging down cookies and milk, because, heck, he's bound to need some nourishment before heading off for the rest of the world.

So be sure to think of Santa when you're doing your holiday baking. Have each of the kids make a single, special cookie or small batch of cookies for the big guy; don't forget the reindeer either. They can be left out on a tray, or the kids can wrap them up as they please; a paper lunch bag with holiday stickers and a simple bow is easy for most kids to do. Make sure Santa leaves a note, acknowledging each of the kids by name, assuring them that these were indeed *the best* cookies he's run into since leaving the North Pole. And make sure he finishes every drop of milk too.

It's All in the Packaging

As much as I think the postal clerks of this nation are a dedicated, conscientious lot, my rule of thumb for packaging baked goods I plan to ship is always to remember that they're probably also underpaid, overworked, and in a hurry on the very days my parcel of Christmas cookies is on its way to Grandmother's house. So I always hope for the best but prepare for the worst.

If your household is anything like ours, then you get a ton of packages around the holidays — toys for the kids, grapefruit from Florida; these parcels are full of good packaging materials you can recycle. Rigid boxes, sheets of puffy plastic, Styrofoam peanuts — put all this stuff aside in a corner for safekeeping.

Anything baked has the best chance of safe delivery if you use the box-within-a-box method; the inner one is carefully packaged, sealed, then placed within a second cushioned box. Of course it looks prettier if the inside box is not a box at all but a decorative tin.

With most of the recipes in this book I have given you some idea whether or not the item is a good shipper; some things are either too loose, fragile, or otherwise inappropriate for sending. So first make sure the item is shippable.

Most of the cookies are perfect for mailing. It's worth taking the extra time to wrap each one individually in plastic wrap or wax paper before you place it in the box or tin. I like to line the container with colorful tissue paper and use more tissue paper between the layers for added cushion. Stack the cookies almost up to the lid, leaving room for a tissue paper cushion on top. Styrofoam peanuts work well for the outer box cushioning, but I don't like to put them right in with the food.

Some of the cakes and fruitcakes are good shippers too. Start by tracking down a tin or box that's basically the same shape, just a little bigger, so there's not much room for shifting. Seal the cake in a plastic bag and place it in the cushioned container; those puffy sheets of plastic work well for cakes.

If you are using a box-within-a-box, bundled-up newspaper is an excellent cushion if you have no other packaging material on hand. Pile it high in the box so you have to push down some on the flaps to close the box.

Then hope for the best and forget about writing messages on the parcel like "Cookies — Please Do Not Crush." Those are the first ones to get sat on.

Rose Water Lemon Curd Cookies

MAKES ABOUT 20 COOKIES

This is an easy variation on Rose Water Almond Nuggets and probably the only way you could improve on that cookie. The combination of lemon and rose water gives these cookies a lovely fragrance and an incredible flavor. You don't need a full recipe of lemon curd to make these, but if you're making lemon curd anyway, it's worth it to double or triple the cookie dough and make a lot of these. They'd be especially suited to a large holiday party; a single layer of these special cookies packed in a small, pretty box would be a sweet gift to send home with each of the women. These don't ship particularly well because the lemon curd is likely to stick to the packaging material.

1 recipe dough for Rose Water Almond Nuggets (following recipe)
1 recipe Lemon Curd (page 217) at room temperature

Prepare the cookie dough as directed and refrigerate for 30 minutes. Preheat the oven to 350°.

When you're ready to bake, shape the dough as directed in the recipe, using floured hands, but make the balls slightly larger, about 1 1/4 inches in diameter. Dip the bottom of a glass in flour and flatten each ball to a thickness of about 1/2 inch.

Using your thumb, make an imprint in the surface of each ball, about the size of a 1/2 teaspoon measuring spoon. When you press down, the sides of the cookie may crack a little, but just mold it back together with your fingers. Bake the cookies as directed, then transfer them to a rack to cool.

Roll the cooled cookies in the confectioners' sugar to cover the tops; do the bottoms too, if you like. Spoon about 1 teaspoon lemon curd into each depression, then lay the cookies directly on a serving tray or plate. Cover and refrigerate, but take them out about 20 to 30 minutes before serving.

Rose Water Almond Nuggets

MAKES ABOUT 24 COOKIES

My wife, Karen, loves roses (both of our daughters have the middle name Rose), so I came up with this little surprise just for her, using her favorite fragrance. She loved these nuggets so much she named them the best cookie of all time. The texture of these bite-size treats is pleasantly dry, with the soft, delicate flavor of roses mingling beautifully with the subtleness of toasted almonds. I think any woman — mother, friend, or wife — would love a little box of these for Christmas. You can find rose water at most health food stores or Middle Eastern stores. For an extraspecial gift, pour rose water into a pretty little glass container, one with a tight-fitting cap or lid, and include it with these cookies. Karen likes to splash a couple of teaspoons on her face and shoulders after a summer shower.

> 1 cup (1/4 pound) shelled almonds
> 1/2 cup (1/4 pound) unsalted butter, softened
> 1/4 cup confectioners' sugar
> 1 1/2 tablespoons preservative-free rose water
> 1/4 teaspoon salt
> 1 cup whole wheat pastry flour
> additional confectioners' sugar for dusting the cookies

Preheat the oven to 350°. Spread the almonds on a large baking sheet and roast for 8 minutes, then tilt them off the sheet and onto a plate to cool. When cool, process the nuts to a fine meal in either a food processor or a blender; if you're using the latter, do it in 2 batches and stop the machine periodically to stir up the nuts so they don't compact under the blades. Set aside.

Using an electric mixer, cream the butter and confectioners' sugar. Beat in the rose water, salt, and almond meal. Stir in the flour 1/2 cup at a time. When the dough is uniformly blended, cover and refrigerate for at least 3 hours or overnight.

When you are ready to bake, preheat the oven to 350°. Meanwhile, if you have chilled the dough overnight, let it sit at room temperature until it is just soft enough to shape. Using your hands — floured, if necessary — roll the dough into balls about 1 inch in diameter. Place them about 1 inch apart on an ungreased baking sheet; they don't spread. Press each one down just a little, using your fingers. Bake for about 15 minutes, until they're just barely beginning to turn golden brown. Cool momentarily on the sheet, then transfer the cookies to a cooling rack. While they are still a little warm, roll each one in confectioners' sugar and return to the rack. Roll them in the sugar one last time before storing in an airtight container.

*Christmas
Cookies
and Bars*

Oatmeal Mincemeat Cookies

MAKES ABOUT 30 COOKIES

*The only thing better than a soft, grainy oatmeal cookie has to be this: one
with mincemeat in it. This dough is unusual in that it calls for heavy
cream, which makes for a very tender, moist cookie with a texture not
unlike rich coffee cake; needless to say, these cookies go down very easily.
If you're making the mincemeat specifically for this recipe, try to cut all
the fruit pieces — apples, dates, and such — on the small side so you don't
end up with huge chunks hanging out of your cookies.*

> 1/2 cup (1/4 pound) unsalted butter, softened
> 3/4 cup packed light brown sugar
> 1 large egg at room temperature
> 1/2 cup heavy cream at room temperature
> 1 teaspoon vanilla extract
> 1/2 cup rolled oats (*not* instant)
> 2 cups whole wheat flour
> 1 teaspoon baking powder
> 1/2 teaspoon salt
> 1 1/2 cups Mincemeat (page 220)
> sugar to roll the dough in

In a large mixing bowl, cream the butter and brown sugar with an
electric mixer, beating for 1 minute. Beat in the egg until smooth,
then add the cream and vanilla and beat for another 10 seconds. Stir
in the oats.

In a separate bowl, mix the whole wheat flour, baking powder,
and salt. Stir the dry ingredients into the creamed mixture half at a
time, just until blended. Fold in the mincemeat. Cover and refrigerate the dough for 15 minutes. Meanwhile, preheat the oven to 375°
and lightly butter 1 or 2 large cookie sheets.

Form the dough into balls about 1 1/2 inches in diameter and
roll them in the sugar. Place the balls about 3 inches apart on the
sheet. Bake for 12 minutes. Cool the cookies on the sheet briefly,
then transfer them to a cooling rack. What you don't eat warm
should be placed in an airtight container, where they'll remain in
good condition for a couple of days.

Coconut Almond Paste Cookies

MAKES ABOUT 30 COOKIES

*This combination of coconut, almonds, and maple syrup works like a
dream. These are my wife Karen's invention; the first time she made these
I ate about seven of them, and I could have eaten that many more again.
They're soft, like an oatmeal cookie, only not quite so chewy, studded
throughout with pieces of almond paste. It's important to blend the dough
thoroughly first, then just stir the almond paste in on the last couple of
turns. Otherwise it breaks into pieces that are too small. You can make
your own almond paste (page 219) or buy the commercial kind in a
specialty food store or the gourmet section of larger supermarkets. A
durable cookie, this one is a good shipper.*

- 1/2 cup (1/4 pound) unsalted butter, softened
- 1 cup pure maple syrup, warmed to body temperature
- 1 teaspoon vanilla extract
- 1/4 teaspoon almond extract
- 1 1/2 cups whole wheat flour
- 1/2 cup unbleached flour
- 1 teaspoon baking powder
- 1/2 teaspoon salt
- 3/4 cup unsweetened shredded coconut (available at health food stores) or sweetened flaked coconut
- 1/2 pound almond paste (1/2 recipe on page 219), crumbled into coarse pieces

Using an electric mixer, cream the butter, gradually adding the
maple syrup in a thin stream. Beat in the vanilla and almond ex-
tracts. Set aside.

Sift the flours, baking powder, and salt into a separate bowl.
Stir the dry ingredients into the creamed mixture in 2 stages, then
blend in the coconut. Stir in the crumbled almond paste using just a
couple of strokes. Cover the dough with plastic wrap and refrigerate
for 15 minutes. In the meantime, preheat the oven to 350° and lightly
butter 2 baking sheets, preferably not dark ones.

After 15 minutes, roll the dough into balls about 1 1/4 inches in
diameter using floured hands. Place the balls about 2 1/2 inches
apart on the sheets. Bake for approximately 15 minutes, until the
tops are just slightly resistant to gentle finger pressure. Store in an
airtight container.

Whole Wheat Chocolate Chunk Fantasy Cookies

MAKES ABOUT 32 COOKIES

If I were ever to start a cookie business, going up against the likes of Mrs. Field, this would be my signature cookie. These cookies might not be the cause of her eventual decline, but they might be of mine — I have almost no control when they're around. They're big and fat, like a Mrs. Field's cookie, and they have the same sweet, right-from-the-oven softness. And no one would ever guess my secret: in addition to the chocolate chunks, these are packed with raisins and sunflower seeds that have been toasted with tamari (or soy sauce). Sounds funny, but the tamari gives the seeds an exotic salty flavor that complements the chocolate and raisins very nicely.

> 1 cup hulled raw sunflower seeds
> 1 scant tablespoon soy sauce or tamari
> 1 cup (1/2 pound) unsalted butter, softened
> 1 1/2 cups packed light brown sugar
> 2 large eggs at room temperature
> 2 teaspoons vanilla extract
> 2 3/4 cups whole wheat flour
> 1 teaspoon baking soda
> 1/2 teaspoon salt
> 1/2 pound semisweet chocolate, chopped into chunks
> 1 cup raisins

Put the seeds in a large skillet and place them over moderate heat. Toast them for about 6 minutes, stirring often, until they turn a rich golden color. Stir in the tamari or soy sauce and immediately turn off the heat. Continue to stir the seeds for 20 more seconds, then scrape them onto a plate to cool.

In a large mixing bowl, cream the butter and brown sugar with an electric mixer on high speed for 1 minute. Add the eggs one at a time, beating well after each addition. Beat in the vanilla. In a separate bowl, mix the whole wheat flour, baking soda, and salt. Stir the dry ingredients into the creamed mixture in 3 stages until uniformly blended. Mix in the chocolate chunks, raisins, and toasted sunflower seeds. Cover the dough and refrigerate for 15 minutes while you preheat the oven to 350°.

To get a good soft cookie, use a heavy but not too dark sheet; tinned steel is good. Even better is one of those "cushion air" sheets, two sheets in one with an airspace in between to buffer the heat. In any case, butter the sheet lightly. Using your hands, make balls of dough about the size of golf balls and place them on the sheet no closer than 3 inches apart. Bake for 15 minutes. The tops will still be soft after 15 minutes, but the cookies will firm up as they cool; they'll stay tender, however, even after they cool. Cool the cookies on the sheet for 5 minutes, then transfer them to a rack to finish cooling. Be sure to wrap these individually if you plan to ship them.

The Best Hot Cocoa

If I am no match for the emperor Montezuma, who is said to have consumed more than 50 cups of his favorite cocoa beverage each day, I love a strong cup of hot cocoa around the holidays. It's one of the best come-in-from-the-cold drinks you can wrap your chilled hands around. After the Snowball Fight of the Century, sledding, skating, or Christmas tree hunting, a hot mug of cocoa lifts the spirits and chases away the chill. Add a plateful of Christmas cookies, and we call that a party. Hot cocoa is so simple to make from scratch, using cocoa powder, there's really no reason to settle for those instant packets; the real thing is so much better.

Cocoa powder is basically just real chocolate minus most of the cocoa butter. It tends to form lumps when added directly to a quantity of milk, lumps that no amount of whisking can smooth; you may have noticed this if you ever tried to wing it making hot cocoa. The best way around this predicament, I've found, is to combine the cocoa powder with sugar and a small amount of water in a saucepan. Bring to a boil, whisking until smooth, then add your milk. Works every time.

As for specifics, for each cup of hot chocolate you want to make, whisk together 1 scant tablespoon unsweetened cocoa and 1 1/2 tablespoons sugar in a saucepan. Whisk in 1/4 cup water per serving and bring to a boil. Reduce the heat to medium, then whisk in 3/4 cup milk for each serving. Heat almost to the boiling point, stirring pretty much continuously. Just before removing from the heat, whisk in 1/4 teaspoon vanilla extract per serving. Pour into mugs and serve piping hot.

Of course, you can top each mug with a dollop of whipped cream and a sprinkle of cinnamon — a finish I think even Montezuma would agree is fit for a king.

Coffee Hazelnut Cookies with Coffee Icing

MAKES ABOUT 36 COOKIES

*These delicate rectangular refrigerator cookies are excellent even without
the icing, but the icing intensifies the coffee flavor and gives them an
attractive finish, flecked with tiny coffee grounds. We often go one step
further, serving these with coffee ice cream and — what else? — hot hazelnut
coffee. These cookies would make a great gift for a serious coffee lover,
packed in a basket with several pounds of his or her favorite javas. You can
hold this dough in the refrigerator for several days — or in the freezer for a
month or more — and then slice and bake at will. That's the beauty of a
refrigerator cookie like this; it's* incredibly *convenient.*

> 1 1/3 cups whole wheat flour
> 3/4 cup confectioners' sugar
> 1/3 cup cornstarch
> 1 1/2 tablespoons finely pulverized coffee beans (I use a coffee mill)
> 1/4 teaspoon salt
> 1 cup (about 1/4 pound) toasted hazelnuts (see page 111 for toast-
> ing instructions), ground to a fine meal
> 1 cup (1/2 pound) unsalted butter at room temperature
> 1 1/2 teaspoons vanilla extract

COFFEE ICING

> 1 cup confectioners' sugar
> 1 tablespoon finely pulverized coffee beans
> 1 tablespoon (approximately) milk

Sift the flour, 3/4 cup confectioners' sugar, cornstarch, 1 1/2 tablespoons coffee, and salt into a bowl. Stir in the ground hazelnuts. In a
separate bowl, cream the butter with an electric mixer and beat in
the vanilla. Using a wooden spoon, stir the dry ingredients into the
butter in 3 stages, until uniform.

Tear off a piece of wax paper about 18 inches long and lightly
flour it. Scrape the dough onto the wax paper and then, using
floured hands, shape it into a brick about 1 inch high, 3 inches wide,
and about 13 inches long; it doesn't have to be precise. Fold the
paper over the top and fold the ends to make the wrapping secure.
Slide the dough onto a small cookie sheet and refrigerate for at least
1 hour or up to 3 days covered with foil. This dough may also be
frozen for up to 1 month.

When you're ready to bake, preheat the oven to 325° and get out 1 or 2 cookie sheets. Unwrap the brick and cut it into slices about 1/3 inch thick. Carefully lay the slices on the sheet about 1 inch apart. Bake for 25 minutes, a little less if you are using a dark cookie sheet. Let the cookies cool for 2 minutes on the sheet, then transfer them to a rack to finish cooling.

While the cookies are cooling, make the icing: In a small bowl, mix 1 cup confectioners' sugar and 1 tablespoon coffee. Stir in almost a full tablespoon of milk. If it seems too dry, stir in a few more drops of milk — just enough to make a thick emulsion. When the cookies are cool, carefully spread a little of the icing over each cookie. Once the icing has firmed up, you can store them in a shallow box, preferably only one layer deep.

N O T E : If you do freeze the dough, let it sit at room temperature for about 30 minutes before slicing.

Orange-Spiked Hazelnut Cookies

MAKES ABOUT 30 COOKIES

These chewy whole wheat cookies use both finely chopped hazelnuts and hazelnut butter, available at health food stores. Just a word about the dough: My experience is that most of these nut butters make the dough grainy, almost crumbly, though this crumbliness pretty much disappears after the cookies are baked. The texture is most workable if you knead the dough 5 or 6 times in the bowl before you begin to shape the cookies. And when you pick up the dough to form balls, give it a good squeeze in your hand to compact it. Resist the temptation to use more chopped hazelnuts in the dough, or it will be too difficult to handle. These cookies ship well.

> 3/4 cup (6 ounces) hazelnut butter
> 1/2 cup (1/4 pound) unsalted butter, softened
> 1 cup sugar
> 1 large egg at room temperature
> 1/2 teaspoon orange extract
> finely grated zest of 1 orange
> 1 3/4 cups whole wheat flour
> 1 teaspoon baking soda
> 1/2 teaspoon salt
> 3/4 teaspoon ground cinnamon
> 1/2 cup (2 ounces) toasted hazelnuts, finely chopped

Lightly butter 1 or 2 large baking sheets, preferably not dark ones, and preheat the oven to 350°.

Using an electric mixer, cream the hazelnut butter and unsalted butter in a mixing bowl. Gradually beat in the sugar, followed by the egg, orange extract, and orange zest. Combine the flour, baking soda, salt, and cinnamon in a separate bowl and stir these dry ingredients into the creamed mixture in 3 stages. Add the chopped nuts and work them into the dough by hand, kneading the dough 5 or 6 times in the bowl.

Using your hands, form balls of dough about 1 1/4 inches in diameter. Lay them on the sheet, about 2 inches apart, and flatten them with the tines of a fork to about 1/2 inch thick. Bake for about 13 minutes, until the tops of the cookies give just a tiny bit of resistance to light finger pressure. Cool the cookies for 2 minutes on the sheets, then transfer them to a rack to cool. As soon as the cookies are cool, store them in an airtight container.

Whole Wheat Cream Cheese Dough

MAKES ENOUGH DOUGH FOR ABOUT
40 CRESCENTS OR 48 RUGELACH

*This melt-in-your-mouth dough makes a wonderful crescent cookie as well
as the Whole Wheat Rugelach (page 82), my adaptation of the traditional
Jewish cookie. I use whole wheat pastry flour here for the exceptionally
tender results it delivers. If your pastry flour has largish pieces of visible
bran, I suggest sifting it first and discarding the bran, which can make the
dough too brittle for these delicate cookies. Measure the flour after you sift.
If at any point when you are rolling the dough it gets too soft and
unmanageable, just slide the dough onto a baking sheet, cover, and
refrigerate it for 10 minutes or so to firm it up. If you don't feel confident
enough at first to use all whole wheat flour here, substitute up to 1 cup
unbleached flour for an equal portion of the whole wheat.*

1/4 pound cream cheese at room temperature
1 cup (1/2 pound) unsalted butter at room temperature
1 1/2 teaspoons vanilla extract
1 teaspoon finely grated lemon zest
2 cups whole wheat pastry flour
1/2 teaspoon salt

In a large mixing bowl, cream the cream cheese, butter, vanilla, and
lemon zest with an electric mixer until smooth and blended. Sift the
flour and salt into a separate bowl, then stir the dry ingredients into
the creamed mixture in 3 stages until evenly blended; the dough will
be pretty firm, almost like a soft pie pastry.

Tear off 2 sheets of wax paper, each about 12 inches long, and
flour them generously. Divide the dough in half, flour each half,
then flatten each on the wax paper into a disk about 3/4 inch thick.
(If you are making the Whole Wheat Rugelach, divide the dough
into quarters and make 4 disks.) Refrigerate the dough for at least
1 1/2 hours; you can refrigerate the dough overnight, but you should
overwrap the wax paper in foil, then let the dough sit at room
temperature for about 10 or 15 minutes or until it is malleable
enough to roll. This dough also freezes beautifully, up to 3 months.

77

Oatmeal Date Pinwheel Cookies

MAKES ABOUT 72 COOKIES

Pinwheel cookies are a little extra trouble to make, but they're worth it for the fun and eye appeal. Kids love the swirl, and they also love to slice the dough log. Even my 3-year-old, Sam, likes to lay the cookies on the baking sheet as I slice the log. This cookie is made with an oatmeal dough and filled with a mixture of finely chopped walnuts, dates, cocoa, and brown sugar. The recipe makes 2 logs, each of which yields about 36 cookies, so you can slice and bake one log and keep the other one in the fridge for up to a week and bake it when you need it. The logs can also be wrapped in plastic and foil and frozen for up to 2 months. A firm-textured cookie, this one ships well.

DOUGH
    1 cup (1/2 pound) unsalted butter, softened
    1 1/2 cups packed light brown sugar
    1 large egg at room temperature
    1 large egg yolk
    1 1/2 teaspoons vanilla extract
    1 cup rolled oats (*not* instant)
    3 cups unbleached flour
    2 teaspoons baking powder
    3/4 teaspoon salt

FILLING
    2 cups (about 1/2 pound) toasted walnuts (see page 111 for toasting
      instructions)
    1 1/2 cups pitted dried dates
    2 tablespoons unsweetened cocoa powder
    2 teaspoons ground cinnamon
    2/3 cup packed light brown sugar
    2 tablespoons unsalted butter, softened

To make the dough, cream the butter with an electric mixer. Beat in the brown sugar, followed by the egg, egg yolk, and vanilla.

    Put the oats into a blender and pulverize them to make a fine flour. Into a separate bowl, sift the oat flour, unbleached flour, baking powder, and salt. If any pieces of oats remain in the sifter, add them to the bowl. Stir the dry mixture into the creamed ingredients in 3 or 4 stages; you may have to use your hands to gently knead in the last batch of dry. Tear off 2 sheets of wax paper, each

about 14 inches long. Divide the dough in half, placing half the dough in the center of each sheet. Shape each one into a square about 3/4 inch thick. Wrap the dough in the wax paper and refrigerate for 1 hour.

Meanwhile, make the filling. Once the toasted walnuts have cooled, place them in a food processor with the dates, cocoa, and cinnamon; process until the mixture resembles fine, damp crumbs. Add the brown sugar and butter and process for a few more seconds. Place the filling in a mixing bowl and set it aside.

When you're ready to assemble the logs, remove one piece of the dough from the fridge. Remove the dough from the wax paper and lightly dust one side of the paper with flour. Roll the dough on the paper into a 12- by 12-inch square. Evenly spread half of the filling on the dough, leaving a margin of about 1 inch on one of the edges. Go over the filling lightly once or twice with a rolling pin to even it out.

Starting at the end opposite the one with a 1-inch margin, roll the dough up tightly, like a carpet. This is a little tricky to explain, but the rolling is best accomplished by grasping both sides of the wax paper and pushing it forward and down to move the log along. This does a more even rolling job than using your hands on the log itself. Just before you reach the end, moisten the margin with a wet fingertip, then complete the roll; it will seal itself. Rewrap the log in the same piece of wax paper and slide it into a large plastic bag. Seal and refrigerate for at least 30 minutes. Repeat the process for the other piece of dough.

When you're ready to bake, preheat the oven to 350° and lightly butter 2 large cookie sheets. Using a sharp serrated knife, saw the log into slices about 1/3 inch thick. Lay the slices on the sheet about 1 1/2 inches apart; they don't spread much at all. Bake for 12 to 15 minutes, just until the edges barely turn brown. Let the cookies cool on the sheet for a minute, then carefully transfer them to a rack to cool. Store the cooled cookies in an airtight container.

A Word About Temperatures

Throughout this book you will find numerous references to the temperatures of various ingredients — cold butter, warm milk, room temperature eggs. There's a reason why: temperatures determine how ingredients behave, and that behavior can make or break a recipe. In bread baking, for instance, liquid ingredients are almost always lukewarm, to provide an environment in which yeast can flourish. Add *cold* milk to your dissolved yeast, and the dough may never rise. Here are a few other temperature guidelines to consider:

• *Butter* — For butter cakes and most cookies, softened or room temperature butter (the terms are often used interchangeably) is the norm. Softened butter should give under light finger pressure, but shouldn't feel squishy soft to the touch. Softened butter creams easily with sugar (it doesn't jump around in the bowl); it holds air that's whipped into cake batter and blends effortlessly with other ingredients.

For pie pastry, cold butter is required. The cold butter is broken into tiny pieces, with a pastry blender or two knives, but remains solid. These tiny bits of butter release steam when the pastry is baked, separating the pastry ever so slightly to create the flakiness prized by pie lovers.

Tart pastry is more crumbly, less flaky, than pie pastry. The butter and flour are blended much more thoroughly, and therefore it's fine to use slightly cool or room temperature butter.

• *Cream Cheese* — Like butter, cream cheese "creams" with sugar and blends more easily with other ingredients if it is first softened to room temperature.

• *Eggs* — In most cases, room temperature eggs are called for; if cold eggs are added to creamed butter, the mixture may congeal, which will alter the volume and texture of butter cakes. Eggs separate most easily when they are cold, so separate them while they are cold if a recipe requires it. To bring cold eggs to room temperature, put them in a small bowl or measuring cup and cover with hot tap water. Let them sit for 3 minutes, then remove them from the water and proceed.

• *Cream* — Heavy cream, which is preferable to whipping cream for whipping purposes because it has more butterfat, whips to its greatest volume in a chilled bowl with chilled beaters.

Opal's Cream Cheese Crescent Cookies

MAKES ABOUT 40 COOKIES

These delicate cookies are from the recipe files of my mother-in-law, Opal Price. Opal sends a dozen or so of these to us each year in her annual box of Christmas cookies, and I've always ranked them near the top of the 10 or so varieties that she sends. Traditionally Opal uses a cream cheese dough made with white flour, but my version uses the Whole Wheat Cream Cheese Dough on page 77. Inside each crescent is a sweet little surprise of preserves, and it's finished with a coating of confectioners' sugar — simple but delicious. Because these cookies are rather fragile, be sure to pack them with care, boxed within a box.

> **1 recipe Whole Wheat Cream Cheese Dough (page 77)**
> **1/3 cup preserves, such as raspberry, peach, or strawberry**
> **confectioners' sugar for coating the cookies**

Form the prepared dough into 4 disks rather than 2; chill.

Working with one disk at a time, roll the dough a little thicker than 1/8 inch on a lightly floured sheet of wax paper. Using a 2 1/4-inch biscuit cutter or glass, cut the dough into circles, keeping the cuts as close together as possible. As you make each cut, transfer the cutout to a lightly floured section of your work area. Before you begin to fill the cookies with the preserves, collect all of the scraps, press them together, wrap, and refrigerate.

Place about 1/2 teaspoon preserves in the center of each circle, then fold the dough in half over the preserves so the edges meet. As you press down along the edge to seal it, also push the ends slightly toward one another so the straight edge becomes arched; now it looks like a crescent. Transfer each cookie to a large ungreased cookie sheet as you shape them, leaving about 1 1/2 inches between them. When the cookie sheet (or sheets) is full, cover loosely with plastic wrap and refrigerate for 15 minutes while you preheat the oven to 350°. Roll and fill the scraps, placing them on another sheet.

When the oven has preheated, bake the cookies for 20 minutes. Allow the cookies to cool on the sheet for 5 minutes, then transfer them to a rack to cool. While they are still barely warm, gently roll them in confectioners' sugar, coating them heavily. Finish cooling the cookies on the rack. Store these crescents flat in single layers, not all jumbled and loose, because they are pretty delicate.

Whole Wheat Rugelach

MAKES 48 COOKIES

Rugelach are bite-size rolled cookies traditionally served on Rosh Hashanah and at Hanukkah. They are most often made with a cream cheese and butter dough, a combination that results in a very tender — and rich! — cookie; here I use the Whole Wheat Cream Cheese Dough on page 77. Rugelach are fun to make, and kids are usually more than happy to help. In fact, since the dough is divided into 4 pieces, you can enlist 4 helpers and let them roll their own piece and use the type of preserves they like. A raisin-date-cinnamon-nut filling goes on top of the preserves, then the dough is cut into wedges and the wedges are rolled up. If you plan to ship these, pack them extra carefully, because they are fragile.

1 recipe Whole Wheat Cream Cheese Dough chilled

FILLING

1 cup (4 to 5 ounces) walnut pieces
1/2 cup raisins
1/2 cup pitted dates
1/3 cup packed light brown sugar
1/2 teaspoon ground cinnamon
1/2 cup thick strawberry, apricot, peach, or other preserves

GLAZE

2 tablespoons milk
2 tablespoons sugar
1/2 teaspoon ground cinnamon

As the dough chills, make the filling. Put the walnuts, raisins, dates, brown sugar, and cinnamon into a food processor and process until the nuts and fruit are chopped into very fine pieces. (Lacking a food processor, chop the walnuts and fruit finely by hand, then mix with the brown sugar and cinnamon.) Lightly butter 2 large, heavy baking sheets.

Working with one piece of dough at a time, roll the dough into a 9-inch circle on a piece of lightly floured wax paper. Stir the preserves to smooth them out, then spread 2 tablespoons preserves over the circle. Sprinkle about one quarter of the nut mixture evenly over the preserves and gently press it in with your hand.

Using a sharp knife, cut the circle into 12 wedges, as you would a pie. Loosen the wedges with a spatula or knife blade and roll each one up, starting at the wide end; keep the roll snug but not overly tight, because you'll force the filling out if you press too hard. Place each one on the sheet with the point (seam) down, keeping them about 1 1/2 inches apart. Cover the rugelach loosely with plastic wrap and refrigerate for 15 minutes while you preheat the oven to 350°.

Just before baking, brush the rugelach lightly with the milk. Mix the sugar and cinnamon in a small bowl and, as you brush each cookie with milk, sprinkle it with a little of the cinnamon and sugar mixture.

Bake the rugelach for 20 minutes; don't be too alarmed if some of the preserves leak out onto the sheet. Let the rugelach cool for about 2 minutes on the sheet, then transfer them to a rack and cool. Store flat, in an airtight container.

Maple Cutout Cookies

MAKES ABOUT 40 COOKIES

In the cutout cookies department, I don't think you can get much better than this. These cookies begin to smell incredibly good a few minutes before you take them out of the oven, and so the real challenge becomes exercising restraint when you finally do take them out. Be firm with yourself, because the maple flavor is more pronounced once they have cooled and crisped. The maple frosting is optional; it can be either spread or piped on the cookies with a pastry bag. Kids love these.

> 1 cup (1/2 pound) unsalted butter at room temperature
> 1 cup packed light brown sugar
> 1/2 cup pure maple syrup, warmed to about body temperature
> 1 large egg at room temperature
> 1 teaspoon vanilla extract
> 2 cups unbleached flour
> 2 cups whole wheat pastry flour
> 2 teaspoons baking powder
> 1/4 teaspoon salt

FROSTING

> 2 cups sifted confectioners' sugar
> 2 tablespoons pure maple syrup
> 1 or 2 tablespoons milk

Using an electric mixer, cream the butter and brown sugar on high speed for 1 minute. Gradually add the maple syrup, egg, and vanilla. Sift the flours, baking powder, and salt into a separate bowl, then gradually stir the dry ingredients into the creamed mixture until uniform in consistency. Flour the dough, divide it in half, and flatten each half into a 1/2-inch-thick disk on a sheet of wax paper. Over-wrap in plastic and refrigerate for 30 to 60 minutes before rolling. (The dough can be refrigerated longer, though you will probably have to let it sit at room temperature for 5 to 10 minutes before it can be rolled.)

About 15 minutes before you're ready to bake, preheat the oven to 350° and get out 1 or 2 large cookie sheets. Working with one batch of dough at a time, roll the chilled dough not quite 1/4 inch thick — about as thick as a thick pie pastry — on a floured work surface. Cut the dough with a knife or use favorite cutters, keeping the cutouts close together. (Gather the scraps, press them together, wrap, and refrigerate; once chilled, roll, cut, and bake.)

Place the cookies on ungreased cookie sheets, leaving 1 inch between them. Bake for 12 to 15 minutes, just until the edges take on the slightest bit of browning — no longer; this will give you crisp cookies when they cool. If, on successive batches, you can catch them just before this point, you'll have a softer cookie when it cools — whatever appeals to you. We all like the crisp. Cool the cookies for a couple of minutes on the sheets, then transfer them to racks to finish cooling. When they are fully cooled, you can frost them if you like.

To make the frosting, whisk together the confectioners' sugar and maple syrup. Whisk in the milk, 1/2 teaspoon at a time, until it reaches the consistency you want — a little thinner for spreading, a little on the thick side for piping on with a pastry bag.

Store the cookies flat, individually wrapped in plastic wrap.

Raisin Date Bars with Mascarpone Topping

MAKES 20 BARS

Since I've discovered mascarpone, the luscious creamy Italian cheese, I've been trying it with just about everything, with an incredibly high success rate: crackers, cookies, fruit — all of it gets put to the mascarpone taste test. One of the best combinations is mascarpone with dates. The rich tartness of the cheese plays just right with the sweet, chewy dates. So I brought the two together in this bar. The bottom layer is a whole wheat and oat cookie, the middle a puree of dates and raisins, the top mascarpone sweetened with a little confectioners' sugar; the combination really hits the spot. When I make a batch of these, the family's repeated requests for "just one more sliver" usually finish the whole thing off in one sitting. These bars are served cold, and they need at least a couple of hours in the fridge for the cheese to firm up after it has been stirred and spread on the bars. So plan accordingly. These bars won't ship well, and if you do take them to a party, make sure you pack them so nothing touches the top layer, or it will stick.

CRUST
- 1 cup whole wheat flour
- 2/3 cup rolled oats (*not* instant)
- 1/2 cup packed light brown sugar
- 1/2 teaspoon baking powder
- pinch of salt
- 1/2 cup (1/4 pound) unsalted butter at room temperature, cut into tablespoon-size pieces

FILLING
- 1 cup chopped pitted dates
- 1 cup raisins
- 1 cup water
- 1/4 cup packed light brown sugar
- juice of 1 lemon
- 1 teaspoon vanilla extract

MASCARPONE TOPPING
- 1 pound mascarpone cheese
- 1/3 cup confectioners' sugar

Preheat the oven to 325° and lightly butter a 7- by 11-inch glass baking pan; set the oven at 350° if you're using a shiny metal pan. Make the crust by mixing the whole wheat flour, oats, 1/2 cup brown sugar, baking powder, and salt in a large bowl. Add the butter and rub it into the dry ingredients with your hands until you have uniformly damp crumbs. Scatter the crumbs evenly in the pan, then press the mixture in. Bake for 30 minutes, then cool on a rack.

To make the filling, combine the dates, raisins, water, and brown sugar in a small saucepan. Bring to a boil, then reduce the heat to a low boil and cook, uncovered, for 13 to 15 minutes, stirring often. When the fruit mixture is fairly thick, with just a little free liquid still in the pan, remove it from the heat and transfer it to a bowl to cool. When the filling has cooled to room temperature, puree it in a food processor or blender, adding the lemon juice and vanilla as you do so.

Spread the fruit mixture evenly on the partially cooled crust, right up to the edges. Bake for another 15 minutes, then transfer the pan to a rack and cool completely.

To make the topping, stir the cheese and confectioners' sugar together in a bowl just until smooth; if you stir too much, it may turn grainy.

After the bars have cooled, spread the mascarpone topping evenly over the fruit mixture using the back of a spoon. Cover and refrigerate for at least 2 hours before slicing into bars.

Chocolate Chip Pecan Brownies

MAKES 16 BROWNIES

Brownies — giving, getting, making — are one of my favorite holiday indulgences; brownies with ice cream a dessert without equal. Some people go in for very fudgy brownies, others for the cakey type. This one is somewhere in the middle, with fudgy leanings; too fudgy and I find that they're a hassle to cut, wrap, and ship. If this recipe isn't quite a model of health consciousness, it does incorporate whole wheat pastry flour, which is good for the fiber but bad because a weak-willed character like me tends to justify eating three or four of these at a time just by waving the whole wheat flag; the calories mount. But heck, these are the holidays.

> 1/2 cup (1/4 pound) unsalted butter
> 1/4 pound semisweet chocolate
> 2/3 cup packed light brown sugar
> 2 large eggs at room temperature
> 1 teaspoon vanilla extract
> 3/4 cup whole wheat pastry flour
> 1/4 teaspoon salt
> 1/2 cup semisweet chocolate chips
> 1/2 cup (2 ounces) chopped pecans, preferably toasted (see page
>   111 for toasting instructions)

Butter and lightly flour an 8- by 8-inch cake pan; I like glass for these brownies. Preheat the oven to 350°.

In a small, heavy saucepan, begin to melt the butter over very low heat. Add the 1/4 pound semisweet chocolate, occasionally swirling the pan so the hot butter runs over the chocolate; this will facilitate the melting. When the chocolate is soft, add the brown sugar, then whisk to smooth it out. Remove from the heat.

Beat the eggs in a medium-size bowl until frothy; stir in the vanilla. Sift the pastry flour and salt into another small bowl. Whisk the melted chocolate into the beaten egg until smooth, then whisk in the flour. Fold in the chocolate chips and pecans.

Scrape the batter into the prepared pan and smooth with a fork. Bake for 40 minutes; it will puff (but eventually settle), and the top will develop very small fissures. Cool the brownies thoroughly on a rack. For easy slicing, you should really cover them with plastic and chill for about 1 hour to firm up the chocolate chips; that's not mandatory, but keep it in mind if you'll be taking these to a party or shipping them out, and you want nice neat squares. Whether or not you are shipping them, wrap individually in plastic wrap and store in an airtight container.

Rich Maple Pecan Rum Bars

MAKES 30 BARS

I love cookies and bars made with oats, and this has to be one of the best I've come across in that category. What you have is a buttery oat dough, half of which is pressed into the pan and then covered with a loose, rum-spiked maple and cream filling. Then the rest of the dough is sprinkled on top. The filling seeps into both the bottom and top crusts, so the bar is very moist, especially in the center. These are good travelers, but whether you are shipping them or just serving them at home, they're easiest to cut if you refrigerate them first; that firms them up enough to cut them cleanly and to wrap them (individually) if necessary. You'll love to eat these out of hand, but try one with a small scoop of vanilla or butter pecan ice cream — it's a dessert you won't soon forget.

CRUST

> 2 cups unbleached flour
> 3/4 cups rolled oats (*not* instant)
> 1 teaspoon baking powder
> 1/2 teaspoon salt
> 3/4 cup (6 ounces) unsalted butter, softened
> 2/3 cup packed light brown sugar

FILLING

> 1 cup heavy cream
> 2/3 cup pure maple syrup
> 1/3 cup packed light brown sugar
> 1/4 cup unsalted butter
> 2 tablespoons rum
> 1/2 cup (2 ounces) finely chopped pecans

Preheat the oven to 375° and lightly butter an 8- by 12-inch baking dish; I use glass for these bars. Make the crust: In a mixing bowl, toss together the flour, oats, baking powder, and salt. In a separate bowl, cream the 3/4 cup butter and 2/3 cup brown sugar with an electric mixer for 1 minute. Add the flour mixture and stir until thoroughly blended. Spread about half of this dough in the prepared dish, then press it into the bottom and only slightly up the sides. (Cover and refrigerate the rest of the dough.) Bake for 15 minutes, then cool on a rack for 15 minutes. Lower the oven temperature to 350°.

After the crust has cooled for 15 minutes, prepare the filling. Combine the cream, maple syrup, 1/3 cup brown sugar, and 1/4 cup butter in a saucepan. Bring to a boil over medium heat and boil vigorously for 2 minutes. Remove from the heat and stir in the rum. Pour the filling over the bottom crust, then sprinkle the pecans evenly over it. Crumble the remaining dough over the filling and bake for 25 minutes. Put the pan on a rack and cool to room temperature. Refrigerate for several hours before slicing into bars. Wrap the bars individually in plastic wrap and store in an airtight container in a cool spot.

Lemon Curd Bars

MAKES ABOUT 20 SMALL BARS

I think a lemon bar should be pretty straightforward, with as few surprises as possible — and that's what I find so appealing about these. There's just a buttery crust and lemon curd for the topping, with a little powdered sugar to finish them off. Even though the lemon curd sets rather firmly, these wouldn't be my first choice for a shipping cookie, since the top can still be squished. But if you can't resist shipping these out to a lemon-loving son, daughter, or friend, wrap them individually in small pieces of wax paper and pack them in a larger flat tin in a single layer. Before you begin baking the crust, have all your lemon curd ingredients ready to go, because you have to pour the hot curd over the crust while it's baking.

> 1 cup unbleached flour
> 1/2 cup whole wheat flour
> 1/2 cup confectioners' sugar
> 9 tablespoons unsalted butter, melted
> 1 recipe hot Lemon Curd (page 217)
> confectioners' sugar for dusting the bars

Preheat the oven to 350° and lightly butter a glass 7- by 11-inch baking pan. In a medium-size bowl, sift the flours and confectioners' sugar. Stir in the melted butter, then rub the mixture with your fingers until you have an even, crumbly mixture. Spread these crumbs around the pan, then press them in; use your fingertips so you leave little peaks and valleys in the crust. Bake for 30 minutes.

As soon as you begin baking the crust, start making the lemon curd. When you're about to add the butter, remove the double boiler from the heat. Take the insert out of the pan, place it on a hot pad, and begin whisking in the pieces of butter. When the butter is all incorporated, push a piece of plastic wrap directly onto the surface of the curd.

When the crust has baked for 30 minutes, take it out of the oven and pour the hot curd on top; it should spread out on its own, but you can coax it with a spoon if it has become a little firm. Bake for 10 more minutes, then transfer the pan to a cooling rack. Give the bars a light dusting of confectioners' sugar while they are still hot, then another dusting once they have cooled. Cut the bars at room temperature, but store them, covered, in the fridge. Bring the bars to room temperature before serving.

Spirited
Cakes

Mention holiday cakes, and the first thing most folks think of — more often than not with trepidation — is fruitcake. For reasons I understand perfectly well, fruitcake in this country has a reputation among the general public close to Velveeta's among cheese connoisseurs. I know because of my own early indoctrination to fruitcake, which began near the front entrance at Woolworth, where the fruitcakes were stacked into pyramids in their snow-scene boxes. Like the 12-packs of tube socks we bought there, they were long on quantity, short on quality, and only slightly more edible.

I haven't been to a Woolworth in some time, so I can't tell you if they're still selling fruitcakes. But I can tell you with certainty that no store-bought cake — fruitcake or otherwise — can match the holiday cakes you can bake at home using fresh, good-quality ingredients. And that goes for most of the fancy, expensive cakes you can buy in decorative tins at gourmet shops: compared to home-made, they don't hold a candle. And homemade fruitcake really *is* terrific.

On the following pages you will find a collection of cakes I enjoy making for my family and friends during

this festive season. Yes, there is a favorite fruitcake — this one made with pears and port — and a ginger honey cheesecake. There are a couple of chocolate cakes, and several more spiked with spirits. Most are made with at least a portion of whole grain flour, much to their advantage.

If these cakes have anything in common, besides being simple to make, it's their way of capturing the celebratory sense of the season in a single bite. It might be a spice or combination of spices. It might be the recognition of a seasonal fruit or the fragrant interplay of rum and maple. And sometimes it isn't even readily apparent just what it is; these things can be hard to put your finger on . . .

. . . and to keep your fingers off. Who can resist the opportunity to fortify one's holiday spirit with a slice of tender buttermilk cake, rich fruitcake, or chocolate almond torte at this time of year? Not me! And why even bother to resist? Holidays are meant for baking and consuming huge slabs of those sinfully rich cakes we only nibble at all the rest of the year. So pick a cake and start baking, and the sooner the better. As my friend Vid's T-shirt says: Life is uncertain . . . eat dessert first!

Chocolate Almond Torte

MAKES 14 TO 16 SERVINGS

This is my kind of cake, one that needs only a light dusting of confectioners' sugar to dress it up. It was inspired by a lovely chocolate cake in Deborah Madison's The Savory Way *(Bantam). This one uses a little more chocolate, some honey in place of the sugar — which helps keep the cake quite moist — Kahlúa, and more ground nuts; it comes out very dense and compact, a one-layer nut-fudge cake fantasy, and therefore it's a good traveling cake, something to take along to a holiday party.*

> 2 cups (about 1/2 pound) shelled almonds
> 2 tablespoons sugar
> 1/2 cup (1/4 pound) unsalted butter
> 1/3 cup strong brewed coffee
> 1/3 cup honey
> 5 ounces semisweet chocolate
> 3 tablespoons unbleached flour
> 1 tablespoon unsweetened cocoa powder
> 1/4 teaspoon salt
> 4 large eggs at room temperature
> 1/3 cup sugar
> 1 tablespoon Kahlúa or Amaretto
> confectioners' sugar for dusting the cake

Preheat the oven to 350°. Spread the almonds on a large baking sheet and toast for 10 minutes. Transfer them to a plate. Once they have cooled, grind them — along with the 2 tablespoons sugar — to a fine meal in a food processor. (You can also do this in a blender, though it is more of a hassle because you must do it in smaller batches and stop often to fluff up the nuts with the handle of a wooden spoon so they don't compact too much.) Set the ground nuts aside. Keep the oven set at 350°.

Over very low heat, combine the butter, coffee, and honey in a small saucepan. When the butter starts to melt, add the chocolate and swirl the pan occasionally to help melt the chocolate; do not let it boil. Once the chocolate has melted, smooth the mixture with a whisk and set aside. While that mixture cools, lightly butter and flour a 9-inch springform pan.

Sift together the flour, cocoa, and salt and set aside. Using an electric mixer, beat the eggs and sugar in a large mixing bowl for about 6 minutes, until pale and thick. Switch to a big whisk, then beat in the Kahlúa or Amaretto, followed by the melted chocolate mixture — add it gradually — and then the sifted ingredients. Stir in the nuts until the batter is evenly blended. Scrape the mixture into the prepared pan and bake for approximately 50 minutes, until the cake has puffed up nicely (it will settle) and a tester inserted in the middle of the cake comes out clean.

Transfer the cake to a rack. When the cake starts to shrink, remove the side of the pan and cool thoroughly. Dust with confectioners' sugar before serving. This cake keeps nicely at room temperature for a couple of days and about twice as long in the fridge. Just keep it covered snugly in plastic wrap or foil.

N O T E : You can, if you wish, add brandy-, bourbon-, or rum-soaked raisins to this cake, a touch I like very much. A few hours or the day before, pour 2 tablespoons of any of those liquors over 3/4 cup raisins. Cover and set aside, stirring occasionally. Fold the raisins, and any liquor which might remain, into the batter after you stir in the nuts.

Spirited
Cakes

Annie's Poppy Seed Cake with Maple Nut Topping

MAKES 2 MEDIUM-SIZE LOAVES,
ABOUT 18 SERVINGS

*I think anything maple makes a great holiday treat, especially this cake
I discovered at a potluck dinner held at our local elementary school. After
finishing off more than my share (I kept claiming the extra slices were for
my greedy kids), I set out to find its contributor. The baker turned out to
be my good friend Annie Valdmanis, who said she got the original recipe
from* Diet for a Small Planet *(Ballantine), the classic that focused
considerable attention on the world hunger problem. I've tinkered just a
little with the original, but this is basically her recipe with the maple
topping she and I both adore; the maple syrup we use comes from right
down the road, from the farm of our mutual friend Maggie Brox.*

CAKE
    3/4 cup milk
    3/4 cup poppy seeds
    finely grated zest of 1 lemon
    1 large egg
    3/4 cup flavorless vegetable oil
    1 cup packed light brown sugar
    1 teaspoon vanilla extract
    1 cup whole wheat pastry flour
    1 cup unbleached flour
    2 1/2 teaspoons baking powder
    1/2 teaspoon salt
    1/2 teaspoon ground cinnamon
    1/2 teaspoon ground nutmeg, preferably freshly grated
    1/3 cup buttermilk or plain yogurt
MAPLE NUT TOPPING
    1/2 cup pure maple syrup
    1/2 cup light cream
    2 tablespoons unsalted butter
    1/2 cup (2 ounces) finely chopped walnuts

In a small saucepan, scald the milk, then stir in the poppy seeds and
lemon zest and remove from the heat. Let the seeds soak for 30
minutes. In the meantime, butter and lightly flour 2 4- by 8-inch loaf
pans and preheat the oven to 350° 15 minutes ahead of baking.

    Using a whisk or an electric mixer, beat the egg, oil, brown
sugar, and vanilla extract. Stir in the poppy seeds and milk.

Sift the flours, baking powder, salt, and spices into a separate bowl, adding any bran particles that won't pass through the sifter. Stir the dry mixture into the liquids in 3 stages, just until smooth. Stir in the buttermilk or yogurt. Turn the batter into the prepared pans and bake on the center rack for 45 to 55 minutes, until the top is springy to the touch and a tester inserted in the center emerges clean. Let the cakes cool in the pans for 15 minutes, then invert them onto separate serving plates.

To make the topping, bring the maple syrup, cream, and butter to a boil in a small saucepan. Boil for 10 minutes, stir in the nuts, then cool in the pan for 2 minutes. Spread the topping evenly over the cakes, letting it drizzle down the sides. To store, cover loosely with foil and refrigerate.

N O T E : This also makes an excellent plain cake without the maple nut topping.

*Spirited
Cakes*

Wheaten Mace Pound Cake

MAKES 1 LARGE CAKE, ABOUT 10 TO
12 SERVINGS

Mace comes from the tough husk of the fruit Myristica fragrans, *the core
of which is the nutmeg kernel. When the husk is dried and ground, you get
the ground mace we use in baked goods, with a flavor similar to — though
milder than — nutmeg. Mace is traditional in buttery pound cakes like
this, though this one breaks with tradition by using brown sugar and a
majority of whole wheat flour. The sour cream helps give the crumb a
wonderfully soft texture. This cake rises beautifully, which is sometimes
not the case with whole wheat cakes; you get a nicely domed, browned top.
It makes a good plain slicing cake, or you can dress it up for a more
formal affair by serving it with sliced or poached fruit (like the figs on
page 221) and whipped cream or mascarpone cheese.*

> 1 cup (1/2 pound) unsalted butter, softened
> 2/3 cup granulated sugar
> 2/3 cup packed light brown sugar
> 5 large eggs at room temperature
> 1 1/2 teaspoons vanilla extract
> 1 1/2 teaspoons lemon extract (or use the zest of 2 lemons and omit)
> finely grated zest of 1 lemon
> 1 1/2 cups whole wheat pastry flour
> 1 cup unbleached flour
> 1 1/2 teaspoons mace
> 1 teaspoon baking powder
> 1/2 teaspoon salt
> 1/3 cup sour cream

Butter a 9- by 5-inch loaf pan, preferably not a dark one, and line it
with wax paper; butter the wax paper. Preheat the oven to 325°.

Using an electric mixer, cream the butter in a large bowl. With
the beater still running, gradually add the sugars, beating until light
and fluffy. Add the eggs one at a time, beating well after each
addition. Beat in the vanilla, lemon extract, and lemon zest.

Into a separate bowl, sift the flours, mace, baking powder, and
salt; add any pieces of bran that may remain in the sifter. Stir half of
the dry ingredients into the creamed mixture until smooth, then stir
in the sour cream. Add the rest of the dry ingredients and stir just
until smooth.

Scrape the batter into the prepared pan. Smooth out the top with the back of a spoon and bake for 1 hour and 15 minutes, until a tester inserted in the center of the cake comes out clean. Cool in the pan for 20 minutes, then remove from the pan and cool on a rack. While the cake is still a little warm, peel off the wax paper. If you're not serving it right away, wrap the cake in plastic wrap once it has cooled to room temperature and slip into a plastic bag.

A Baking Day Checklist

Mistletoe, carolers, family gatherings — it's easy to get caught up in the spirit of holiday baking. But the spirit alone, we have learned, won't move you very far without some basic preparations and considerations *before* baking day. Among them:

• Practice makes perfect. By practice I mean simply trying out a recipe at least once before you decide this is something you want to bestow on your friends and family. Practice lets you know whether *you* like the cookie or whatever, which indeed you should if you'll be making 10 dozen. Practice also lets you learn the little tricks and techniques inherent in almost every baking recipe — the little fold or twist of the dough that makes for a graceful touch.

• Shop ahead. Baking day can turn into a nightmare when you're looking around for dried cherries at the last minute, only to find they have to be ordered specially. Check your ingredient list carefully and have everything on hand before baking day. This goes for the obvious stuff too; too many times I've assumed I had plenty of flour or baking powder on hand, only to find out otherwise. Do you have the right pan?

• Delegate. Many baking recipes involve steps or procedures, like chopping nuts or grating lemon zest, that any willing set of hands can help with. With children — because you often have to explain a procedure patiently — there may be no actual time saving for you. But efficiency on baking day sometimes has to take a backseat to conviviality if we hope to nurture the holiday spirit.

• And to wrap up . . . don't forget all the tins, boxes, tissue paper, bags, stickers, shipping tape, and greeting cards you might need to get your goods in the mail or down the road without delay.

Ginger Honey Cheesecake

MAKES 12 TO 14 SERVINGS

Cheesecake is a festive dessert at any time of year, but this one — flecked with little pieces of golden raisins and candied ginger — packs the holiday mood into every creamy bite. It would be just the thing to serve on Christmas Eve when friends and family stop by or to take along to a Christmas dinner; either way, remember you have to make this, and just about any cheesecake, the day ahead so it has plenty of time to chill and mellow.

CRUST

  1 cup (about 8 full crackers) fine graham cracker crumbs
  1 tablespoon sugar
  1/4 cup cold unsalted butter, cut into 1/4-inch pieces

FILLING

  1 pound cream cheese at room temperature
  1/2 cup honey
  1/2 cup sugar
  2 large eggs at room temperature
  1 1/4 cups sour cream
  1 tablespoon fresh lemon juice
  1 1/2 teaspoons vanilla extract
  2/3 cup finely minced golden raisins
  1 to 2 tablespoons (to taste) finely minced candied ginger

Butter the sides only of an 8-inch springform pan. Make the crust by mixing the cracker crumbs and 1 tablespoon sugar in a bowl. Add the butter and rub it in until all of the crumbs are dampened by the fat. Distribute the crumbs loosely but evenly in the pan and press them in, pushing them slightly up the sides. Cover and chill while you make the filling; preheat the oven to 350°.

Using an electric mixer, cream the cream cheese, honey, and sugar until light and fluffy. Beat in the eggs one at a time, then add the remaining ingredients and continue to beat until evenly blended; use the greater amount of ginger if you want a pronounced ginger flavor, the lesser amount for a subtle effect. Scrape the filling into the pan and bake for 1 hour and 15 minutes. Cool the cake thoroughly on a rack — it will take several hours — then cover, still in the pan, and refrigerate for 12 hours before unmolding and slicing.

NOTE: I have played around some with baking cheesecakes in a water bath, curious to see if it made any difference in the final cake. It seems to improve the texture a little bit, making it creamier. And I'm not sure if this is just a coincidence, but my water bath cakes don't split on top after they come out of the oven, perhaps because they don't rise as much. In any case, if you would like to experiment on your own, simply wrap the bottom of your springform pan in a single sheet of aluminum foil, pushing it snugly up the sides. Pour a scant inch of hot water into a large, shallow casserole and place the springform pan in it. Bake as usual, leaving the pan in the water after you take it out of the oven, until the water cools off. Cool and chill as usual.

Spirited
Cakes

Bourbon Pecan Cake

MAKES 14 TO 16 SERVINGS

This cake turns whole wheat flour to its advantage like no other; with the whole wheat you get just the right amount of firmness and compactness to soak up the maple bourbon glaze that gets brushed on after the cake is cooked. This cake is quite dark and pretty, with a texture like pound cake. The outside is studded with chopped pecans, with more pecans inside. This cake is excellent on its own, with coffee, or served with a mound of maple-sweetened whipped cream — or butter pecan ice cream — on the side. If you don't want a big hit of bourbon, you can simply omit the glaze or boil off the alcohol as described on page 105.

>1 1/2 cups (about 6 ounces) finely chopped pecans, preferably toasted (see page 111 for toasting instructions)
>1 cup whole wheat flour
>1/2 cup whole wheat pastry flour
>1 teaspoon baking powder
>1/2 teaspoon ground nutmeg, preferably freshly grated
>1/4 teaspoon salt
>3/4 cup (6 ounces) unsalted butter, softened
>2/3 cup packed light brown sugar
>3 large eggs at room temperature
>1 teaspoon vanilla extract
>1/2 cup pure maple syrup at room temperature
>1/3 cup bourbon

GLAZE
>2 tablespoons pure maple syrup
>2 tablespoons bourbon
>1 tablespoon fresh lemon juice

Generously butter a 9-inch kugelhopf pan and sprinkle about 1/2 cup nuts; cover as much territory as you can and expect many to fall to the bottom (actually top) of the pan. With the pan still bottom up, dust the interior, including the center tube, with a little flour — not whole wheat — then turn the pan over and *gently* tap it against the counter. Put back in any nuts that fall out. Preheat the oven to 350°.

Sift the flours, baking powder, nutmeg, and salt into a bowl; set aside.

Using an electric mixer, cream the butter and brown sugar in another bowl until fluffy. Add the eggs one at a time, beating well after each one; add the vanilla. Mix together the 1/2 cup maple syrup

and 1/3 cup bourbon, gradually adding about half of it to the creamed mixture in a thin stream. With the mixer on low speed, beat in about half of the dry ingredients, followed by the remaining maple bourbon, then the rest of the dry; beat just until smooth. Fold in the reserved pecans.

Distribute the batter evenly in the prepared pan and bake for about 45 minutes. When done, the cake will be springy to the touch and a tester inserted into the cake will come out clean. Cool the cake in the pan for 20 minutes, then put a cake plate over the pan and invert. If the cake doesn't drop right out, gently rap the pan and plate on the counter.

Make and apply the glaze while the cake is still warm. Simply heat the 2 tablespoons maple syrup, 2 tablespoons bourbon, and lemon juice in a small saucepan and brush it all over the cake with a pastry brush; lacking one, just spoon it on. Serve at any temperature, wrapping the cake snugly in plastic wrap after it has cooled. This will keep up to a week in the fridge.

Burning Off Alcohol

Cakes soaked in rum, brandy, and other spirits are part of the holiday tradition. Some people, however, like the flavor but prefer theirs without a heavy hit of alcohol. You can't eliminate every last trace of alcohol, but you can burn off most of it by heating your rum, brandy, or whatever in a nonreactive skillet and then igniting it with a match — a *long* match. Turn the heat off, then let the flame burn out on its own. Dim the lights; the blue flame can be hard to see in bright light. If you want to reduce the alcohol content further, you have to do it by reducing the liquid that remains in the skillet; there's not enough alcohol left to burn it off at this point. As you reduce the liquid, you intensify the flavor, so you may want to dilute the remaining liquid essence with water.

Pear and Port Fruitcake

MAKES 1 LARGE CAKE,
ABOUT 16 SERVINGS

*I love cooking with fresh pears, so when I first saw the recipe this cake was
modeled after — developed by Bob Chambers, former executive chef of
American Express Publishing Corporation — it caught my eye
immediately. The fresh pears are cooked down to a thick sauce in a little
sugar and port. They're combined with molasses and dried cherries, among
other things, to give the cake a lustrous, almost mahogany color. It's
really pretty. Extra port is brushed on the finished cake, so it is quite
moist and keeps very well. A basket of fresh pears, with this gorgeous cake
sitting in the center, is a gift any pear lover would appreciate.*

> **3 large ripe pears (I use Anjou), peeled, cored, and cut into smallish
> chunks**
> **1 cup ruby port**
> **1/4 cup sugar**
> **1/2 cup (1/4 pound) cold unsalted butter, cut into 1/2-inch pieces**
> **1/2 cup packed light brown sugar**
> **1/4 cup unsulfured molasses or pure maple syrup**
> **3 large eggs, lightly beaten**
> **finely grated zest of 1 lemon**
> **finely grated zest of 1 orange**
> **1 1/2 cups dried sour cherries**
> **1 cup dried currants**
> **1 1/2 cups whole wheat pastry flour**
> **3/4 cup unbleached flour**
> **2 teaspoons baking soda**
> **2 teaspoons ground cinnamon**
> **1/4 teaspoon salt**
> **1 cup (about 1/4 pound) shelled walnuts, coarsely chopped**
> **additional 1/2 cup ruby port to brush on the cake**

In a medium-size saucepan, combine the pears, 1/2 cup port, and
sugar. Bring to a boil, then cook at a not-too-vigorous boil for about
20 minutes, until the pears are quite soft. Using a potato masher,
mash the pears into a sauce; do this right in the pan. Cook for about
5 minutes more, stirring occasionally, until the pears have the approximate consistency of applesauce. Scrape the pear sauce into a
bowl and stir in the butter. When it has melted, stir in the brown
sugar, molasses, eggs, lemon zest, and orange zest. Set aside.

As that mixture cools, steam the dried cherries and currants for 5 minutes in a covered saucepan. Transfer them to a bowl, then pour the remaining port over them and set aside. Preheat the oven to 300°, then butter and lightly flour a 9-inch tube pan; I like my kugelhopf pan for this cake. Don't forget to butter and flour the center tube as well.

Sift the flours, baking soda, cinnamon, and salt into a bowl. Stir the dried cherries and currants, along with the liquid, into the pear mixture. Stir in the dry mixture, about half at a time, into the liquids, stirring until evenly blended. Fold in the walnuts. Spoon the batter into the prepared pan, then bake for approximately 1 hour and 20 minutes, until a tester inserted into the center of the cake comes out clean. Cool the cake in the pan for 15 minutes, then invert it onto a plate; if it doesn't drop right out, bring the cake pan and platter down on the counter with a little force (but don't use a breakable plate!).

Cool the cake thoroughly, then brush 1/4 cup port over the entire surface of the cake. Cover well with plastic wrap, let sit overnight, and brush with another 1/4 cup port on the following day. Wrap thoroughly in plastic wrap. This cake will keep at room temperature for up to a week, longer if kept in the fridge, but bring the slices to room temperature before serving. If you like, you can brush individual slices with port just before serving.

Wheaten Savarin with Rum Maple Syrup

MAKES 1 LARGE CAKE,
ABOUT 14 SERVINGS

I have long been fond of the individual rum-soaked cakes the French call babas au rhum. I once worked at an inn where we made the rich, yeasted babas in muffin tins, then completely immersed them in rum syrup for hours to become totally saturated—as did some of the guests who ate them; they can be rather heady. This savarin is a larger version of those babas, baked in a kugelhopf pan. After it is baked, the cake is left in the pan, the crusty bottom is sliced off, and the maple rum syrup is poured over the cake and down the sides of the pan. Once the cake is cooled, it is inverted onto a plate and served either at room temperature or slightly chilled. You can fill the hole in the center of the cake with sweetened whipped cream or, if you want to get really fancy, with Lemon Curd (page 217) cut with whipped cream as for the Light Lemon Tart (page 135). This is a regal dessert, suitable for one of your main holiday meals or a New Year's party.

> 1/3 cup lukewarm water
> 2 1/4-ounce packages (about 2 tablespoons) active dry yeast
> 3/4 cup (6 ounces) unsalted butter
> 1/2 cup light cream or milk
> 4 large eggs at room temperature
> 1/2 cup sugar
> finely grated zest of 1 lemon
> 1 1/2 cups whole wheat flour
> 1 teaspoon salt
> 1 cup unbleached flour

RUM MAPLE SYRUP

> 1/3 cup water
> 1/3 cup pure maple syrup
> 1/4 cup dark rum

Pour the lukewarm water into a small bowl and stir in the yeast. Set aside for 5 minutes. While the yeast dissolves, melt the butter in a small saucepan, pour it into a large mixing bowl, and stir in the cream or milk. In another bowl, beat the eggs, then add them to the liquid along with the dissolved yeast, sugar, and lemon zest.

Using an electric mixer, gradually beat the whole wheat flour into the liquid, beating for 2 minutes once all of the whole wheat has

been added. Cover this sponge with plastic wrap and set it aside in a warm, draft-free spot for 15 minutes.

After 15 minutes, stir in the salt. Using the mixer, gradually beat in the unbleached flour, beating the batter for 2 minutes after the last bit of flour has been added. Cover the bowl with plastic wrap and set aside in a warm, draft-free spot until doubled in bulk, 45 minutes to 1 hour. While the batter is rising, butter and lightly flour a 9-inch kugelhopf pan.

Once it has doubled, scrape the batter into the pan. Cover with plastic wrap and set aside in a warm, draft-free spot. When the batter is well on its way to doubling in bulk — perhaps after 30 minutes — preheat the oven to 375°.

When the batter almost reaches the rim, bake the savarin for 45 minutes; the visible part of the dough should be well browned. Cool *in the pan* on a rack.

As the savarin begins to cool, make the syrup by bringing the water and maple syrup to a boil. Boil for 1 minute, then remove from the heat and stir in the rum. Using a sharp, serrated knife, cut off the crusty part of the cake that rose above the rim; use the rim as a guide for your knife. Spoon the hot syrup over the cake and down the sides of the pan; it will soak right in. Set the pan aside and let the cake cool to room temperature.

When the cake has cooled, unmold onto a serving plate. Cover with plastic wrap until ready to serve. It can stay at room temperature if you plan to serve it that day, but refrigerate it if you aren't serving it until the following day; remove from the fridge about 15 minutes before serving.

N O T E : This cake will easily absorb more syrup than the amount called for here if you like a wet, syrupy slice. The way I do it, the syrup penetrates the outer areas, but the center stays dry. If you want to saturate the cake, double the syrup ingredients and spoon half over the cake. Wait 15 minutes, then apply the rest.

Beehive Cake with Mascarpone Filling

MAKES 10 SERVINGS

This beehive cake was inspired by a Julia Child recipe I found in her great book The Way to Cook *(Knopf). The beehive itself is a dome of brioche dough; in this case I use the Whole Wheat Brioche on page 168. It has an outer coating of chopped nuts — those, I think, are supposed to approximate the little bees. The cake is assembled by halving it, sprinkling the halves with a little rum syrup, then spreading the bottom with a filling of lightly sweetened mascarpone cheese; it ends up looking like a big cheese sandwich on a bun. This is very much a celebration cake, fit for a holiday party, and it is rugged enough to transport to someone's house without upsetting it.*

> 1 recipe Whole Wheat Brioche (page 168)
> egg wash: 1 large egg beaten with 1 tablespoon milk
> 2 tablespoons honey
> 1/2 cup (2 ounces) chopped walnuts or almonds
>
> RUM SYRUP
> 3 tablespoons rum (I use dark, but any type is fine)
> 3 tablespoons honey
> 1 tablespoon water
> ground nutmeg, preferably freshly grated
>
> MASCARPONE FILLING
> 1 pound mascarpone cheese
> 1/2 cup plain yogurt
> 1/3 cup confectioners' sugar

Once the brioche dough has risen, punch it down and divide it in half. Knead half of it into a ball (bake the other half as a loaf) and place the ball in the center of a buttered baking sheet, preferably a dark one. Pat the dough into a disk about 5 inches across, then cover it with lightly buttered plastic wrap. Wait about 8 minutes to relax the dough, then pat the dough again to make a disk 9 inches in diameter. Cover with the plastic wrap and set the dough aside in a warm, draft-free spot until quite swollen and puffy to the touch; this should take 45 to 55 minutes. About 10 minutes before it reaches that point, preheat the oven to 375°.

A few minutes before baking the dough, brush it *very gently* with the egg wash. Put the 2 tablespoons honey into a small saucepan and heat it until it is runny. Brush the honey all over the surface of the

cake, very gently, then sprinkle the chopped nuts on top. Ever so gently pat them into the dough with your palm to embed them slightly. Bake the brioche for 35 minutes, then slide it onto a rack to cool.

When you're ready to assemble the cake, up to an hour ahead, slit the cake in half like a bun; you'll need a sharp serrated knife with a long blade. Make the rum syrup by heating and stirring the rum, 3 tablespoons honey, and water in a saucepan. Turn over the top section of brioche — you'll lose some nuts; don't worry — and spoon the syrup equally over both halves. Give the bottom half a good dusting of nutmeg.

To make the filling, stir — don't beat — the mascarpone, yogurt, and confectioners' sugar in a bowl until smooth. Spread it evenly over the bottom half of the cake, right up to the edge, then put the top back on. Refrigerate if not serving right away. Serve alone, with a wedge of sliced fruit, or a spoonful of good out-of-season berries.

Toasting Nuts

Many of the recipes in this book call for toasting nuts before using them in a recipe. The reason is that toasting brings out the delicate flavor of most nuts. This is easy to do, and once you've tried it you'll appreciate the difference it makes.

Spread the nuts on an ungreased baking sheet and place them in a 350° oven for about 7 to 10 minutes. If the oven is preheated, it's likely to take less time; if you're preparing a recipe and the oven is in the process of preheating — as is usually the case when I do it — expect it to take 10 minutes or a little more.

How can you tell when they're done? Trust your nose; it's usually the point at which you catch the first whiff of nutty fragrance in the air. Noses have been known to be distracted by kids, phone calls, and stolen kisses with one's spouse, so just in case I always use a timer to back me up; the nuts can go from golden brown to burned surprisingly fast, so check them often. Dump them right onto your work counter, because if they stay on the sheet they can continue to cook. Cool, then chop.

Hazelnuts (filberts) have a papery, bitter skin that's best removed after they're toasted. When the skins have split from the nuts, after 8 to 10 minutes in the oven, dump the nuts directly into a tea towel. Fold the towel over, covering them. Wait a minute, then rub the nuts vigorously through the towel. Most of the skins should come right off. Don't worry, however, if some of the skins remain — and they will; they won't ruin the recipe.

Dark and Dense Rye Honey Cake

MAKES 1 LARGE LOAF CAKE,
12 TO 14 SLICES

Here is an excellent holiday cake for those with any number of dietary restrictions: there's no fat, eggs, milk products, or refined sugar. You might think that such a cake would taste pretty grim, but on the contrary, this is a great cake even if one isn't on a special diet. The taste is a little like that of Boston brown bread, with a very firm coarse texture; even thinly sliced it can stand up to a spreading of cold, firm cream cheese — if that's not on the forbidden list. This cake can be eaten as soon as it's cooled, but it definitely improves in both texture and flavor if you can wait 24 hours.

1 3/4 cups rye flour
1 1/2 cups unbleached flour
1 1/2 teaspoons baking soda
1 teaspoon unsweetened cocoa powder
1 teaspoon ground cinnamon
1 teaspoon ground ginger
1/2 teaspoon salt
1 cup honey *or* 3/4 cup honey plus 1/4 cup unsulfured molasses
1 cup hot water
1/4 cup dark rum
1 teaspoon vanilla extract
1 cup (about 1/4 pound) chopped walnuts
3/4 cup raisins

Preheat the oven to 300° and lightly butter and flour a 5- by 9-inch loaf pan, preferably not a dark one. Into a large bowl, sift all of the dry ingredients (flours through salt); add to the bowl anything that won't go through the sifter. In a separate bowl, whisk the honey, hot water, rum, and vanilla. Stir the dry ingredients into the liquid in 2 stages, then fold in the walnuts and raisins.

Scrape the batter into the prepared pan and bake for 80 to 90 minutes; a tester inserted in the center of the cake should come out clean. (Don't be alarmed if the cake develops a bit of a crack in the center; mine often does.) Let the cake cool in the pan for 20 minutes, then turn it out and finish cooling on a rack. As soon as it no longer feels warm, wrap the loaf in plastic wrap and seal it in a plastic bag. Store overnight before cutting into thin slices.

Banana Rum Cake

MAKES 10 SERVINGS

This is a simple snacking cake, rich and moist, what you might imagine a banana pound cake would taste like. There are rum-soaked raisins and a little extra rum in the batter, but the rum is still very subtle; it adds a pleasant accent to the banana flavor without overpowering it. It is excellent alone, or you can spiff it up for your guests by serving slices piled with whipped cream and sliced bananas.

1 cup raisins
1/3 cup plus 2 tablespoons light or dark rum
1 cup whole wheat flour
1 cup unbleached flour
2 teaspoons baking powder
1/2 teaspoon salt
1/2 teaspoon ground nutmeg, preferably freshly grated
1/2 teaspoon ground cinnamon
1/2 cup (1/4 pound) unsalted butter, softened
2/3 cup sugar
2 large eggs at room temperature
1 teaspoon vanilla extract
1 cup (about 2 large) mashed very ripe bananas

At least 3 hours before making this, put the raisins in a small bowl and pour on 1/3 cup rum. Set aside, stirring every hour. Preheat the oven to 350° and butter a 5- by 9-inch loaf pan, preferably a shiny metal one. In a medium-size bowl, mix the flours, baking powder, salt, nutmeg, and cinnamon. In a separate bowl, cream the butter with an electric mixer. Gradually add the sugar and continue to beat for another 2 or 3 minutes, until light and fluffy in texture. Beat in the eggs one at a time, beating well after each addition. Add the vanilla.

Stir half of the dry ingredients into the creamed mixture until smooth. Blend in the mashed bananas, the remaining 2 tablespoons of rum, then the rest of the dry mixture. Fold in the raisins and stir just until the batter is smooth. Scrape the batter into the buttered pan and smooth the top with a fork. Bake for 55 to 60 minutes, until a tester inserted in the center of the cake comes out clean.

Cool the cake in the pan for 10 minutes, then invert it onto a rack to finish cooling. This is excellent warm or at room temperature. Store leftovers in a sealed plastic bag or wrapped in foil.

113

Buttermilk Spice Cake with Apricot Wine Glaze

MAKES 1 LARGE CAKE,
12 TO 14 SERVINGS

This is an old-fashioned cake with a buttermilk-soft crumb and a gorgeous golden brown exterior. It tastes just how you'd expect it would with 2 sticks of butter, 5 eggs, plenty of brown sugar, and just the right amount of spice: incredible! The finishing touch is a sweet glaze made by blending apricot jam and white wine, heating it, then brushing it over the still-warm cake. The glaze is so good that you may want to double the proportions and use the extra to spoon over individual slices. What works very well is to put a little whipped cream half on and half off each slice, then drizzle the glaze over both the slice and the cream. If you really want a fancy holiday party touch, fill the hollow center of the cake with fresh berries — if you can find good imported ones — and serve some with each slice.

> 1 cup (1/2 pound) unsalted butter at room temperature
> 1/2 cup honey
> 1 1/2 cups packed light brown sugar
> 5 large eggs at room temperature
> 1 teaspoon vanilla extract
> finely grated zest of 1 lemon
> 2 cups unbleached flour
> 1 1/2 cups whole wheat pastry flour
> 1 teaspoon baking soda
> 1 teaspoon ground cardamom
> 1 teaspoon ground nutmeg, preferably freshly grated
> 1 teaspoon ground cinnamon
> 1/2 teaspoon salt
> 1 cup buttermilk

GLAZE
> 1/2 cup dry white wine
> 1/3 cup apricot jam

Preheat the oven to 350° and butter a 10-inch Bundt pan. Using an electric mixer, cream the butter and honey on high speed. Gradually add the brown sugar and beat for another minute after all of it has been added. Add the eggs one at a time, beating well after each one. Beat in the vanilla and lemon zest.

In a separate bowl, sift the flours, baking soda, spices, and salt. Stir the dry ingredients into the creamed mixture in 3 stages, alternating with the buttermilk, beginning and ending with the dry.

When the batter is evenly blended, scrape it into the buttered pan. Bake for 60 minutes, until a tester inserted in the center of the cake comes out clean. Cool the cake in the pan for 15 minutes.

Meanwhile, make the glaze. Puree the wine and apricot jam in a blender. Pour the glaze into a small saucepan and heat gently for 5 minutes, stirring occasionally. Remove from the heat. Invert the cake onto a large cake plate. While the cake is still quite warm, brush or spoon the glaze over the entire surface. Store the cake in a cool location, covering it snugly with plastic wrap.

Harvest Carrot Cake

MAKES 1 LARGE CAKE,
16 TO 20 SERVINGS

Whether you use your own organic carrots from the root cellar or buy them at the market, you'll find a good use for them in this moist harvest cake. The predominant flavor here is neither the oats nor the carrots but the orange, the whole of which is chopped in a food processor before being added to the batter; that and the generous, lively mix of spices makes this a good holiday snacking cake. This is a moist, substantial cake — not heavy, but somewhat compact because there are oats, chopped nuts, and raisins. I like this the first day, but it is even better the second. Be sure to cover it tightly with plastic wrap as soon as it has cooled, to trap the moisture, which will help to soften the exterior.

- 1 1/2 cups (about 6 ounces) toasted walnuts (see page 111 for toasting instructions)
- 1 cup rolled oats (*not* instant)
- 1 cup raisins
- 2 cups unbleached flour
- 2 teaspoons baking powder
- 1 teaspoon baking soda
- 1/2 teaspoon salt
- 1 1/2 teaspoons ground cinnamon
- 1/2 teaspoon ground cardamom
- 1/2 teaspoon ground nutmeg, preferably freshly grated
- 4 large eggs
- 3/4 cup (6 ounces) unsalted butter, melted
- 1 cup packed light brown sugar
- 2 teaspoons vanilla extract
- 1 orange, scrubbed under running water and dried
- 1 tablespoon granulated sugar
- 1/3 cup buttermilk or plain yogurt
- 2 cups finely grated carrots

Butter a 10-inch Bundt pan, preferably one with a nonstick finish, and preheat the oven to 350°.

Put the oats and half of the toasted walnuts in a food processor or blender and process to a fine meal; if you're using the latter, you may have to stop periodically to stir up the mixture so it doesn't compact under the blades. Transfer to a large mixing bowl. Coarsely chop the remaining walnuts with the raisins and set them aside in a small bowl.

Sift the flour, baking powder, baking soda, salt, and spices into the bowl with the oat mixture and mix them together. In a separate mixing bowl, beat the eggs with an electric mixer for 1 minute. Beat in the melted butter, brown sugar, and vanilla. Cut the orange in half and remove the seeds. Cut each half into two quarters, then place them in a food processor with the tablespoon of sugar. Process until you have a slightly chunky, but pretty smooth consistency — almost like pickle relish. Beat the orange into the liquid along with the buttermilk.

Make a well in the dry mixture and stir in the liquids. Fold in the chopped raisins and nuts, then the carrots.

Scrape the batter into the prepared pan and even it out. Bake for 45 to 50 minutes, until a tester comes out clean. Cool the cake in the pan on a rack for 10 minutes, then put a cake plate over the pan and invert the cake onto it; it should slip right out. Cool before slicing. Store the cake in a cool location, covered with plastic wrap.

Chocolate Banana Bundt Cake

MAKES 20 TO 24 SERVINGS

A big, dark party Bundt cake, this one is rich and moist, sweetened with brown sugar, honey, and a little molasses. The outside is a coating of walnuts sprinkled on the sides of the buttered pan; they toast perfectly in the baking, leaving a pretty exterior of amber walnuts set against the dark chocolate. This is the cake to think of when you've let some bananas sit around for too long. Serve it at your tree-trimming party, with hot chocolate or cold milk.

> 1 cup (about 1/4 pound) shelled walnuts
> 1 cup (1/2 pound) unsalted butter at room temperature
> 1 cup packed light brown sugar
> 2/3 cup mild-tasting honey, such as orange blossom
> 1/3 cup unsulfured molasses
> 2 teaspoons vanilla extract
> 4 large eggs at room temperature
> 2 cups (4 large) mashed ripe bananas
> 1 1/2 cups unbleached flour
> 1 1/2 cups whole wheat flour
> 3/4 cup unsweetened cocoa powder
> 1 tablespoon baking powder
> 1 teaspoon salt
> confectioners' sugar for dusting the cake (optional)

Chop the walnuts by hand into small pieces. Generously butter a 10-inch Bundt pan and sprinkle 1/2 cup of the walnuts into it; get the nuts on all the surfaces, including the center tube, and expect some of them to fall into the bottom of the pan. Place the pan down on the counter softly so all the nuts don't fall out of place. Set the remaining nuts aside. Preheat the oven to 350°.

In a large mixing bowl, cream the butter with an electric mixer until soft. Separately beat in the brown sugar, honey, molasses, and vanilla. Beat in the eggs one at a time, adding each one when the batter becomes soft and fluffy. Beat in the mashed bananas.

Into a separate bowl, sift the flours, cocoa, baking powder, and salt. Stir the dry ingredients into the creamed ones in 3 stages, stirring after each addition until evenly blended. Scrape the batter into the prepared pan and smooth the top with a fork. Sprinkle the top of the cake with the remaining nuts.

Bake the cake for 60 to 70 minutes or until a tester inserted in the center of the cake comes out clean. Cool the cake in the pan on a rack for 15 minutes, then turn it out onto a cake platter and finish cooling. Slice when cooled. You can, if you wish, give the cake a light dusting of confectioners' sugar before serving. Store the cake in a cool spot, covered with plastic wrap.

Vanilla Sugar

Many of the recipes in this book and elsewhere call for a light dusting of confectioners' sugar as a finishing touch on yeasted coffee cakes, cookies, and other pastries. I love it for my holiday baking: It looks like snow, and it gives a sweet bite to every mouthful.

But you can do one better with your holiday baking by keeping a jarful of vanilla sugar on hand at this time of year. Vanilla gives a gorgeous perfume to the sugar; sometimes I inhale the fragrance of vanilla sugar just for the fun of it, even when I'm not baking with it. . . .

To make vanilla sugar, you will need one vanilla bean per pound of confectioners' sugar. If you do a lot of holiday baking, better to make two or three pounds at a time; at least you'll have it on hand if you need it, and if not it will last indefinitely anyway. Or you can always give a pound of it to a baking friend, packed in a pretty tin.

Slit the vanilla bean in half lengthwise and bury the halves in the sugar. Cover and set aside for a week at room temperature before you use it. It's okay to use it before that, but the longer the vanilla sugar sits, the better the vanilla suffuses the sugar. Use the vanilla sugar anywhere a dusting of confectioners' sugar is called for or to sweeten whipped cream. As your supply dwindles, replenish it by adding more confectioners' sugar to the container.

Maple-Glazed Gingerbread

MAKES 8 LARGE SERVINGS

Everyone who's tasted it agrees that gingerbread has taken a great step forward here: the bottom is sticky maple, like the glaze on upside-down cake; the middle is the moistest, spiciest rendition of gingerbread ever; and the top has a crunchy sugar and candied ginger coating. This gingerbread goes right to the table in the iron skillet you bake it in, so it makes a fun snack during an informal tree-trimming party or other holiday happening. We love it with sweetened whipped cream or coffee or vanilla ice cream, served with Hot Spiced Cider (page 223).

MAPLE GLAZE
    2 tablespoons unsalted butter
    2 tablespoons sugar
    1/3 cup pure maple syrup
CAKE
    2 large eggs, lightly beaten
    1/2 cup packed light brown sugar
    2/3 cup unsulfured molasses
    6 tablespoons unsalted butter, melted
    1 1/2 teaspoons vanilla extract
    1 1/4 cups whole wheat pastry flour
    3/4 cup unbleached flour
    1 teaspoon baking soda
    1/2 teaspoon salt
    1 1/2 teaspoons ground ginger
    1 teaspoon ground cinnamon
    1/2 teaspoon ground mace
    1/2 teaspoon ground cardamom
    3/4 cup milk
    1/3 cup minced candied ginger
    1 tablespoon sugar

To make the glaze, melt the 2 tablespoons butter over medium heat in a 10-inch cast-iron skillet. Stir in the 2 tablespoons sugar and the maple syrup and cook over high heat just until it bubbles across the whole pan. Remove from the heat. Preheat the oven to 350°.

    To make the cake, whisk the eggs in a large bowl just until frothy. Whisk in the brown sugar, molasses, melted butter, and vanilla. In a separate bowl, sift together the flours, baking soda, salt, and spices. Whisk half of the dry ingredients into the liquid until smooth. Blend in the milk, then stir in the rest of the dry ingredients until the batter is uniform; don't overbeat.

Scrape the batter into the skillet, then scatter the candied ginger evenly over the top. Sprinkle the 1 tablespoon of sugar over the batter and bake for about 40 minutes, until a tester inserted in the center of the cake comes out clean. Slice and serve hot or warm, right from the pan.

Tree Trimming, Family Style

We think if you're going to take the life of a tree, you should honor it by having fun decorating it. How? Simply by getting everyone involved in the process, and focusing on their individual talents. For instance, Tess, our oldest girl, loves handwork; she's happy to make felt ornaments all day long. Ben, our oldest boy, likes a little more variety: changing the Christmas music, making spiced cider, and baking cookies. Alison loves to string beads or popcorn, and help with making cookies. Our little Sam likes to hang dog bones as ornaments. And of course the big advantage of focusing on each kid's interest is that they stay happy longer, so Mom and Pop are more relaxed too.

We usually allow the better part of a day for tree trimming, because we make most of what goes on it by hand. Yes, we have a few bulbs and special ornaments, but the attrition rate of such precious things is so rapid when you have four youngsters that the collection has been weeded down to a sturdy few. If the better part of a day seems like a lot of time to trim a tree, perhaps it is. But little hands work slowly sewing up felt snowmen and stringing popcorn. The payback is that the kids can revel in the gratification of being a key part of the process. In that respect the tree becomes something extraspecial, an extension of themselves and not just the place they find presents.

Our definition of ornament is pretty loose and has included such hot finds as bird nests, big pinecones, and an overdone batch of cookies we forgot to put the baking powder into anyway. (Our dog, Stina, didn't seem to mind, however; when we came down on Christmas morning that year, all we found left of them were the loops of ribbon we'd hung them by.)

Aside from any personal treasures — a favorite stuffed toy or little charm — the kids love to make felt ornaments, one of our mainstays. Two perennial favorites in this category are the aforementioned snowmen and Christmas trees. Beavers and lambs were big last year too.

We don't get too fancy. The tree is just your basic long triangle with a box for the trunk; the snowman, a simple series of graduated circles. Just draw the pattern on a piece of paper, cut it out, and pin it to a piece of felt. Cut around the edge, then do a second one. Give the kids small wooden beads to sew on for the eyes and nose or as ornaments for the trees; we've also used tiny buttons and little bells as ornaments. Simple stitching will do for the snowman's mouth. And don't worry about crooked snowman smiles or droopy bead noses; too much "help" can turn the kids off real quick. Sew the two halves together using embroidery

floss, stuffing your ornament with wool or cotton balls before you sew it closed. Finally, sew an embroidery floss loop onto the top to hang it from the tree by.

Another favorite kid tree ornament is strings of popcorn and cranberries. Our experience is that kids lose patience with those long strands that go around the tree — takes forever — so we now do just short strands, about six or eight inches long, and hang them over the branches as you would tinsel. We do some with just cranberries, some with just popcorn, and some alternating the two.

Kids have their own ideas about how to decorate a tree. Our littlest ones, for instance, operate on the principle that if one dog bone looks good hanging from a branch, then 16 on the same branch will look 16 times as good. You can try to teach them the subtle art of balance and suggest that Spot will like it just as well if they're spread out; but don't fight it too much. Tree-trimming power struggles with two- and four-year-olds are a dead-end street.

In addition to lights, we now put candles on the tree. Our kids love the natural glow of the candles, and lighting them — then singing carols before we blow out the candles and head off to bed — has become one of our family traditions.

Taking the tree down is never easy, and I suspect we have a little more trouble than most families in letting go of the holiday spirit; last year, in fact, our tree came down the day before Valentine's Day. The needles on the tree at that point were so brittle that a sneeze would precipitate a shower of brown needles. Even so, we dragged the tree outside the living room window, propped it up in the snow, and hung half a dozen pinecone bird feeders from it. It was like Christmas all over again for the chickadees.

Lemon Lime Pudding Cake

MAKES 8 SERVINGS

I have tried many combinations of orange, lemon, and lime juice in pudding cakes; this honey-sweetened one stands out. The texture is different from that of many cakes of this sort, the cake part taking on the creamy texture of a cheesecake — it's almost like eating a cheesecake with lemon curd underneath. The orange zest is optional; including it makes this a triple-citrus pudding cake. I much prefer the cake chilled for at least several hours before serving, with unsweetened whipped cream.

> 3/4 cup sugar
> 1/4 cup unbleached flour
> 1/8 teaspoon salt
> 1/4 cup unsalted butter
> 1/2 cup honey
> 1/4 cup fresh lime juice
> 1/4 cup fresh lemon juice
> 4 large eggs, separated, at room temperature
> grated zest of 1 orange (optional)
> 1 cup light cream

Preheat the oven to 350° and butter a 9-inch deep-dish ceramic pie pan. You will also need a larger shallow casserole to hold the first one and serve as a water bath. Bring a pot of water to a boil.

In a medium-size bowl, mix 1/2 cup of the sugar with the flour and salt. Set aside. Over gentle heat, melt the butter in a small saucepan. Stir in the honey and turn off the heat.

Make a well in the dry ingredients and add the lime and lemon juices, the butter and honey mixture, and the egg yolks. Whisk just until smooth. Stir in the orange zest if you're using it, then the light cream. Beat the egg whites until they're almost to the point where they hold soft peaks, then add the remaining 1/4 cup sugar and continue to beat until they reach that point. Fold them into the batter — it will be quite soupy — then pour the batter into the buttered dish.

Place the cake dish in the larger casserole and add enough boiling water to the casserole to come halfway up the sides of the smaller dish. Bake for 40 minutes; the top will just be starting to brown. Carefully remove the cake dish from the hot water bath and cool on a rack. When cooled, cover and refrigerate for at least a couple of hours before serving.

Indian Pudding Cake

MAKES 6 TO 8 SERVINGS

In my travels about New England, I'm always looking for good Indian pudding — a modest enough pursuit and one that's turned up variations both satisfying and underwhelming. Indian pudding, you may know, is a simple dish of eggs, milk, and sweetening; when the colonists decided to thicken the English hasty pudding of their homeland with cornmeal instead of flour, the former being easier to come by, Indian pudding was born. This version is actually more pudding than cake, but I include it here because I think it preserves the basic idea without the heavy texture of Indian pudding that always leaves me feeling stuffed. The cake part is spongy and thin; the pudding that forms underneath it is thick and creamy, with a spicy molasses flavor.

- 1 cup sugar
- 1/8 teaspoon salt
- 2 tablespoons unbleached flour
- 2 tablespoons yellow cornmeal, preferably stone-ground
- 1/2 teaspoon ground ginger
- 1/2 teaspoon ground cinnamon
- 1/4 teaspoon ground cloves
- 1/4 cup unsalted butter, melted
- 1/4 cup unsulfured molasses
- 3 large eggs, separated, at room temperature
- 1 1/3 cups milk

Preheat the oven to 350°. Butter a shallow 8-inch square casserole or a 9-inch round one. You will need a second, slightly larger casserole to hold the first one, filled with about 1/2 inch of boiling water.

Mix 3/4 cup of the sugar, the salt, flour, cornmeal, and spices in a bowl. Whisk the melted butter, molasses, egg yolks, and milk — in that order — into the dry ingredients.

Put the egg whites in a bowl and beat them until they hold soft peaks. Add the remaining sugar and beat a little more, until they are stiff but not dry. Fold the egg whites into the first mixture; it will be soupy. Pour the batter into the buttered casserole and place it in the water bath. Bake for 45 minutes, then remove the casserole from the water bath and place it on a rack. Serve warm, at room temperature, or chilled, with whipped cream or vanilla ice cream.

Seasonal Pies

and

Sweet Tarts

When Labor Day comes and goes, and summer fades into fall, the baker in me always experiences a certain sense of loss. Pie lovers will know what I mean. Gone, for what looks like an eternity, are all the sun-kissed fruits and berries that have followed on the heels of one another for the past several months, the peach pies with crumb topping I love so much, the mixed berry tarts. Of course you can try your hand at winter versions, with produce from distant points on the globe. But the quality of the fruit is never quite the same as the real summer thing.

Fortunately my sense of loss is soon replaced with the expectation of pies and tarts to come. As we work into fall, the air takes on a sharpness that lures us back to the stove. It slowly begins to charge with the electricity and excitement of the season ahead. Small animals scurry about, cheeks full of nuts against a long winter. The woodbox, vacant for many weeks, erupts with the clatter of kindling and logs. The first of the new crop apples appear, and we pie makers are back in business.

Personally, I always feel a little sad when I see shopping carts, right before the big holidays, crammed with four or five store-bought pies. As tradition would have it, they're always the same: apple and pumpkin. But why bother with tradition, I always wonder, if you're going to dispense with good taste? Especially when a good home-made pie or tart takes such a small effort. You make a crust, you make a filling. And that's all there is to it. Sure, it takes a little time. But not that much. And what you get is so much better than anything out of a box.

The holiday pies and tarts on the following pages rely on the full roster of fall and winter staples. That includes apples, in what I consider the perfect apple pie, and pears — in one case combined with port and dried cherries and in another mixed with winter squash. Many include dried fruits, nuts, and even bananas, in a playful pairing with chocolate. In certain ways these pies and tarts tend to be more complex than those of summer, when a single fruit — judiciously sweetened — will suffice. That is neither good nor bad but simply the challenge of working with what is available.

A lot of people, I've noticed, seem to think that making tarts is more difficult than making pies. This isn't true. A tart is really nothing more than a single-crust pie with a French accent. If you can make a pie — and you can — you can make a tart. I think the stumbling block with tarts is mainly a mental one: people think of tarts as French cooking, and that gives them an aura — a false aura — of inaccessibility.

I tend to make more tarts than pies during the holidays because, visually, you can't beat them — and I like my desserts to look good, especially for company. And frankly, I think they're easier than pies, because you don't have to fiddle with the top crust. Also, pies are sometimes too heavy after a big holiday feast; tarts are a little lighter on the stomach.

Pie or tart, I think you'll find some inspiring and novel ideas on these next few pages. You may not get to all of them *this* season, but my guess is — once you've tried a few — you'll be looking forward to *next* holiday season.

Seasonal Pies
and
Sweet Tarts

129

Foolproof Spiced Apple Pie

MAKES 8 SERVINGS

If you're willing to take a few extra little steps for the sake of an incredibly good apple pie, try this recipe; this would be the pie to make if you wanted to serve the one best traditional pie for Thanksgiving dessert. The first step is prebaking the bottom crust, which essentially guarantees you won't end up with a soggy bottom. And the other step is pouring off the liquid from the apples and boiling it down a little, which not only intensifies the apple flavor but also makes a thickish syrup that's less likely to dampen the bottom crust than the straight juice would. This is a little fussy but, as I said, worth it. For the topping I like this whole wheat streusel, which adds a natural nutty flavor and textural contrast with the soft apples.

> **1 recipe Whole Wheat Tart Pastry (page 240) or Basic Tart Pastry (page 234), chilled**

FILLING

> **6 large Granny Smith or other tart juicy apples, peeled, cored, and sliced not quite 1/4 inch thick**
> **2/3 cup sugar**
> **juice of 1 lemon**
> **1 teaspoon ground cinnamon**
> **1 teaspoon ground cardamom**
> **pinch of salt**
> **1 1/2 tablespoons cornstarch**
> **2 tablespoons unsalted butter**

WHOLE WHEAT STREUSEL

> **1 cup whole wheat flour**
> **2/3 cup packed light brown sugar**
> **1/2 teaspoon ground cinnamon**
> **1/4 teaspoon salt**
> **1/2 cup (1/4 pound) cold unsalted butter, cut into 1/4-inch pieces**

On a sheet of lightly floured wax paper, roll the pastry into a 12-inch circle and line a 9-inch pie pan with it. Fold the overhang back, at the same time forming a blunt, somewhat flattened rim. Refrigerate for 15 minutes while you preheat the oven to 400°.

Put the apples in a large mixing bowl and stir in the sugar, lemon juice, spices, and salt. Set aside for 1 hour.

Line the pie shell with aluminum foil. Add enough dried beans or rice to weight the crust down; it should almost reach the top rim, to keep the sides from falling down. Bake for 20 minutes, then

carefully remove the foil with the weights still in it. Poke the pastry 4 or 5 times with a fork, then bake another 8 minutes. Check the shell periodically to see if it is puffing up in the pan; if so, poke it once with a fork to deflate it. Cool the shell on a rack.

When the hour is up, set the oven at 425°. Pour the juices off the apples into a small saucepan and set the pan aside. Stir the cornstarch into the apples, then pile the apples into the pie shell, dotting the top of the apples with the 2 tablespoons butter. Drape a piece of aluminum foil over the pie, pulling it down around the rim. Bake for 30 minutes while you make the topping.

Mix the flour, brown sugar, cinnamon, and salt in a bowl. Add the 1/2 cup butter and cut or rub it in until the mixture resembles fine, evenly textured crumbs. Set aside.

When the 30 minutes are almost up, bring the juice to a boil and boil until reduced by about half, probably about 5 minutes. Pull the pie out of the oven, place it on a baking sheet, and pour the hot juice all over the apples. Spread the topping evenly over the apples, patting it down a little with your hands. Lower the heat to 375°, then put the pie — on the sheet — back in the oven for another 40 to 45 minutes. Check the pie midway through this last stretch, and if the topping is getting dark — and it probably will be — cover it loosely with the foil. When done, you will probably be able to see thick juices bubbling near the edge. Cool the pie on a rack for at least 45 minutes before slicing. Store the pie in a cool place, covered with plastic wrap.

Boiled Cider Pie

MAKES 8 SERVINGS

This is one of my all-time favorite Thanksgiving pies, one that originated with the Shakers, who used boiled cider as a sweetening in many baked goods. A few years back, my curiosity about boiled cider led me to the Vermont farm of Willis and Tina Wood, one of the few remaining families who make it. It was very interesting to see their operation; in one building the apples are ground and pressed to make the cider, which is then fed into their maple syrup evaporator — fitted with a special pan — to boil it down to the syrup stage (about one-seventh the original volume) or jelly stage (about one-eighth). As you would imagine, this condensed cider has a very intense apple flavor just about perfectly matched here with maple syrup. This pie is pretty sweet, and it has a smooth, puddinglike texture. Serve it at room temperature or slightly chilled with lightly sweetened whipped cream. You can order boiled cider directly from the source I mentioned above or make your own (see note at end of recipe).

1 9-inch pie shell (I often use Three-Grain Butter Pastry, page 242)

FILLING

3/4 cup pure maple syrup
3/4 cup boiled cider (see note below)
2 tablespoons unsalted butter
1/4 teaspoon salt
3 large eggs, separated
dusting of ground nutmeg, preferably freshly grated, or mace

Partially bake the pie shell as directed in the pastry recipe and let it cool on a rack. Set the oven temperature to 350°.

To make the filling, gently heat the maple syrup, boiled cider, and butter in a small saucepan just until the butter melts. Pour the mixture into a bowl, stir in the salt, and cool to lukewarm.

Whisk the egg yolks and blend them into the liquid. Beat the egg whites in a separate bowl until they hold soft peaks, then thoroughly fold them into the liquid. Pour the filling into the pie shell and bake for 35 to 40 minutes, just until the pie is set; the center may still seem a bit wobbly, but it will firm up as the pie cools. Cool the pie on a rack, giving it a dusting of nutmeg or mace before serving. Store the pie in a cool location, covered with a domed foil "tent"; the topping will stick if the foil touches it.

NOTE: Boiled cider can be ordered directly from Wood's Cider Mill, RFD 2, Box 477, Springfield, VT 05661. Write for a current price list. Or you can make your own by boiling your own fresh, preservative-free cider down to one-seventh the original volume. Be sure to use a large nonaluminum and nonreactive pot. Measure the height of the cider when you start so you have a reference point; if you start at 3 1/2 inches, for instance, you would be done when the liquid is reduced to 1/2 inch. You will have to remove the pan from the heat to measure.

About Pie Apples

If apple pies always seem to taste best around the holidays, that's because they probably do: The less time your apples have spent in storage, the better they are for eating *and* for baking. A freshly picked apple is crisp and juicy and full of flavor; stored apples get mealy and often taste flat.

There is much debate over which apples make good pies. I'd rather eat apple pie than debate any day, but I have made some observations on the matter. A good pie apple, generally speaking, is one that's tart, juicy, crisp, and holds its shape in the oven; it shouldn't turn to applesauce. If you live in or near the country, within an easy drive of apple growers, you may find some unusual and superb pie apples available at a local orchard. Talk with the people who grow them; *they'll* know something about good pie apples.

Of the more common market varieties, I try to avoid the Red Delicious, which is pretty disappointing no matter how you eat it. The Granny Smiths from New Zealand make a good apple pie, but they sometimes get a little soft after an hour in the oven. I've recently been pleased with the pies I've made with another New Zealand apple, the Royal Gala.

For several autumns running, apple-picking friends would bring us big boxes of Baldwins and Northern Spys, and we made some wonderful pies with them. Pippins, Gravensteins, Staymans, and Cortlands all make good apple pies too.

Remember that a good apple is just one piece — albeit an important one — of the perfect apple pie puzzle. If you want to read about the other pieces, check out the Foolproof Spiced Apple Pie on page 130. It's my idea of the perfect apple pie.

133

Apple Butter Maple Pie

MAKES 8 SERVINGS

I came up with this pie to see how closely I could duplicate the Boiled Cider Pie (preceding recipe) without using boiled cider, it being something you'll either have to make yourself or mail-order (see page 133). Apple butter, on the other hand, is everywhere. This is a great pie for procrastinators, because even if you've committed yourself to bringing a pie to a party or potluck, you could make this at the last minute, almost in your sleep if you had to — that's how easy it is. You would have to have a piecrust on hand, however, and I recommend the Three-Grain Butter Pastry on page 242 — it's perfect for this.

1 9-inch pie shell made with Three-Grain Butter Pastry (page 242)

FILLING

- **3/4 cup pure maple syrup**
- **3 tablespoons unsalted butter**
- **1/2 cup apple butter**
- **1 teaspoon vanilla extract**
- **3 large eggs, lightly beaten**
- **pinch of salt**

Partially bake the pie shell as directed in the pastry recipe. Preheat the oven to 375° while you make the filling. In a medium-size saucepan, gently warm the maple syrup and butter just until the butter melts. Transfer to a large mixing bowl, then stir in the apple butter, vanilla, eggs, and salt. Slowly pour the filling into the pie shell and bake for 10 minutes. Reduce the oven temperature to 350° and bake for another 20 minutes or so. When done, the pie will just be starting to puff up; the center may quiver, but it shouldn't be soupy. Transfer the pie to a rack to cool. Serve warm or at room temperature with lightly sweetened whipped cream. Store the pie in a cool spot, covered with plastic wrap.

Light Lemon Tart

MAKES 10 SERVINGS

This is a lemon curd tart, but it's not made with straight lemon curd, which I find too intense in a tart. What I have done here is spread just a little of the lemon curd on the bottom of the tart shell, then blended the rest with some sweetened whipped cream to cut the intensity and lighten the filling (in texture only; don't even think about the calories). Once it's been chilled, this is a good traveling tart because it becomes quite firm; as long as someone doesn't sit on it on the way to Christmas dinner at Grandma's, a little jostling in the car won't hurt it. If the tart has been chilled, let it sit at room temperature for maybe 10 or 15 minutes before serving, to make the crust less brittle.

1 9-inch tart shell made with Whole Wheat Tart Pastry (page 240)
1 recipe Lemon Curd (page 217), chilled
2/3 cup heavy cream, chilled
3 tablespoons confectioners' sugar

Fully bake the tart shell and cool to room temperature. About 15 minutes before you whip the cream, put a medium-size ceramic mixing bowl and your beaters or whisk in the refrigerator.

To assemble the tart, spoon about one third of the lemon curd into the tart shell and spread it evenly with a spoon. Using the chilled bowl and beaters, beat the heavy cream until it holds soft peaks, then add the confectioners' sugar and continue to beat until quite firm; if you notice any signs of graininess, stop beating. Add the remaining lemon curd to the whipped cream and beat just until thoroughly blended. Spoon the filling over the lemon curd and spread it evenly with the back of a spoon. Cover the tart with a foil tent and refrigerate for at least 1 hour before serving, letting it stand at room temperature for 10 minutes before serving. Serve with lemon tea.

Pear Pie with Sour Cherries in Port

MAKES 8 SERVINGS

Pear pies, I find, are always an unexpected treat, not to mention a welcome change for somebody who really likes to make pies, simply because you can only make so many apple ones before the creative spirit longs for something different. This one is very different. First I take dried sour cherries and soak them overnight in port. Then I mix them and some of the port with sliced pears, a minimum of sugar, and a little lemon juice. If I happen to have some on hand, I'm likely to add a few sprigs of dried lavender from our herb garden — but just a few sprigs, because the flavor can be quite dominating. All of this makes for a very pretty pie, shaded light pink, not to mention absolutely delicious.

 3/4 cup dried sour cherries, available at health food stores
 1/2 cup ruby port
PASTRY
 1 recipe Three-Grain Butter Pastry (page 242)
FILLING
 5 large ripe but firm Bartlett or Anjou pears
 1/2 cup sugar
 1 tablespoon fresh lemon juice
 2 1/2 tablespoons instant tapioca

The night before — or at least 3 hours ahead — combine the dried cherries and port in a small bowl. Cover and set aside. In the meantime, refrigerate the pie pastry for at least 30 minutes. Roll half of the pastry into a 12-inch circle on a sheet of lightly floured wax paper and line a 9-inch pie pan with it, letting the edge hang over. Cover and refrigerate. Preheat the oven to 425° while you make the filling.

 Peel, core, and slice the pears, then combine them in a large bowl with the sugar, lemon juice, and tapioca. Using a slotted spoon, add the cherries to the filling, then measure and add 1/4 cup of the port they soaked in. Roll the other half of the pastry into an 11-inch circle on a sheet of wax paper.

 Turn the filling into the shell and lightly moisten the edge with a finger or pastry brush dipped in water. Lay the top pastry over the filling, pressing around the edge to seal. Trim off all but 1/2 inch of

the overhang and shape it into an attractive, upstanding edge. Poke several steam vents in the crust, then bake for 20 minutes. Lower the oven temperature to 375° and bake for about another 45 minutes or until any visible juices bubble thickly. Cool the pie on a rack. Serve barely warm, or at room temperature. Store the pie in a cool spot, covered with plastic wrap.

Seasonal Pies
and
Sweet Tarts

Cranberry Apricot Tart with Sour Cream Topping

MAKES 8 TO 10 SERVINGS

Here is a light cranberry tart, very easy to make. You just boil some cranberries and sweetening, fold in some apricot jam, and spread in a tart shell. The sour cream topping — the sourness nicely balancing out the sweetness of the filling — can be made in seconds. Other types of preserves would work here as well, such as peach, cherry, or strawberry.

1 9-inch tart shell made with Whole Wheat Tart Pastry (page 240)
FILLING
2 cups cranberries
1/2 cup water
1/2 cup sugar
1/2 cup golden raisins
3/4 cup apricot preserves (a 10-ounce jar is enough)
SOUR CREAM TOPPING
1 1/4 cups sour cream
2 tablespoons confectioners' sugar
1/2 teaspoon vanilla extract

Fully bake the tart shell as directed in the pastry recipe, leaving it in the pan to cool. To make the filling, put the cranberries and water in a nonaluminum saucepan and bring to a boil. Reduce the heat, cover, and cook at a gentle boil for 3 to 4 minutes, until they start to break down. Stir in the sugar and raisins and cook, uncovered, for about 5 minutes more, until thickened. Transfer to a large bowl and stir in the apricot preserves. Spread the filling up the sides of the bowl so it cools off more quickly. Preheat the oven to 425°.

While the filling cools, whisk the sour cream, sugar, and vanilla together in a mixing bowl.

When the filling has cooled, spread it evenly in the shell, being careful not to break the edge of the shell with your spoon. Carefully spread the sour cream topping over the filling so it almost touches the pastry. Bake the tart for 6 or 7 minutes; this will loosen the sour cream just enough to settle it over the topping. You'll probably notice that it will also run into the sides, which is fine.

Cool the tart on a rack, then cover with a foil tent so it doesn't touch the top of the tart and chill for about 30 minutes before serving. Store leftovers, covered, in the fridge, but let the tart sit at room temperature for about 30 minutes before serving.

Chocolate Almond Kahlúa Tart

MAKES 10 SERVINGS

One of my wife Karen's favorite liqueurs is Kahlúa, so I try to work it into my baking when the opportunity presents itself and generally around the holidays. In this case I was trying to use up the last of a bottle we had left over from the holidays; I was on a tart binge at the time, and we thought it would work well in a tart with chocolate and goo — as in the kind of goo you get in pecan pie. We were right; the coffee and chocolate flavors are wonderful together, strong and luxurious partners, and the almonds add a complementary crunch. I think of this as a grown-up tart, something to be shared with your love in front of a cozy fire after the kids are safely tucked into bed, with visions of sugarplums dancing in their heads.

1 9-inch tart shell made with Whole Wheat Tart Pastry (page 240)

FILLING

    1 cup (about 1/4 pound) shelled almonds
    6 tablespoons unsalted butter
    1/2 cup honey
    1/2 cup packed light brown sugar
    4 large eggs, lightly beaten
    1/3 cup Kahlúa
    1 teaspoon vanilla extract
    1/2 cup semisweet chocolate chips

Partially bake the tart shell as directed in the pastry recipe and set aside to cool. Preheat the oven to 375°. Spread the almonds on a baking sheet and toast them in the oven for about 8 minutes, then transfer them to a plate to cool. Chop them coarsely and set aside.

Meanwhile, melt the butter in a small saucepan, stir in the honey, and remove from the heat. Scrape the honey mixture into a mixing bowl, then whisk in the brown sugar, eggs, Kahlúa, and vanilla. Carefully ladle this liquid into the tart shell, then drop in the chocolate chips and almonds evenly throughout the tart. Bake for approximately 40 minutes, until the tart puffs and is evenly browned on top.

Cool the tart in the pan on a rack for at least 1 hour before serving. This tart is best served barely warm or at room temperature. Store the tart in a cool spot, covered with plastic wrap.

Free-Form Date and Apple Tart

MAKES 8 SERVINGS

This sort of free-form tart, called a crostata in Italy, is great for informal entertaining when a fancier tart might seem out of place. In this version you roll the pastry into a large circle and cover it with a date puree. The puree is then covered with chopped apples and a brown sugar and cinnamon mixture and baked in a very hot oven. There's lots of crust, because the excess gets folded over the top of the puree. This tart is good eaten out of hand, though it's a bit fragile, so I prefer slices served on plates with a little sweetened whipped cream.

1 recipe Basic Tart Pastry (page 234) or Whole Wheat Tart Pastry (page 240)

FILLING

2 cups chopped dried dates, preferably Medjool

1 cup water

juice of 1 lemon

1 tablespoon honey

1 teaspoon vanilla extract

TOPPING

1 cup chopped peeled apples

3 tablespoons packed light brown sugar

1 teaspoon ground cinnamon

1 tablespoon cold unsalted butter

Chill the pastry while you make the filling. Combine the dates and water in a small saucepan. Bring to a boil, reduce the heat to an active simmer, and cook the dates for about 13 minutes, stirring often. When the mixture is thick, with just a little free liquid visible, remove from the heat and transfer to a plate to cool. Using a food processor or blender, puree the cooled dates with the lemon juice, honey, and vanilla extract.

When you're ready to bake, preheat the oven to 425° and butter a large baking sheet, preferably a dark, heavy one. On a sheet of lightly floured wax paper, roll the dough into a 13-inch circle. Invert the pastry onto the sheet and peel off the paper. At this point, if the pastry has started to soften and is difficult to handle, place the entire baking sheet in the fridge for 5 to 8 minutes.

Spread the date puree over the pastry, leaving a 2-inch margin around the entire perimeter. Fold the uncovered edge of the pastry

over the filling, using a spatula or dough scraper to help lift the pastry if necessary. You will have to do this in sections, and the pastry may break as you fold it. But this is not a problem, since the breaks will simply determine where the next section should be folded. When you are done, the folded-over edge will have a pleated look. Put the baking sheet back in the fridge for 8 minutes.

Sprinkle the chopped apples over the filling. Mix the brown sugar with the cinnamon and sprinkle that over the apples. Cut the butter into small pieces and dot the surface of the tart with it. Bake for 35 minutes, until the crust is golden brown. Cool the tart right on the sheet on a cooling rack. Serve slightly warm or at room temperature, cut into wedges. Store the tart in a cool spot, covered with plastic wrap.

Gingerbread Tart

MAKES 10 SERVINGS

I love gingerbread and tarts, so I came up with this unlikely combination of the two. The gingerbread filling is like a moist torte, with finely chopped walnuts used in place of much of the flour. Spiced with ginger, cinnamon, and cloves, it rises above the rim of the tart shell and then settles some as it cools. It's good warm, but I think the flavor is better at room temperature, with coffee ice cream on the side. This tart keeps well overnight, wrapped in plastic wrap, so it can easily be made ahead without any loss of quality.

**1 9-inch tart shell made with Whole Wheat Tart Pastry (page 240)
or Basic Tart Pastry (page 234)**

FILLING

1 cup (about 1/4 pound) walnut pieces

1/3 cup unbleached flour

1/2 teaspoon baking powder

1 1/4 teaspoons ground ginger

1/2 teaspoon ground cinnamon

1/4 teaspoon ground cloves

1/4 teaspoon salt

1/2 cup (1/4 pound) unsalted butter, softened

1/3 cup packed light brown sugar

1/4 cup unsulfured molasses

2 large eggs at room temperature

1 teaspoon vanilla extract

Partially bake the tart shell as directed in the pastry recipe and set it aside to cool. Preheat the oven to 350°. Spread the walnuts on a large baking sheet and toast them in the preheated oven for 8 minutes; transfer to a plate and cool. When the nuts are cool, process them briefly in a food processor or blender, then add the flour and continue to process until you have a very fine meal. (If you're using a blender, stop often to fluff up the nuts with the handle of a wooden spoon, since they tend to compact under the blades.) Put the nuts aside in a small bowl and stir in the baking powder, spices, and salt. Set the oven at 375°.

Using an electric mixer, cream the butter, brown sugar, and molasses in a medium-size bowl. Beat for about 2 minutes, then beat in the eggs one at a time, then add the vanilla. Gradually stir the dry ingredients into the creamed mixture until smooth.

Spread the filling evenly in the tart shell and bake for 30 minutes. The filling will rise above the top of the pan, then settle back down once the tart starts to cool. Cool the tart in the pan on a rack for 15 minutes, then remove the side of the pan and cool to room temperature. Store the tart in a cool spot, covered with plastic wrap.

Banana Chocolate Tart with Coconut Crumb Topping

MAKES 10 SERVINGS

Most of us don't take the banana too seriously as a pie or tart ingredient, but here is a tart that could change all that and become a regular in your winter baking repertoire. Once you have the prebaked tart shell, the rest is simple — just slice a few bananas into the shell, scatter some chocolate over that, then cover with a coconut crumb topping that you can assemble in 5 minutes. Baked, the bananas and chocolate get soft, and the top turns golden brown and chewy. I think it tastes best slightly warm or at room temperature, after the chocolate has firmed up a little. Serve with vanilla or butter pecan ice cream.

> 1 9-inch tart shell made with Basic Tart Pastry (page 234) or Whole Wheat Tart Pastry (page 240)
>
> 2 large egg whites
>
> 1/3 cup packed light brown sugar
>
> 1 cup (about 1/4 pound) chopped toasted walnuts (see page 111 for toasting instructions)
>
> 2/3 cup unsweetened shredded coconut (available at health food stores) or sweetened flaked coconut
>
> 2/3 cup (about 6 whole crackers) graham cracker crumbs
>
> 2 large ripe bananas
>
> 1/4 pound semisweet chocolate, coarsely chopped

Partially bake the tart shell as directed in the pastry recipe and set it aside to cool. Preheat the oven to 350°. To make the topping, beat the egg whites in a mixing bowl just until frothy. Whisk in the brown sugar. Stir in the walnuts, coconut, and graham cracker crumbs. Set aside.

Peel the bananas and slice them into 1/4-inch slices, letting them fall right into the cooled crust; spread them out in the shell. Scatter the chocolate over the bananas, then scrape the walnut and crumb topping over the top and spread it around with your fingers or a fork. Bake the tart for 40 minutes, until the top is golden brown; if it starts to get too dark, cover it loosely with foil. Cool the tart for 10 minutes on a rack, then remove the side of the pan and cool further. Serve slightly warm or at room temperature. Store the tart in a cool spot, covered with plastic wrap.

Chocolate Buckwheat Tart

MAKES 10 TO 12 SERVINGS

Chocolate is one of the best matches for buckwheat, since both are quite assertive. Here we combine the two in this rich, velvety tart that's meant to be served in thin slices at a somewhat formal dinner; it's a sophisticated, show-off tart for those with adventurous palates. The texture of the filling is very moist, something like a flourless brownie. It's good warm or at room temperature, served with almond cream: lightly sweetened whipped cream with a few drops of almond extract beaten in.

 1 9-inch tart shell made with Buckwheat Cocoa Tart Pastry
    (page 236)

FILLING

 3/4 cup heavy cream
 1/4 cup milk
 1/3 cup plus 2 tablespoons sugar
 6 ounces unsweetened chocolate, coarsely chopped
 1 1/2 teaspoons vanilla extract
 1 large egg, lightly beaten

Fully bake the tart shell as directed in the pastry recipe. As it cools, make the filling. Heat the cream, milk, and sugar in a small saucepan over medium heat until very hot. Add the chocolate, turn off the heat, and whisk until smooth; it will take 15 seconds or so to melt the chocolate. Stir in the vanilla. Let the mixture sit in the saucepan for 15 minutes while you preheat the oven to 350°.

After 15 minutes, whisk the egg into the chocolate mixture just until smooth. Scrape the filling into the tart shell and bake for 20 to 25 minutes, just until the surface looks set and the edge looks slightly dry. Transfer to a rack and cool in the pan. Slice and serve warm or at room temperature with the almond cream. Store the tart in a cool spot, covered with plastic wrap.

Prune Tart with Coffee Cream

MAKES 12 SERVINGS

Dried fruits give depth and character to one's holiday baking. Of all the dried fruits I can think of, prunes don't have much of a public image, for reasons I don't have to explain. Actually, plain prunes don't do much for me, but I love this: prunes cooked in port, pureed, then baked in the middle of a yeasted pastry. This tart also sports a festive touch of coffee cream — just sweetened whipped cream with some pulverized coffee to flavor it. Try this out on a party of adventurous eaters for breakfast or a late dessert.

> 1 recipe Wheaten Yeasted Pastry (page 245)
> 1 pound pitted prunes, cut in half
> 2 1/4 cups ruby port
> 1/2 cup water
> 1/4 cup honey
> up to 1/2 cup orange juice, fresh or prepared frozen

COFFEE CREAM
> 1 cup cold heavy cream
> 1/3 cup confectioners' sugar
> 1 tablespoon finely pulverized coffee beans
> 1/4 teaspoon vanilla extract

Chill the prepared pastry. Put the prunes, port, water, and honey into a medium-size nonaluminum saucepan. Bring to a boil, reduce the heat, then cook the prunes at a gentle boil for 30 to 40 minutes, until they are very tender. Pour the prunes and their juice into a bowl, cover, and cool to room temperature. If you aren't making this the same day, refrigerate the prunes overnight.

When you're ready to prepare the tart, put the prunes in a food processor and process to a smooth puree, adding as much of the orange juice as necessary to keep the texture damp enough to spread easily without becoming loose-wet; if the prunes have just cooled, it could be as little as 1/4 cup. If they have been refrigerated overnight, you might need the 1/2 cup. Preheat the oven to 350° and get out a large, heavy cookie sheet.

On a sheet of lightly floured wax paper, roll the dough into a 14-inch circle. Invert the pastry over the sheet and peel off the paper. Spread the prune puree in the center of the tart, leaving a 2-inch margin all around. Fold the margin up over the filling, taking care to enclose all of the puree. Refrigerate the tart and sheet for 5 minutes.

Bake the tart for 30 minutes; as it bakes make the coffee cream. Cool it slightly on the sheet while you make the coffee cream. Whip the cream until it holds soft peaks. Add the remaining ingredients and whip until it becomes a little stiffer. Slice the tart and serve with some of the coffee cream on the side. Store the tart in a cool spot, covered with plastic wrap.

Seasonal Pies
and
Sweet Tarts

Poached Fig and Pear Pie with Walnut Streusel

MAKES 8 SERVINGS

I'm really wild about this pie — but of course figs, pears, and walnuts are an autumn trio that's hard to beat. If you're tempted to skip the poaching step for the figs, don't; it's easy, and it really makes a difference because it enables the wine essence to permeate the entire filling, imparting an incredible flavor. Try to plan this a few days ahead so the figs have time to absorb the poaching liquid. Serve with vanilla ice cream or lightly sweetened whipped cream or mascarpone cheese.

1 recipe Whole Wheat Tart Pastry (page 240)

FILLING

2 cups Poached Calimyrna Figs (page 221)
4 large ripe but firm pears, peeled, cored, and sliced
1/3 cup sugar
1/3 cup poaching liquid from the figs
2 tablespoons quick-cooking tapioca

WALNUT STREUSEL

1/2 cup sugar
1/2 cup unbleached flour
pinch of salt
1/4 cup cold unsalted butter, cut into 1/4-inch pieces
1 cup (1/4 pound) finely chopped walnuts

Chill the prepared pastry. Once it has chilled, roll it into a 12-inch circle on a sheet of lightly floured wax paper and line a 9-inch pie pan with it, tucking it into the bottom crease without stretching it. Trim the overhang to a fairly even 1/2 inch all around, then fold it back and under, sculpting it into an upstanding ridge. Refrigerate the pastry while you make the filling. Preheat the oven to 425°.

Cut each fig into quarters. Place them in a large bowl and stir in the pears, sugar, poaching liquid, and tapioca. Scrape the filling into the pie shell and place the pie in the oven. Bake the pie for 20 minutes while you make the walnut streusel.

Mix the sugar, flour, and salt in a medium-size bowl. Add the butter and cut or rub it in until the mixture resembles damp, clumpy crumbs. Add the walnuts and rub them in.

After the pie has baked for 20 minutes, take it out and spread the streusel evenly over the surface. Reduce the heat to 375° and bake for another 50 to 55 minutes, until any visible juices bubble thickly. If the top starts to get too dark, cover it with a piece of aluminum foil.

Cool the pie on a rack for at least 1 hour before slicing and serving. Store the pie in a cool spot, covered with plastic wrap.

*Seasonal Pies
and
Sweet Tarts*

Home

for the

Holidays

Mugging for Your Friends

When friends gather 'round the holiday hearth and the sundry desserts are divided and passed, there's no better way to extend the pleasure of the evening than by serving a special hot toddy. A hot nightcap, served in tall, narrow mugs, keeps the hands warm and gives one's mouth an intermission from — and appreciation of — the dessert at hand.

The hot drink I like most is coffee based and flavored with hazelnut.

Coffee Hazelnut Nightcap

MAKES 6 SERVINGS

3 tablespoons sugar
1 1/2 tablespoons unsweetened cocoa powder
1 cup water
1 cup light cream or milk
3 cups freshly brewed coffee
3/4 cup Frangelico (hazelnut liqueur)
lightly sweetened whipped cream and cinnamon for garnish

Whisk together the sugar and cocoa in a medium-size saucepan. Stir in the water and bring to a boil over moderate heat. Boil, stirring, for 1 minute, then stir in the cream and coffee. Bring almost to a boil, stirring occasionally. Remove the saucepan from the heat.

Pour 2 tablespoons of the Frangelico into each of 6 coffee mugs, then add enough of the toddy to reach within 3/4 inch of the rim. Top each serving with whipped cream and a sprinkling of cinnamon. Serve at once.

Provençal Fig Tart

MAKES 8 TO 10 SERVINGS

I've been a fig fan ever since I tasted my first Fig Newton, so I'm always on the lookout for new ways to use figs in my baking. Here I use the dried figs whole after simmering them in red wine and honey, an idea I borrowed from Lindsey Shere's Chez Panisse Desserts *(Random House). The figs are arranged in a tart shell, with the remainder of the poaching liquid poured over the top. Slices are served with lightly sweetened mascarpone cheese—a better accompaniment there isn't—with the option of sprinkling toasted hazelnuts over the top.*

1 9-inch tart shell made with Whole Wheat Tart Pastry (page 240) or Basic Tart Pastry (page 234)

FILLING

1 recipe Poached Calimyrna Figs (page 221)

1 cup (about 1/4 pound) toasted hazelnuts (see page 111 for toasting instructions) (optional)

SWEETENED MASCARPONE

1 cup mascarpone cheese

1/4 cup confectioners' sugar

Fully bake the tart shell as directed in the pastry recipe and set it aside to cool. As it cools, prepare the figs if you haven't already. When they are tender, remove the figs to a plate with a slotted spoon and let them cool. Boil down the remaining poaching liquid until it equals about 1/3 cup; pour it into a measuring cup to check, then set the liquid aside.

When you're almost ready to serve the tart, assemble it by cutting the figs in half from tip to base. Arrange the figs in the shell in concentric circles—on their sides—with the flat cut side of one pushing into the curved part of the one next to it; keep them very tight. Drizzle the poaching liquid over the top of the figs, spooning it here and there.

To make the sweetened mascarpone cheese, blend the mascarpone and sugar in a small bowl, stirring just until smooth; do not beat, or it may curdle.

Cut the tart with a sharp knife and serve individual slices with the sweetened mascarpone. Sprinkle with chopped hazelnuts if you like. Store the tart in a cool spot, covered with plastic wrap.

151

Maple Hazelnut Cream Tart

MAKES 8 SERVINGS

The filling for this tart is made like the filling for a banana cream pie: thickened with egg yolks and flour and cooked on top of the burner. But that's where the resemblance ends. This filling is made with maple syrup, never in short supply here in New Hampshire, and flavored with hazelnut butter — maple and hazelnut are perfect companions. I love the tart just like that — with the filling poured into the prebaked crust — but you can, and should, dress up the top with the toasted coconut topping. It takes only a few minutes to make. Sprinkled over the top of the tart, it gives a pretty, festive finish and blends nicely with the hazelnut flavor.

> **1 9-inch tart shell made with Whole Wheat Tart Pastry (page 240) or Basic Tart Pastry (page 234)**

FILLING
> **1 cup light cream**
> **1 cup milk**
> **1/3 cup sugar**
> **2 1/2 tablespoons unbleached flour**
> **1/2 teaspoon salt**
> **3 large egg yolks**
> **2/3 cup pure maple syrup**
> **2 tablespoons unsalted butter**
> **2/3 cup hazelnut butter (available at health food stores)**
> **1 teaspoon vanilla extract**

TOASTED COCONUT TOPPING
> **2/3 cup unsweetened shredded coconut (available at health food stores)**
> **1 tablespoon pure maple syrup**

Fully bake the tart shell as directed in the pastry recipe. While it cools, make the filling. In a small saucepan, gently heat the cream and milk until hot to the touch. Remove from the heat. In a large saucepan, mix the sugar, flour, and salt; do not heat yet. In a small bowl, whisk the egg yolks and maple syrup. Whisk a little of the hot milk mixture into the egg yolks and maple syrup, then whisk the yolk mixture into the larger saucepan containing the sugar. Cook the mixture over medium-low heat, whisking almost continuously, until it thickens, gradually adding the remaining cream and milk.

When the mixture starts to boil, turn the heat down a little and cook for about 2 minutes; use a spoon as well as a whisk to scrape down into the crease of the pan. After 2 minutes, remove the pan from the heat and whisk in the butter a tablespoon at a time. Whisk in the hazelnut butter and vanilla until smooth. Place a piece of plastic wrap directly on the surface of the filling to prevent a skin from forming; let cool for 30 minutes.

After 30 minutes, whisk the filling once more, then scrape it into the tart shell. Cool to room temperature. Cover loosely with wax paper and chill for at least 2 hours.

To make the topping, put the coconut in a heavy skillet and turn the heat to medium-low. Toast the coconut for about 5 minutes, stirring almost constantly with a wooden spoon, until it becomes a light golden brown. Transfer to a bowl and cool to room temperature. Add the maple syrup to the cooled coconut and rub it in with your fingers until evenly distributed.

Just before serving, spread the toasted coconut over the top of the tart. This tart is best eaten within 12 hours.

Once the pie has cooled to room temperature, cover with plastic wrap and store in the fridge.

Pearsauce Squash Tart

MAKES 8 TO 10 SERVINGS

This is one of the best variations on squash pie I have ever eaten, maybe the best. The whole idea started one evening when we had a box of fresh pears, from the orchard of our friends Sandy and Dan Dunfey, sitting on our kitchen table. I had been wondering what to do with them, and the sheer quantity suggested pearsauce, which ended up combined with some squash we had baked that evening. The pearsauce turned out to be the magic ingredient, the fruitiness that gives this an extra autumnal layer of flavor that makes it just right for the Thanksgiving season. The flavors are delicate, so I keep the spices toned down instead of playing them up as you would for the usual pumpkin or squash pie. Don't let the extra step of making the pearsauce deter you; it isn't much of a chore, and this tart makes it all worth it. Serve with lightly sweetened whipped cream.

**1 9-inch tart shell made with Whole Wheat Tart Pastry (page 240)
   or Basic Tart Pastry (page 234)**

FILLING

1 cup mashed cooked winter squash
1 1/2 cups Pearsauce (page 218)
2 large eggs, lightly beaten
1/2 cup heavy cream
1/2 cup sugar
1/4 teaspoon ground ginger
1/4 teaspoon salt (omit if the squash is already salted)
1 teaspoon vanilla extract

Partially bake the tart shell as directed in the pastry recipe. As the shell cools on a rack, preheat the oven to 400° and prepare the filling.

Using a food processor or food mill, puree the squash and pearsauce and blend them in a bowl. Stir in the remaining ingredients until evenly blended. Scrape the filling into the shell and bake for 10 minutes. Lower the heat to 350° and bake for another 40 minutes. Cool the tart in the pan on a rack to room temperature before serving. I like this tart best slightly chilled. If you aren't serving it right away, cover loosely with foil and refrigerate. As with any refrigerated tart, it is best to let it sit at room temperature for about 15 minutes before serving, or the crust will be rather hard.

A
Holiday
Bread
Miscellany

Here's a hodgepodge of my favorite holiday breads that don't fit neatly into any other chapter. They aren't strictly breakfast items, though I would gladly grab a slice of any of these when I roll out of bed. And they aren't necessarily Thanksgiving candidates, though — again — such determinations are so personal, who is to say otherwise? Some have definite and traditional associations, like the stollen. And still others are multipurpose, like the mixed grain Cuban bread I use for the pizzas and bruschette I seem to make so often in November and December.

Looking back on some 20 years of home baking, I can say without hesitation that the holidays have never failed to bring with them a magic and energy that spills over into my breads. In summer, frankly, it sometimes takes an effort to make a yeast bread. The beach and garden beckon. We balk at turning on the oven and heating up the house. But during the holidays one is almost swept away by the spirit of the season. The oven radiates an extra measure of warmth we cherish in the colder weather. Like splitting and carrying wood, the energetic rhythm of kneading warms us from within. We turn to bread making instinctively when the weather gets cold.

This section includes mainly yeast breads but a few quick ones also. Yeast bread was my first love in the kitchen, the thing I taught myself to bake while I was still in my teens. Since then I have taught literally hundreds of people in baking classes what I know about making bread. I think one of the most valuable lessons anyone

learned from me is that bread making can be terrific fun. I've always tried to emphasize that bread making is intrinsically rewarding in that it allows us to learn something new, no matter how old we are. This learning is deeply satisfying not only because the end product tastes good but also because it restores our faith in ourselves as intelligent human beings. Because bread making is so varied, the potential for new learning is always there. And what better time to give yourself the gift of new knowledge than now, during the holidays?

If you have never made yeast bread before, and you would like a thorough indoctrination in the basics, I suggest you refer to a copy of my earlier *Ken Haedrich's Country Baking.* If you are an adventurous neophyte, you can probably find your way along with just a few pieces of advice. First, be sure that none of your liquid ingredients is hotter than 115°, or you may kill your yeast. Add the flour to the liquid gradually so you don't end up with a stiff lump of dough to knead. Be patient with the rising; give it ample time to double in bulk. And if you aren't sure if it's done, give your bread a little extra time in the oven.

A gift of homemade whole grain bread attractively wrapped or just adorned with a simple ribbon is perhaps the most welcome of holiday gifts. But I do like to acknowledge the limitation of time. Ideally I prefer to hand out most of my breads on the day they are made, and certainly no later than the next day. (The exception is the stollen, which keeps quite well.) I think of breads as gifts for friends and family in the immediate area; for traveling, cookies are a much better choice.

A Holiday Bread Miscellany

157

Pearsauce Walnut Bread

MAKES 1 LARGE LOAF,
ABOUT 12 SERVINGS

This mostly whole wheat quick bread begins with making pearsauce, just as you would make applesauce. The toasted walnuts give the bread a bit of texture; I sometimes add chopped dried figs too, which turns this into something like a fruitcake. This big loaf would be a nice gift for a family. Wrap the loaf in plastic wrap and place it in the center of a large wicker basket, surrounded by several different types of pears and walnuts.

> 1 1/2 cups Pearsauce (page 218)
> 2 cups whole wheat flour
> 1/2 cup unbleached flour
> 1 tablespoon baking powder
> 3/4 teaspoon salt
> 1 teaspoon ground ginger
> 1 teaspoon ground cinnamon
> 1/2 cup (1/4 pound) unsalted butter, melted
> 3/4 cup packed light brown sugar
> 2 large eggs
> 1 1/2 teaspoons vanilla extract
> 1 cup (about 1/4 pound) shelled walnuts, preferably toasted, chopped (see page 111 for toasting instructions)

If you haven't already, prepare the pearsauce and allow it to cool to room temperature. Preheat the oven to 350° and lightly butter a 4- by 10-inch loaf pan. Line the pan with wax paper and butter it.

Sift the flours, baking powder, salt, and spices into a bowl. In a separate bowl, whisk together the butter, brown sugar, eggs, and vanilla extract. Stir half of the pearsauce into the liquid, followed by half of the dry ingredients, the rest of the pearsauce, then the rest of the dry; stir just until combined, folding in the walnuts on the last few strokes.

Scrape the batter into the prepared pan and bake for about 1 hour, until a toothpick inserted in the center of the cake comes out clean. Cool the bread in the pan for 15 minutes, then turn it out and cool on a rack. While the bread is still slightly warm, peel off the wax paper. Wrap the bread in plastic wrap when it has cooled completely. The flavor and texture improve if this bread has a chance to sit overnight.

Cranberry Cornmeal Soda Bread

MAKES 2 LOAVES,
ABOUT 8 SERVINGS EACH

This is one of the prettiest holiday breads around, golden brown spheres with deep crusty fissures, offset by cranberry-red protrusions of that highly acidic fruit. Here I temper the acidity by first mixing the chopped cranberries with a little sugar and an uplifting amount of orange zest. Just before baking I brush the tops of the loaves with milk and sprinkle with a few pinches of sugar; that gives the top crust a great crunchy contrast to the soft inside.

> 1 1/2 cups cranberries, coarsely chopped
> 1/3 cup sugar
> finely grated zest of 1 orange
> 2 cups unbleached flour
> 1/2 cup yellow cornmeal, preferably stone-ground
> 1 teaspoon baking soda
> 1/2 teaspoon salt
> 1/2 teaspoon ground nutmeg, preferably freshly grated
> 5 tablespoons cold unsalted butter, cut into small pieces
> 1/2 cup sour cream, yogurt, or buttermilk
> 1/2 cup milk
> a little extra milk and sugar for the top

Combine the cranberries, sugar, and orange zest in a small bowl and set aside for 15 minutes. Preheat the oven to 400° and lightly butter a large baking sheet.

Mix the flour, cornmeal, baking soda, salt, and nutmeg in another bowl. Add the butter and cut it in until it is broken into fine pieces. Mix the sour cream and milk, then make a well in the dry ingredients and add the liquid all at once. Stir until the dough starts pulling together, then stir in the cranberries. When you have a cohesive ball of dough, turn it out onto a floured surface and divide in half.

Briefly knead each half of dough into a ball, then place the balls on the sheet, leaving ample space between them. Brush the tops of the loaves with a little milk and sprinkle each one with several big pinches of sugar. Bake for 40 to 45 minutes, until the tops are a rich golden brown. Cool the loaves on a rack. These loaves should be almost entirely cool before being sliced; use a sharp serrated knife.

Currant Rye Tea Bread

MAKES ABOUT 10 SERVINGS

This light rye bread is compact and moist like pound cake, shot throughout with bourbon-soaked currants and a lift of orange zest. It's an easy-to-make, highly portable holiday bread and one whose texture and flavor only seem to improve over the course of several days — why I am not sure. It may have something to do with the bourbon in the currants slowly being reabsorbed into the bread, but for that to happen the currants must have soaked long enough for the liquor to soak in; that goes for any bread or cake of this nature. Best to soak dried fruits overnight, but if you can't, an hour or so in a very warm spot will do. Wrap this bread in plastic wrap as soon as it has cooled, then overwrap in foil. Very nice served with tea.

>1 cup dried currants
>3 tablespoons bourbon or brandy
>6 tablespoons unsalted butter, softened
>1/4 pound cream cheese at room temperature
>3/4 cup packed light brown sugar
>2 large eggs at room temperature
>1 teaspoon vanilla extract
>finely grated zest of 1 orange
>1 1/2 cups unbleached flour
>1/2 cup rye flour
>2 teaspoons baking powder
>1/2 teaspoon salt

The night before or at least several hours ahead, combine the currants and bourbon. Cover and set aside, stirring occasionally. When you're ready to proceed, butter and lightly flour a 4 1/2- by 8 1/2-inch loaf pan, preferably not a dark one. Preheat the oven to 350°.

Using an electric mixer, cream the butter and cream cheese until light and airy. Beat in the brown sugar and then the eggs, one at a time, followed by the vanilla and orange zest.

Sift the flours, baking powder, and salt into another bowl, then stir the dry ingredients into the creamed mixture in 2 stages. Stir in the currants and their liquid, if any, when a few streaks of flour are still visible, continuing to stir until evenly blended.

160

Scrape the batter into the prepared pan, evening it out with a fork. Bake for 50 to 55 minutes, until a tester inserted into the center of the bread comes out clean. Cool for 20 minutes in the pan on a rack, then turn the bread out. Line a plate with wax paper and put the bread directly on it. As soon as it has cooled, lift the bread — on the wax paper — onto a long piece of plastic wrap and wrap it up. Overwrap the bread in foil. It is best to let this mellow overnight before slicing; use a sharp serrated knife.

A
Holiday
Bread
Miscellany

Yeasted Pastry Candy Canes

MAKES ABOUT 14 CANDY CANES

I call these pastry candy canes, but that's only one shape you can turn this simple yeasted dough into. You can do wreaths (a circle with the ends in a half-knot), stars, bells, or almost anything with simple lines. My kids are much more imaginative and daring than I am with these; I usually just stick with candy canes. No matter what shape you make, you will love the way they taste: a little like a plain doughnut, but with a texture more like a biscuit—hard to describe, easy to eat. If you make shapes other than candy canes, you can loop a piece of ribbon through them and hang them from the Christmas tree.

> 1 recipe Wheaten Yeasted Pastry (page 245), modified as outlined
> 1 teaspoon vanilla extract
> finely grated zest of 1 lemon
> egg wash: 1 large egg beaten with 1 teaspoon milk
> poppy seeds to sprinkle on top (optional)
> a little sugar to sprinkle on top

Prepare the pastry as directed, making the following changes: Use 3 tablespoons of sugar instead of 2; add the vanilla extract and lemon zest to the beaten egg before combining it with the dry ingredients. Mix the dough as directed and shape it into an approximate 5- by 6-inch rectangle. Dust the rectangle with flour, wrap in wax paper, and refrigerate for 1 hour. While the dough rests, lightly butter 2 large baking sheets and set them aside. Line a third baking sheet or tray with wax paper and flour it lightly.

After an hour, dust a work surface with flour and roll the dough into an approximate 10- by 8-inch rectangle. Cut the dough into strips (the long way) a little wider than 1/2 inch; this is best accomplished with a pastry or pizza cutter and a ruler as a guiding straight edge. A knife will do, but unless it is very sharp it tends to pull the dough, and you end up with uneven strips. Lay the strips on the wax paper–lined sheet, close but not touching, and cover with wax paper. Refrigerate for 15 minutes while you preheat the oven to 350°.

Brush any flour from the strips and shape them into candy canes, then lay the canes on the buttered sheets. You'll get a better result if you twist the strips as you shape them; otherwise they just look a bit flat. Lay the candy canes alternately head to toe so they take up less space on the sheets. If you are making other shapes and you find you need longer strips, roll them gently under your palms first. Brush the candy canes lightly with the egg wash, sprinkling each one with some poppy seeds and a big pinch of sugar.

   Let the canes rest at room temperature, uncovered, for 5 minutes, then bake for about 20 minutes, until lightly browned on top. Cool briefly on the sheets, then transfer the candy canes to a rack to finish cooling. Store in a covered container for up to 4 days. Handle carefully.

A
Holiday
Bread
Miscellany

Conquering the Fear of Yeast Bread

At the risk of oversimplifying the issue, I can sum up most of what you need to know about yeast in one phrase: Hot liquids will kill it. Not long ago, I talked to my brother in New Jersey, who called with yet another long-distance tale of baking woe. His bread dough wasn't rising, and he wanted to know why. As we went over the process, everything seemed to check out until I asked him about the type of fat he used. Butter, he said — "I just melted it and poured it over the dissolved yeast."

While it was hot?

"Yep."

Problem solved: He had killed the yeast with hot butter.

So, most important, be sure none of the liquids that come into contact with your yeast is hotter than 115°. It isn't necessary to use a thermometer to check the temperatures unless you really need to be reassured. If you are using tap water, it should feel lukewarm, comfortable on your wrist like the milk in a baby's bottle. If you are using milk, which is easily overheated, just pour it into a bowl and wait until it cools.

Yeast is commonly sold in two forms: *active dry yeast* and *compressed cakes.* Dry yeast comes in 1/4-ounce packets, measuring just under a tablespoon, and cake yeast in 3/5-ounce cakes that look something like bouillon cubes. (To substitute cake yeast for active dry yeast, use one 3/5-ounce cake for one 1/4-ounce packet. Crumble the fresh yeast into the liquid — where you would normally sprinkle on the dry yeast — and stir to dissolve.)

I find there's little difference in whole grain baking in the results you get using active dry yeast as opposed to compressed cakes. However, since active dry yeast can be stored in the freezer, tightly sealed, for up to a year, this is the one I normally recommend. Compressed yeast must be used within 4 to 6 weeks from the date of manufacture, though it will keep in the freezer for up to 2 months. If you bake with yeast infrequently, it makes more sense to use active dry yeast. I recommend buying bulk active dry yeast at a health food store — it's cheaper that way — and keeping it in a sealed jar in the freezer.

As for the new fast yeasts, they can cut your rising times in half, but there's a trade-off: The flavor of your bread suffers because your dough has less time to mature; allowing doughs to ripen slowly greatly enhances their flavor.

You've probably heard the expression "proofing yeast." Proofing is simply a way to find out if your yeast is still alive, or active, before you go through the entire bread-making process, only to find all your efforts have been for naught.

To proof active dry yeast, pour 1/4 cup lukewarm water into a small bowl and sprinkle the full amount of yeast over it. Add a pinch of sugar, stir with a fork, and set the bowl aside. Well within 10 minutes the yeast water should become visibly frothy and bubbly. If you see no activity at all, the yeast is no longer good and should be discarded. Remember to deduct 1/4 cup of liquid — usually water or milk — from the total amount specified in the recipe if you proof yeast in this manner.

To proof compressed cake yeast, the procedure is a little different: Crumble one 3/5-ounce cake into the water and use a small wooden spoon to stir it in with the pinch of sugar. It too should froth and bubble.

Yeast does not dissolve easily in milk or milk products; always use water.

If indeed your yeast is good, and you've handled it correctly, your bread baking should proceed without a glitch. But here are a few other tips to smooth the way.

• Always add flour gradually, especially as the dough becomes more cohesive. This will guard against adding too much flour, which can result in a dry loaf.

• When you knead, press gently on the dough as you roll it under your palm; you can press more firmly as the dough becomes elastic. Knead until the dough is smooth and elastic. It is almost impossible to overknead by hand, but pretty common to underknead, which gives your bread a weak structure and prevents a good rise in the oven.

• Choose a warm but not hot spot for the rising. On top of the fridge is good, *under* the woodstove, or in a gas oven where the pilot stays lit.

• To check whether a yeast bread is done, turn it out of the pan (if you used one) and tap the bottom with a finger; it should give a hollow retort. (The exception here is filled breads like coffee cakes). If you don't get a hollow sound, bake for another 10 minutes.

Cornmeal Sage Breadsticks

MAKES ABOUT 18 BREADSTICKS

*I've always thought these made an excellent gift, even for another baker,
because breadsticks aren't the sort of thing one usually makes for oneself.
And they're just right for that somebody on your holiday list — we all know
someone like this — who claims not to like sweets or is on a perpetual diet.
Crisp and chewy, with the subtle flavor of sage, these are perfect with
Italian foods, marinated vegetables, salad and soup meals, thick garlicky
dips, or just as a between-meals nibbler — a good thing when you have
kids, whose first impulse is to reach for the cookie jar. To gift wrap, just
tie a pretty ribbon around a fistful of these or fill a long narrow basket,
maybe lined with a colorful cloth, with them.*

> 1 1/2 cups lukewarm water
> 1 1/2 teaspoons active dry yeast (half of a 1/4-ounce package)
> 1 teaspoon honey
> 1 1/2 teaspoons salt
> 1 2/3 cups whole wheat flour
> 1/3 cup yellow cornmeal, preferably stone-ground
> 2 tablespoons good quality olive oil
> 1 tablespoon crushed dried sage
> a few grinds of black pepper
> 2 cups (approximately) unbleached flour
> egg wash: 1 large egg white beaten with 1 teaspoon water
> 2 tablespoons sesame seeds for sprinkling on breadsticks

Pour the water into a large mixing bowl and stir in the yeast and
honey. Set aside for 5 minutes. After the yeast is dissolved, stir in the
salt, whole wheat flour, and cornmeal. Beat vigorously with a
wooden spoon for 1 minute, then cover the bowl with plastic wrap
and place in a warm, draft-free spot for 15 minutes.

After 15 minutes, stir the oil, sage, and pepper into the sponge.
Beat in enough of the unbleached flour, about 1/2 cup at a time, to
make a soft, kneadable dough. Turn the dough out onto a floured
surface and knead for about 8 minutes, using as much of the remaining flour as necessary to keep the dough from sticking. Shape the
dough into a narrow loaf and lay it on a floured section of your work
area. Cover loosely with plastic wrap and let the dough rest for 5
minutes. While you're waiting, lightly oil 2 large baking sheets.

Flour an approximate 2-foot by 6-inch section of your work table. Place the dough in the middle of this area, flour the surface, and roll it into a long rectangle, roughly 24 by 6 inches; the exact size is less important than the thickness, which should be about 3/4 inch, no less. Using a very sharp knife — or preferably a pastry or pizza cutter, because it won't pull the dough out of shape — cut the dough in half; you now have 2 sections about 12 inches long.

Now cut each section into lengthwise strips 3/4 inch wide. Immediately move each strip onto the sheet, leaving about 1 1/2 inches between them; try not to stretch the strips as you pick them up, and straighten them up a little on the baking sheet, but don't try to make them look too perfect. Part of the charm of these is their little irregularities. Set the sheets aside, uncovered, in a warm, draft-free spot for 20 minutes. Meanwhile, preheat the oven to 400°.

After 20 minutes, brush each strip of dough with a little of the egg wash and sprinkle with sesame seeds before brushing the next one. (If you brush all of them first, the glaze will tend to dry out, and the seeds won't adhere as well.) Bake for 25 minutes, until dark brown and crusty. Transfer the sticks to a rack and cool. Store the cooled breadsticks in a sealed plastic bag.

A
Holiday
Bread
Miscellany

Whole Wheat Brioche

MAKES 2 LOAVES, ABOUT 12 TO
14 SLICES PER LOAF

*I first fell in love with brioche at a bakery called Mrs. London's in
Saratoga, New York, once run by my friends Michael and Wendy London.
Among the wonderful items on their breakfast menu was a French toast
made from brioche; it was so light it almost hovered over the plate, and I
haven't had such good French toast since. I still make French toast with
brioche, but there are lots of other special holiday things you can do with it
too, all of them based on this whole wheat brioche dough. I have never seen
a recipe for whole wheat brioche, and perhaps some will find the whole idea
heretical. But one taste will convince you this is not a bad idea at all. If
you have never had it, brioche is a very light bread, enriched with lots of
eggs and butter. The large amount of butter makes it very difficult to mix
by hand, and this is one case where I wouldn't even bother without using a
heavy-duty mixer; the dough is simply too sticky to work with. This basic
recipe will make 2 loaves to enjoy as is or for the Brioche Cinnamon Bread
Custard (page 226) or the Crumb Croûte of Pears (page 228).*

STARTER
> 1/3 cup lukewarm water
> 1 1/4-ounce package (about 1 tablespoon) active dry yeast
> 1 tablespoon sugar
> 1/2 cup unbleached flour

DOUGH
> 1 3/4 cups whole wheat flour
> 1 1/2 cups unbleached flour
> 1 1/2 teaspoons salt
> 5 large eggs at room temperature, lightly beaten
> 1/2 cup milk at room temperature
> 3/4 cup (6 ounces) unsalted butter at room temperature

To make the starter, pour the lukewarm water into a small bowl or a
2-cup measure. Whisk in the yeast and sugar. Wait 2 minutes, then
whisk in the 1/2 cup flour. Cover the starter with plastic wrap and
set aside for 15 minutes.

Meanwhile, mix the whole wheat flour, unbleached flour, and
salt in a large bowl. When the 15 minutes have elapsed, make a well
in the dry ingredients and add the eggs, milk, and starter. Using a
wooden spoon, stir the dough vigorously for 1 minute; at least try to

be vigorous — the dough may be quite thick at this point. Cover the dough with plastic wrap and set it aside in a warm, draft-free spot for 45 minutes.

After 45 minutes, transfer the dough to the bowl of a large, heavy-duty mixer fitted with the flat beater. Holding the butter in hand, cut it into approximate 1/4-inch pieces, letting them drop right on top of the dough. Start out mixing the dough on slow speed for 2 minutes, then increase to medium speed and mix for about 5 minutes more. You may have to stop occasionally to push the dough down off the beater.

When the dough is fully kneaded, it will be smooth and satiny, and it will tend to ride up on the beater without letting loose. But it will have less spring or elasticity than a yeast dough usually does. Turn the dough out onto a lightly floured surface and knead, with floured hands, for 1 minute. Place the dough in a buttered bowl, turning to coat the entire surface. Cover with plastic wrap and place in a warm, draft-free spot until doubled in bulk, probably about 1 1/2 hours. Generously butter 2 4 1/2- by 8 1/2-inch loaf pans.

Punch the dough down and turn it out onto a lightly floured surface. Divide the dough in half and let the halves rest briefly. Using a rolling pin, roll each into an oblong about 1/2 inch thick, a little wider at one end. Starting at the narrow end, roll the dough up, jelly roll style, keeping it somewhat taut. Pinch the seam to seal, then place in the pan seam down. The dough will seem small in relation to the pan, but it needs plenty of rising space. Cover the pans with lightly buttered plastic wrap and set them aside in a warm, draft-free spot until the center of the dough comes about 1 inch above the top of the pan. Preheat the oven to 375° about 15 minutes before the dough reaches that point.

When the loaves are fully doubled, bake them for 40 minutes; when you turn the bread out of the pan and tap the bottom crust, it should sound hollow. Cool the loaves on a rack or slice with a sharp serrated knife and eat warm. Store in sealed plastic bags.

A
Holiday
Bread
Miscellany

Baked Pumpkin Doughnuts

MAKES ABOUT 2 DOZEN DOUGHNUTS

Baked doughnuts are definitely the way to go if, like me, you don't want the hassle of deep-frying. Naturally, baked doughnuts are breadier than deep-fried cake doughnuts, but they're delicious, tender, and a lot more fun to make if you plan to involve the kids. We get in the doughnut mood around Halloween. One of our favorite Halloween party games is a blindfolded version of bobbing for doughnuts. We hang them on string from the ceiling, then the blindfoldee is spun around and sent gobbling into the air to get a bite of doughnut; it can get very silly, and the kids have a blast. Once we're in the spirit, we usually continue to make doughnuts throughout the holiday season. These favorites use a pumpkin base, which gives them a pretty orange cast and plays well with the nutmeg. We finish them with a maple glaze or melted butter and cinnamon sugar, both of which are outlined here. Serve them warm.

> 1 small sugar pie pumpkin (about 2 pounds) *or* 1 cup
>   canned pumpkin
> 1/3 cup lukewarm water
> 1 1/4-ounce package (about 1 tablespoon) active dry yeast
> 1 large egg at room temperature, lightly beaten
> 1/2 cup packed light brown sugar
> 1/4 cup sour cream
> 1/4 cup unsalted butter, melted
> 1 1/4 teaspoons ground nutmeg, preferably freshly grated
> 2 cups whole wheat flour
> 1 1/2 teaspoons salt
> 1 1/2 cups (approximately) unbleached flour

Bake the pumpkin and process 1 cup of the flesh as described for the Pumpkin Spice Muffins on page 20. Set aside. Pour the lukewarm water into a mixing bowl and stir in the yeast; set aside for 5 minutes. Once the yeast has dissolved, whisk in the pumpkin, egg, brown sugar, sour cream, butter, and nutmeg. Stir in the whole wheat flour a cup at a time, beating well with a wooden spoon after each cup. Cover the bowl with plastic wrap and set it aside in a warm, draft-free spot for 15 minutes.

After 15 minutes, stir the salt into the dough. Work in enough of the unbleached flour, about 1/3 cup at a time, to make a soft, kneadable dough. Turn the dough out and knead for 10 minutes —

gently at first, because the pumpkin makes this a little sticky — until the dough is smooth and somewhat elastic; it will remain pretty soft and delicate, however. Place the dough in a lightly oiled bowl, turning to coat the entire surface. Cover with plastic wrap, and set aside in a warm, draft-free spot until doubled in bulk, about 1 hour. Butter 2 large baking sheets, preferably not dark ones, and set them aside.

Once the dough has doubled, punch it down and turn it out onto a floured surface. Knead for 1 minute, then dust the dough lightly with flour and let it rest for 5 minutes.

After the rest, roll the dough about 3/4 inch thick on a floured surface. Using a 3-inch doughnut cutter — or a larger one, which of course will give you fewer doughnuts — cut as many doughnuts as you can, keeping the cuts close together. Transfer the doughnuts and holes to the sheets, leaving about 1 1/2 inches between them. Handle the doughnut dough carefully, because if the rounds stretch too much, they won't rise nicely. Knead the scraps together and cut them too. Lightly oil 2 sheets of plastic wrap and cover the doughnuts carefully. Set them aside in a warm, draft-free spot until soft, swollen, and nearly doubled in size, 30 to 40 minutes. Preheat the oven to 400°.

When the doughnuts appear doubled, bake them for 20 to 25 minutes, until golden brown. Transfer them to a large sheet of wax paper and finish with one of the following glazes while still hot.

MAPLE SUGAR GLAZE
1/2 cup confectioners' sugar
2 1/2 to 3 tablespoons pure maple syrup

Put the sugar in a small bowl and briskly stir in 2 1/2 tablespoons of the maple syrup. Use enough of the remaining maple syrup to make a runny but still slightly thick glaze. Brush it on the hot doughnuts with a pastry brush.

CINNAMON SUGAR GLAZE
1/4 cup unsalted butter, melted
1/2 cup sugar
2 teaspoons ground cinnamon

Brush the hot doughnuts generously with butter. Mix the sugar and cinnamon and sprinkle plenty of it over each one.

Store the doughnuts in a sealed plastic bag, in a cool spot.

Mashed Potato Bread

MAKES 2 LOAVES,
ABOUT 12 SLICES EACH

For anyone who likes to bake, Thanksgiving week is hectic. There are the pies, the rolls, not to mention the old favorite recipes we fall back on when family members arrive from distant points. I've always taken special pleasure from incorporating the leftovers into my post-Thanksgiving baking, and here is one example: a perfectly light, tender, and delicious potato bread made with leftover mashed potatoes. For those who can rise to the occasion, the bread should be made the morning after the big day, so it's still barely warm when the first call goes up for turkey sandwiches. This is a fine all-purpose loaf to have on hand for a busy week.

> 2 cups milk
> 1/4 cup unsalted butter
> 1 cup leftover mashed potatoes
> 1/4 cup lukewarm water
> 1 1/4-ounce package (about 1 tablespoon) active dry yeast
> 1 tablespoon sugar
> 2 1/2 teaspoons salt
> 1 large egg, lightly beaten
> 3 cups whole wheat flour
> 3 cups (approximately) unbleached flour

Heat the milk and butter in a small saucepan until the butter melts. In a large mixing bowl, stir together the milk mixture and mashed potatoes. Set the bowl aside. Pour the lukewarm water into a small bowl or measuring cup and stir in the yeast; set aside for 5 minutes.

When the milk mixture has cooled to about body temperature, stir in the dissolved yeast, sugar, salt, and egg. Add the whole wheat flour 1 cup at a time, beating well with a wooden spoon after each addition. Stir in enough of the unbleached flour, about 1/2 cup at a time, to make a soft, kneadable dough. Turn the dough out onto a floured surface and knead — gently at first because the dough is very soft — for 10 minutes, using as much of the remaining flour as necessary to keep the dough from sticking. When the dough is soft, smooth, and somewhat elastic (the presence of the potato makes it less elastic than some doughs), place it in a lightly oiled bowl, turning to coat the entire surface. Cover the dough with plastic wrap and set it aside in a warm, draft-free spot until doubled in bulk, 1 to 1 1/2 hours. In the meantime, butter 2 4- by 8-inch loaf pans.

When the dough has doubled, punch it down and turn it out onto a lightly floured surface. Divide the dough in half and knead each half briefly; let the halves rest, loosely covered with plastic wrap, for 5 minutes.

Working with one piece of dough at a time, roll the dough on a lightly floured surface into a tapered oblong about 12 inches long; it should look something like a guitar pick, with the narrow part pointing toward you. Starting at the narrow end, roll the dough up like a carpet, keeping it snug but not so tight that you rip the surface of the dough. Just before you finish rolling, moisten the long edge with a fingertip dipped in water. Finish rolling up the dough and pinch the seam to seal. Place the dough, seam side down, in one of the pans. Repeat for the other piece of dough. Put the pans side by side in a warm, draft-free spot and cover loosely with plastic wrap. When the loaves have almost doubled in bulk, preheat the oven to 375°.

Once the loaves have doubled, bake them for approximately 50 minutes; when done, they'll be nicely browned on top. Take one out of the pan and tap the bottom with a fingertip; if it's done, it will give a faint hollow retort, but it will not be as evident as with other breads without potato in them. Remove the bread from the pans and cool the loaves on a rack. Wait until they are almost cooled before slicing. Store in sealed plastic bags.

Mixed Grain Cuban Bread

MAKES 1 LARGE LOAF

I don't know why this bread is called Cuban, but Cuban bread recipes have been floating around for years. Variations exist — this favorite uses both cornmeal and rye flour — but the basic idea is always an abbreviated version of crusty traditional French bread. And it's the time-saving factor that makes this a good bread for this busy time of year. In addition to serving this plain, just as you would French bread, there are a few other uses for it: for White Pizza (page 196), and as the foundation for the variety of toasts known as bruschette (page 210) that make wonderful finger food for your holiday parties.

> 1 1/4 cups lukewarm water
> 1 1/4-ounce package (about 1 tablespoon) active dry yeast
> 1 teaspoon sugar
> 1 teaspoon salt
> 1/4 cup yellow cornmeal, preferably stone-ground
> 2 tablespoons rye flour
> 2 1/4 to 2 1/2 cups unbleached flour

Pour the water into a medium mixing bowl and stir in the yeast and sugar. Set aside for 5 minutes, to dissolve. Once the yeast has dissolved, stir in the salt, cornmeal, and rye flour. Beat in enough of the unbleached flour, about 1/2 cup at a time, to make a soft dough; it may seem a little sticky, but once the dough is too heavy to stir, turn it out onto a floured surface and begin kneading it with floured hands.

Knead the dough for 6 minutes, using as much of the remaining flour as necessary to keep the dough from sticking. Scrape and rub your mixing bowl clean with your hands, flour it lightly, and place the dough in it. Cover the bowl with plastic wrap and set it aside in a warm, draft-free spot until the dough has doubled in bulk. In the meantime, get out a large baking sheet and dust it generously with cornmeal.

Once the dough has doubled, punch it down and knead briefly on a lightly floured surface. Let the dough rest for a few minutes, then roll it into an oblong about 14 inches long. Gently stretch one long side of the oblong, to square off the edges, then start rolling it from the other long edge. Keep your roll a little tight but not too tight. Before you finish rolling, moisten the edge of the dough with a fingertip dipped in water, finish the roll, and pinch the seam to seal. Pinch each end to give them a rounded-off look. Place the dough on the sheet, seam side down, and straighten the loaf out with cupped hands. Let the dough rest for 15 minutes, uncovered; do not preheat the oven.

After 15 minutes, brush the surface of the dough lightly with water. Using a sharp, serrated knife, make 5 diagonal slashes in the top of the dough, about 1/2 inch deep. Put the sheet into a *cold* oven and turn the heat up to 425°. Bake for 35 minutes, until the loaf is golden and crusty on all sides. If you are not slicing the loaf right away, cool on a rack. To reheat, put the loaf — unwrapped — in a 400° oven for 10 minutes. Reheating brings the crust right back.

A
Holiday
Bread
Miscellany

Walnut Bread

MAKES 4 GIFT-SIZE OR
2 LARGE LOAVES

*This bread is full of walnuts — inside and outside — with walnut oil to
accentuate the dominant theme. It bakes up dark and dense and slices nice
and thin for sandwiches. It would be right at home on a holiday buffet table,
next to a cold cut platter or some cream cheese spreads. This bread makes
great toast too. If you plan to use this bread as a family loaf, not for gifts or
parties, you might want to skip the extra step of the walnut crust.*

> 2 1/2 cups lukewarm water
> 1 1/4-ounce package (about 1 tablespoon) active dry yeast
> 2 tablespoons honey
> 5 1/2 cups whole wheat flour
> 2 teaspoons salt
> 1/3 cup walnut oil
> 4 cups (about 1 pound) walnuts, 2 of the cups toasted (see page
>   111), finely chopped
> 1/2 cup (approximately) unbleached flour for kneading
> egg wash: 1 large egg white beaten with 1 teaspoon water

Pour the lukewarm water into a large bowl and sprinkle on the
yeast. Wait 5 minutes, then stir in the honey and 3 1/2 cups of the
whole wheat flour. Stir the mixture vigorously for 1 minute, then
cover it with plastic wrap and set this sponge aside in a warm, draft-
free spot for 15 minutes.

    After 15 minutes, stir the salt, oil, and the 2 cups of finely
chopped toasted walnuts into the sponge. Stir in the remaining
whole wheat flour 1/2 cup at a time until you have a kneadable
dough; you may have to work the last bit of whole wheat flour into
the dough with the back of a wooden spoon.

    Flour your work surface with some of the unbleached flour and
turn the dough out onto it. With floured hands, knead the dough for
10 minutes, using as much of the unbleached flour as necessary to
keep the dough from sticking; don't knead too roughly, because this
dough is a little sticky. Place the dough in a lightly oiled bowl,
turning it to coat the entire surface. Cover the bowl with plastic
wrap and set the dough aside in a warm, draft-free spot until doubled in bulk, 1 to 1 1/2 hours. Lightly butter 2 large, heavy baking
sheets, preferably dark ones, and set them aside.

Once the dough has doubled, punch it down and knead briefly, then divide the dough into quarters (or half if you're making 2 larger loaves). Working with one piece of dough at a time, knead it into a ball. Put 1/2 cup of the remaining untoasted chopped walnuts on a piece of wax paper. Brush the entire surface of the dough with the egg white wash, then roll the dough in the nuts, coating the whole thing. Place the ball seam side down on the baking sheet. Repeat for the other pieces of dough, coating each one with 1/2 cup nuts. It isn't necessary to cover the loaves, but put them aside in a warm, draft-free spot until doubled in bulk, 40 to 50 minutes. About 15 minutes before that point, preheat the oven to 375°.

Bake the loaves for 45 minutes, then transfer them to a rack to cool before slicing. Store leftovers in a plastic bag.

N O T E : If you're making 2 loaves, use 4 1/2- by 8 1/2-inch loaf pans. Coat each with 1 cup of untoasted nuts, if you like, before placing them in the pans. Or knead the halves into balls, coat them with walnuts, and bake free-form on a baking sheet.

*A
Holiday
Bread
Miscellany*

Whole Wheat Julekake

MAKES 2 FREE-FORM LOAVES,
ABOUT 12 SLICES EACH

*Variations on this cardamom-scented bread are found throughout
Scandinavia. This one is somewhat unusual in that the dough contains
half of an orange — peel and all — ground in a food processor. Contrary to
what you might expect, the skin leaves no bitter taste but adds only a
pleasant chewiness. The top is coated with an egg glaze and dusted with
sugar, which gives the crust a gritty, crunchy texture I love. I first read
about this bread in Jane Watson Hopping's* The Pioneer Lady's
Country Christmas *(Villard Books). She tells a story of her friend,
Edvard Amundsen, who came to this country from Norway as a young
man. His family had saved for years to send him here, realizing that his
ancestral farm would never produce enough to sustain the next generation.
He worked for 8 years after his arrival, clearing the land, planting, and
building a home, before finally sending for a hardworking wife from his
native land. Thus arrived 18-year-old Inger, whose holiday julekake was
perfect, a little piece of home for Edvard and his fellow homesick
countrymen who didn't yet have a family in the new land. Good story.
Good bread!*

1/4 cup lukewarm water
1 1/4-ounce package (about 1 tablespoon) active dry yeast
1/2 navel orange
1/4 cup sugar
1 1/4 cups lukewarm milk
1/3 cup honey
finely grated zest of 1 lemon
1 1/2 teaspoons vanilla extract
2 cups whole wheat flour
1 teaspoon ground cardamom
1 large egg, lightly beaten
1/4 cup unsalted butter, softened
2 teaspoons salt
3 1/4 to 3 1/2 cups unbleached flour
egg wash: 1 large egg beaten with 1 tablespoon milk
4 teaspoons sugar to sprinkle on top

Pour the lukewarm water into a small bowl and stir in the yeast. Set
it aside for 5 minutes. While the yeast dissolves, cut the half orange
into a few smaller chunks and place them in a food processor along

with the sugar. Process until the mixture is reduced to very small pieces; it should have some texture and not turn into a puree.

Pour the lukewarm milk into a large mixing bowl and stir in the orange, dissolved yeast, honey, lemon zest, and vanilla. Add the whole wheat flour and cardamom and beat vigorously for 1 minute with a wooden spoon. Cover this sponge with plastic wrap and set it aside in a warm, draft-free spot for 15 minutes.

After 15 minutes, stir in the egg, butter, and salt. Stir in enough of the unbleached flour, 1 cup at a time, to make a soft, kneadable dough. Turn the dough out onto a floured surface and knead with floured hands for 10 minutes, using enough of the remaining flour to keep the dough from sticking; this is a soft dough, so knead gently at first to keep it from sticking to your hands. The dough will not get terribly springy, but it will become somewhat elastic and smooth when fully kneaded. Place the dough in an oiled bowl, turning to coat the entire surface. Cover the bowl with plastic wrap and set it aside in a warm, draft-free spot until the dough is doubled in bulk, 1 to 1 1/2 hours. In the meantime, lightly butter a large, heavy baking sheet, preferably a dark one.

When the dough has doubled, punch it down and turn it out onto a floured surface. Divide the dough in half, then knead each half into a ball. Place the balls on the sheet, leaving plenty of room between them for expansion. Cover the balls loosely with lightly oiled plastic wrap and set the sheet aside in a warm spot until the balls are almost doubled in bulk, 35 to 45 minutes. About 15 minutes before this point, preheat the oven to 375°.

When the loaves are almost doubled, brush them liberally with the egg wash. As soon as you put the wash on, sprinkle the top of the loaf with 2 teaspoons of the sugar. Repeat with the other loaf. When the loaves have doubled, bake them for 55 minutes, until the top is a rich golden color and quite crusty. Transfer the loaves to a rack to cool or slice and serve warm with hot tea or coffee. Store leftovers in sealed plastic bags.

*A
Holiday
Bread
Miscellany*

Braided Egg Bread

MAKES 2 LONG BRAIDED LOAVES OR
WREATHS, ABOUT 14 SLICES EACH

To make an attractive braided bread you need to use plenty of eggs in the dough so it swells and bakes up looking full and round; this dough — which has 6 eggs — is just the one. A braid automatically gives a loaf of bread a visual boost, making it look all decked out, perfect for the holiday season. A straight braid is pretty, but for Christmas I like to take the dough and wrap it around a bowl to form a wreath. This wreath can then become the centerpiece of a buffet table. (You'll have to encourage your guests to dig in, because this looks too pretty to cut.) A very light bread, and not really sweet, this goes with anything you care to serve it with — from cold cuts to savory spreads to cheeses.

    1/2 cup lukewarm water
    2 1/4-ounce packages (about 2 tablespoons) active dry yeast
    1 1/2 cups lukewarm milk
    1/4 cup honey
    6 large eggs at room temperature, lightly beaten
    4 cups whole wheat flour
    1 tablespoon salt
    6 tablespoons unsalted butter, softened
    3 1/2 to 4 cups unbleached flour
    egg wash: 1 large egg beaten with 1 tablespoon milk

Pour the lukewarm water into a small bowl or measuring cup and mix in the yeast. Set aside for 5 minutes. Pour the lukewarm milk into a large mixing bowl and stir in the honey and dissolved yeast. Add the eggs and then the whole wheat flour. Using a wooden spoon, beat the batter vigorously for about 2 minutes. Cover the bowl with plastic wrap, then set it aside in a warm, draft-free spot for 15 minutes.

    After 15 minutes, beat the salt and butter into the dough. Beat in enough of the unbleached flour, about 1 cup at a time, to make a soft, kneadable dough. Turn the dough out onto a floured surface and knead for 10 minutes, using as much of the remaining un-bleached flour as necessary to keep the dough from sticking. Place the dough in a large oiled bowl and rotate it to coat the entire surface. Cover the bowl with plastic wrap and set it aside in a warm, draft-free spot until doubled in bulk, 1 to 1 1/2 hours. In the meantime, butter 2 large heavy baking sheets; for wreaths, large square sheets are ideal.

Once the dough has risen, punch it down and turn it out onto a floured surface. Divide the dough in half, then knead each half for about 1 minute to force out any air bubbles. Put one half back in the bowl and cover; divide the other half into 3 equal pieces and shape them into balls.

On a lightly floured surface, roll each of the 3 pieces under your palms — stretching the dough out as you do — to make even strands about 2 feet long. Rolling the pieces a little at a time works better than trying to stretch a piece to its limit right off the bat. So keep switching from one piece to the next. Lay the strands right next to one another at one end, from which you will start to braid, but let them flare out at the other end, away from one another. Press the 3 strands together at the end where they are close, keeping the center strand on top; tuck that end under a little. Braid the loaf, twisting the strands a little as you go; this will help to keep them tight. Press the strands together at the other end and tuck them under too.

If you're making a straight braid, just lift the dough onto the sheet and center it. If you're making a wreath, place an 8-inch bowl in the center of the sheet to keep the dough round. Wrap the braid around it and remove the bowl just before you join the ends. Moisten one of the ends with a fingertip dipped in water, then butt the ends together. Using a pastry brush, brush the entire surface of the dough with the egg wash. Repeat for the other half of the dough. Set the braids aside in a warm, draft-free spot until quite swollen and puffy, though perhaps not quite doubled in bulk, 30 to 40 minutes. About 15 minutes before the dough reaches this point, preheat the oven to 375°.

When the dough is swollen and puffy, bake the loaves for 45 minutes, until the surface turns a deep, dark golden brown. Slice and serve hot from the oven or transfer the loaves to a rack to cool. Once the loaves have cooled, carefully wrap them in plastic wrap or slip them into large plastic bags.

Whole Wheat Fig Swirl Bread

MAKES 2 LARGE LOAVES,
ABOUT 14 SLICES EACH

*This is a very versatile holiday bread, something like a fig coffee cake but
not so sweet or rich. It's made almost entirely with whole wheat flour, with
a thick swirl of fig puree running through it. It makes an excellent
breakfast bread — you could easily make it the day before — and I
particularly like it with whipped cream cheese or plain mascarpone cheese.
Don't overlook the possibility of serving this bread with a stew or soup for
dinner, however, because the fig filling would complement any number of
meat dishes, including chicken. These are long, dark, handsome loaves,
and they look great served presliced in a long narrow basket lined with an
off-white cloth.*

> 1 recipe Poached Calimyrna Figs (page 221)
> 2 1/2 cups milk
> 3/4 cups rolled oats (*not* instant)
> 1/3 cup packed light brown sugar
> 3 tablespoons cold unsalted butter, cut into tablespoon-size pieces
> 1/4 cup lukewarm water
> 1 1/4-ounce package (about 1 tablespoon) active dry yeast
> 4 1/2 cups whole wheat flour
> 1 large egg, lightly beaten
> 2 1/2 teaspoons salt
> 1/3 cup (approximately) unbleached flour
> egg wash: 1 large egg beaten with 1 tablespoon milk

To prepare the fig filling, place the poached figs in the bowl of a food
processor. Bring the poaching liquid to a boil and reduce it to a little
less than 1/2 cup. Process the figs to a smooth puree, gradually
adding all of the poaching liquid. Transfer the puree to a plate, cover
with plastic wrap, and allow to cool.

To make the dough, heat the milk until hot to the touch. Put the
oats, brown sugar, and butter in a large mixing bowl and pour the
hot milk over them. As that mixture cools, pour the lukewarm water
into a measuring cup and sprinkle the yeast over it. Stir and set aside
to dissolve.

When the milk mixture has cooled to about body temperature,
stir in the dissolved yeast and 2 1/2 cups of the whole wheat flour.
Beat vigorously with a wooden spoon for 1 minute, then cover with
plastic wrap and set aside in a draft-free spot for 15 minutes.

After 15 minutes, stir the egg and salt into the sponge. Stir in enough of the remaining whole wheat flour, about 1/2 cup at a time, to make a kneadable dough. Turn the dough out onto a lightly floured surface and knead it for about 8 minutes, using any remaining whole wheat flour and then the unbleached flour to knead with. After about 8 minutes the dough should be smooth, soft, and springy. Place the dough in a lightly oiled bowl, turning to coat the entire surface. Cover with plastic wrap and place the bowl in a warm, draft-free spot until doubled in bulk, 1 to 1 1/2 hours. In the meantime, lightly butter a large, heavy baking sheet.

When the dough has doubled, punch it down and knead for a minute on a floured surface. Divide the dough in half and knead each half into a ball. Cover the halves with plastic wrap and let rest for 5 minutes.

Working with one ball of dough at a time, roll it into a rectangle measuring about 14 inches by 11 inches. Using your hands, smear half of the fig puree over the surface, leaving a 1-inch margin around the entire perimeter. Lightly moisten the edges with a fingertip or pastry brush dipped in water, then roll up the rectangle, starting on one of the long sides; keep it somewhat tight as you roll. Pinch the seam to seal the dough, then pinch the ends and tuck them under. Transfer this long log to one side of the baking sheet, seam side down. Repeat for the second ball of dough. When both logs are on the sheet, cover them with lightly oiled plastic wrap and set aside in a warm, draft-free spot until they are quite swollen, probably about 45 minutes; they won't actually look doubled in size, however. About 30 minutes into this rising, preheat the oven to 350°.

Just before the loaves go into the oven, brush the entire surface of each one with the egg wash. Using a sharp serrated knife, make a series of 5 or 6 diagonal slashes on top of each one, deep enough to expose the top layer of fig puree. Bake the loaves for 45 minutes. (Because of the thick filling, these loaves won't give a hollow echo when you tap them with a finger.) Slide the loaves onto a rack to cool. This bread is excellent warm or at room temperature. Store leftovers in sealed plastic bags.

N O T E : For smaller, gift-size loaves, divide the dough and filling into quarters and make 4 loaves. Bake them on 2 sheets so they have plenty of room.

Vanilla-Scented Pear Bread

MAKES 1 LARGE RING,
ABOUT 20 SERVINGS

Yeasted pear breads are uncommon, though I know of a French bread that teams pears with black pepper, and it's very good. But for the holidays I prefer this combination of pears in a soft, vanilla-flavored dough. The aroma is wonderful, and a loaf of this bread in the oven adds a warm and festive air to any intimate Christmas gathering. Ideally, you'd bake this just before your company arrived and serve it still warm — dusted with vanilla sugar — with plenty of good strong coffee. If you're having only a small family or a couple over, you could make 2 loaves and send one home with your guests. If you don't have vanilla sugar on hand, just use plain confectioners' sugar.

> 1 cup milk
> 1/4 cup honey
> 1/4 cup lukewarm water
> 1 1/4-ounce package (about 1 tablespoon) active dry yeast
> 1 cup whole wheat flour
> 3 1/2 cups unbleached flour
> 2 teaspoons salt
> 1 large egg at room temperature, lightly beaten
> 2 1/2 teaspoons vanilla extract
> 3 tablespoons unsalted butter, softened
> 1 1/2 cups finely chopped peeled pears
> 2 tablespoons unsalted butter, melted
> vanilla sugar (page 119) for dusting the bread

In a small saucepan, heat the milk just until hot, then pour into a large mixing bowl and stir in the honey. While that mixture cools, pour the lukewarm water into a small bowl or measuring cup and stir in the yeast. Set aside for 5 minutes.

When the milk has cooled to body temperature, stir in the dissolved yeast, whole wheat flour, and 1 cup of the unbleached flour. Beat vigorously with a wooden spoon for 1 minute, cover with plastic wrap, and set aside in a warm, draft-free spot for 15 minutes.

After 15 minutes, stir in the salt, egg, vanilla, and softened butter. Stir in enough of the remaining unbleached flour, about 1/2 cup at a time, to make a soft, kneadable dough, beating well after each addition. Turn it out onto a lightly floured surface and knead for about 7 minutes, using as much of the remaining flour as needed to keep the dough from sticking; the dough will become smooth-surfaced but only moderately elastic. Place the dough in an oiled bowl, turning it to coat the entire surface. Cover the bowl with plastic wrap and set aside in a warm, draft-free spot until doubled in bulk, 1 to 1 1/2 hours.

Sprinkle about half the chopped pears over the fully risen dough and punch it down; turn the dough out onto a lightly floured surface and knead in the remaining pears. Knead the dough into a ball, cover, and let rest for 5 minutes. Lightly butter a large baking sheet.

Using a floured thumb, poke a hole through the center of the dough to make a big doughnut. Flour your hands, then pick up the dough, sliding your hands into the hole. Rotate the dough so the hole increases in size by the weight of the dough pulling itself down. Lay this big doughnut down on the baking sheet and shape it into the best ring you can manage, so that the center hole is about 6 inches in diameter. Cover the dough loosely with lightly oiled plastic wrap and set aside in a warm, draft-free spot. About 15 minutes before the ring has doubled in size—which should take about 40 to 50 minutes—preheat the oven to 375°.

When the ring is ready to bake, make about 8 diagonal slashes on the surface of the dough, using a sharp serrated knife; the slashes will make the ring look like a wreath. Bake for about 40 minutes, until nicely browned on the entire surface. Slide the ring onto a cooling rack and brush the surface with the melted butter. Cool for about 10 minutes, then dust generously with the vanilla sugar. Slice and serve right away or cool thoroughly and store in plastic bags.

Whole Wheat Ricotta Cheese Stollen

MAKES 4 MEDIUM-SIZE LOAVES,
10 SERVINGS EACH

I am an inveterate reader, and maker, of stollen recipes, ever seeking new techniques or ingredients that might bring me closer to the perfect stollen; this is as close as I've gotten thus far. The ricotta cheese dough is one step away from the cottage cheese dough that, I learned from one source, is not uncommon in some parts of Germany; I like the way it contributes to a soft, light dough that stays moist longer than others I've tried. The vanilla, raisins, and citrus zests make a nice festive statement, as does the dusting of confectioners' sugar. There is enough dough here to make 4 loaves, requiring 2 large baking sheets. If your oven won't hold that much at once, don't shape 2 of the loaves until the first 2 have baked for 30 minutes.

> 1/3 cup lukewarm water
> 2 1/4-ounce packages (about 2 tablespoons) active dry yeast
> 1 cup ricotta cheese
> 3/4 cup milk
> 1/2 cup sugar
> 1/3 cup honey
> 1 tablespoon vanilla extract
> 3 large eggs at room temperature, lightly beaten
> 2 1/2 cups whole wheat flour
> finely grated zest of 2 lemons
> finely grated zest of 2 oranges
> 1 tablespoon salt
> 1/2 cup (1/4 pound) unsalted butter, softened
> 3 1/2 to 4 cups unbleached flour
> 2 cups golden raisins
> 2 cups dark raisins
> 1 1/2 cups (6 ounces) toasted almonds or walnuts, chopped
> 1/4 cup unsalted butter, melted
> confectioners' sugar for dusting the loaves

Pour the lukewarm water into a small mixing bowl and stir in the yeast. While that dissolves, gently heat the ricotta cheese, milk, and sugar in a small saucepan until lukewarm. Pour the heated mixture

into a large mixing bowl and stir in the honey, dissolved yeast, vanilla, and eggs. Beat in the whole wheat flour, then cover with plastic wrap and set this sponge aside for 15 minutes in a warm, draft-free spot. (While the sponge sits, grate the zests and steam your raisins if they are on the dry side.)

After 15 minutes, stir the lemon and orange zests and salt into the dough. Add the softened butter, then stir in enough of the unbleached flour, 1 cup at a time, to make a soft, kneadable dough. At this point, turn the dough out onto a lightly floured surface and knead for 8 minutes, using as much of the remaining flour as necessary to keep the dough from sticking. After 8 minutes the dough will be smooth, though it will still be a little slack and sticky; that's fine. Place the dough in a large, lightly buttered bowl, turning the dough to coat the entire surface. Lightly butter 2 large baking sheets, preferably not dark ones.

When the dough has doubled — approximately 1 1/2 hours — flour a large work surface or counter and turn the dough out onto it *without punching it down.* Flour the top of the dough lightly and then roll it into a large rectangle about 1/4 to 1/2 inch thick; it needn't be perfect. Mix the raisins and nuts and spread them over the dough; run over them lightly with a pin to gently embed them. Starting at a short end, roll the dough up like a carpet, using a spatula or dough scraper if it sticks.

Cut the dough log into 4 even sections and knead each section into a ball. Flour a section of your work area and lay the balls on it, loosely covered with plastic wrap. Let them rest for 10 minutes.

Working with one ball at a time, roll it into an oval about 3/4 inch thick. Fold the dough not quite in half, lengthwise; it should look like a giant pair of lips, with the upper one set back from the lower one by about 1 inch. Repeat for the other loaves, placing them evenly spaced on the sheets. Cover loosely with sheets of plastic wrap and set aside in a warm, draft-free spot until doubled in bulk, about 45 to 50 minutes. Preheat the oven to 325° when the loaves appear nearly doubled.

When loaves look doubled, bake for 50 minutes; the entire surface will turn dark brown. When done, transfer to a rack and immediately brush the loaves generously with the melted butter. As soon as they're cool, dust the loaves amply with the confectioners'

sugar and wrap in foil before slipping the loaves into plastic bags. If you're shipping these, send them out right away. Otherwise, refrigerate for up to a week or 10 days or freeze for up to several months.

N O T E : I've gotten out of the habit, because the flavor often turns my kids off, but if you want a more sophisticated stollen, you can combine the raisins and douse with brandy or rum — about 1/3 cup. Cover and let stand at room temperature overnight, stirring them up when you think of it. If you do this, there's no need to steam them.

Savory Baking
for
Holiday
Entertaining

When I think about holiday entertaining, I imagine something big and baked at the center of the dinner table. This holds true whether I'm taking it to a party, having a few friends over for a meal, or throwing a huge New Year's Eve bash. Seductive tarts, bold and colorful pizzas, saucy pot pies — these are the heartwarming, satisfying foods that fit the season, flatter the cook, and make for cherished holiday memories.

Almost all of the baked entrées in this section are designed to be the focal point of the meal. I think it's better, and certainly easier, to serve one well-executed baked dish and round it out with a creative salad, a good wine, and a simple dessert than to serve a lot of different dishes. Too many courses can be distracting, and uncomfortably filling, and most of us just don't have the time to pull such a feast off anyway without feeling pressured. When you bite off more than you can chew, holiday entertaining soon becomes a chore.

The foundation for most of these entrées is a crust, yeasted or pastry, made with at least a portion of whole grain flour. I love crusts, and I love whole grains, and the combination of the two makes an incredibly satisfying lid, support, or wrapping for the panoply of entrées here.

If you've been fearful of crusts up until now, make an early New Year's resolution to put your fears aside and try your hand. Crusts are easy if you just remember a few important basics. With yeast doughs, make sure your yeast is active (see directions for proofing yeast, page 165) before you begin. Work your flour in gradually so the dough doesn't get stiff and difficult to knead. And be casual about your kneading if the process is new to you; you'll catch on to the rhythm.

With pastry doughs, add only enough water to make them cohere; otherwise you'll activate the gluten, a protein that will make your pastry tough. Chill the dough before you roll it, to give it some stability, and roll your dough on floured wax paper unless otherwise specified. You'll prevent a lot of sticking problems that way.

A closer look at any of these recipes will reveal how easily they can be broken down into manageable steps so you aren't pressed for time at the last minute when your guests are expected to arrive. Any yeasted dough can be made hours ahead and refrigerated; any pastry, a day or two in advance. Other preparations, such as chopping or cooking vegetables, can be made at your leisure. The more organized you are, the more smoothly your recipe will progress.

Savory Baking
for
Holiday
Entertaining

Deep-Dish Lamb Pie with Mint Gremolada

MAKES 6 TO 8 SERVINGS

If you like lamb, you'll love this version of lamb pot pie. The meat, wine, and tomatoes make a lovely, rich broth, infusing the parsnips and potatoes with their essence. Each portion is topped with a little of the gremolada — a mixture of parsley, mint, garlic, and lemon — which gives a fresh, fragrant finish to the dish. Enjoy this with a glass of white wine, tossed salad, crusty French bread, and a simple fruit dessert.

> 1 recipe Basic Tart Pastry (page 234) or Whole Wheat Tart Pastry (page 240)
> 2 tablespoons flavorless vegetable oil
> 2 pounds boned lamb shoulder, trimmed of fat and cut into 1 1/4-inch cubes
> 2 tablespoons unsalted butter
> 2 large onions, chopped
> 2 garlic cloves, minced
> 3 tablespoons unbleached flour
> 2 cups dry white wine
> 1 1/2 cups chicken broth
> 1 bay leaf
> 1 teaspoon dried thyme
> 1/2 teaspoon dried rosemary
> 1 teaspoon salt
> freshly ground pepper to taste
> 1/3 cup tomato puree
> 1 pound (about 3 large) parsnips, peeled and sliced 1/4 inch thick
> 2 large potatoes, peeled and cut into 3/4-inch cubes
> 2 cups shelled fresh or frozen peas

GREMOLADA
> 1/4 cup minced fresh parsley
> 1 1/2 tablespoons minced fresh mint
> 2 garlic cloves, minced
> finely grated zest of 1/2 lemon

This dish requires a deep casserole, such as an 8- by 12-inch one or — the one I use — a 14-inch oval gratin dish. Form the prepared pastry into the same shape as your baking dish, keeping it about 3/4 inch thick. Chill the pastry.

To make the stew, heat the oil in a large, heavy enameled pot or Dutch oven. Pat the lamb pieces between layers of paper towels to dry them thoroughly, then add half of the lamb to the pot; the pieces should not be crowded, or they won't brown properly. Brown the first batch on all sides over medium heat for 3 to 4 minutes. Transfer the lamb to a plate using a slotted spoon. Brown the second batch and transfer it to the plate. Discard the fat in the pot.

Put the pot back on the stove and melt the butter over medium-high heat. Add the onions and sauté them for 4 to 5 minutes, stirring them often. Stir in the garlic and the reserved lamb pieces, then shake the flour over everything. Stir briefly, then add the wine, chicken broth, herbs, salt, and a generous amount of black pepper.

Bring the stew to a boil, then reduce to a simmer, cover, and cook for 10 minutes. Stir in the tomato puree, parsnips, and potatoes, cover, and simmer for 20 more minutes. Add the peas, cook for another minute, then pour the stew into the baking dish. Let the stew cool for 30 minutes, preheating the oven to 400° 15 minutes before you plan to bake.

When you're ready to bake, roll the pastry on a sheet of lightly floured wax paper until the pastry is a little bit larger than the top of your baking dish. Lay the pastry over the filling, tucking it down the sides. Poke 4 or 5 steam vents in the top crust with a fork. Bake for 50 minutes, until the top crust is browned.

Meanwhile, make the gremolada by combining the ingredients in a small bowl. Serve the stew piping hot with some of the gremolada sprinkled over each portion.

Pastry Pizza with a Whole Wheat Crust

MAKES 12 SERVINGS

Anybody who loves a piecrust would eventually hit on the idea by serendipity: Why not put a traditional pizza topping on a pastry base instead of a bready one? That's essentially all this is, and it makes a fantastic addition to any holiday party. While this pizza can be assembled using almost any unsweetened pastry, I think the whole wheat variation makes these rectangular pizzas all the more interesting, adding a depth of flavor you wouldn't find with an all-white crust. You can make the pizzas round, but I prefer rectangular tarts because the slices are easier to hold and less likely to break, since the crust doesn't taper off as it would on a triangular slice. Notice that I use some cherry tomatoes on top to give the pizza a chunky tomato texture. It would be ideal to use a homemade sauce here, made from either crushed tomatoes or whole chopped ones, but you can simplify this operation even more by substituting a good brand of chunky tomato sauce. These pizzas are best when baked shortly before being served.

PASTRY

    1 1/4 cups whole wheat flour

    1 cup unbleached flour

    1/2 teaspoon salt

    3/4 cup (6 ounces) cold unsalted butter, cut into 1/4-inch pieces

    4 to 5 tablespoons ice-cold water

TOPPING

    2 tablespoons good-quality olive oil

    1 large onion, halved lengthwise and thinly sliced

    1 large green bell pepper, thinly sliced

    salt to taste

    1 clove garlic, minced

    2 cups thick, chunky-style tomato sauce

    12 cherry tomatoes, quartered

    3 cups grated cheese (mozzarella, provolone, or Cheddar, alone or combined)

    1/4 cup chopped fresh parsley

Make the pastry: Mix the flours with the salt in a large bowl. Add the butter and cut it in quite thoroughly, until the mixture resembles fine crumbs. Sprinkle 3 tablespoons of the water over the mixture, tossing and compacting it with a fork as you do so. Add another tablespoon of water, toss, then check to see if the dough coheres when packed. If it still seems a bit dry, add the final tablespoon of water.

When the dough coheres, pack it into a ball and knead it twice in the bowl. Divide the dough in half, then flatten the dough — directly onto sheets of plastic wrap — into rectangles measuring about 5 inches by 6 inches. Wrap the rectangles and refrigerate for about 30 minutes to firm. The pastry can be refrigerated overnight if you like and rolled the next day; let it sit at room temperature for about 15 minutes before attempting to roll.

When you're ready to assemble the pizzas, preheat the oven to 400° and get out 2 large baking sheets, preferably dark ones. While the oven is heating, heat the olive oil in a large skillet over medium heat. Add the onion and pepper and a pinch or two of salt and gently sauté them for 5 minutes — stirring occasionally — until wilted. Add the garlic, cook for a few more seconds, then remove from the heat.

Working with one piece of pastry at a time, roll it into an approximate 6- by 16-inch rectangle on a sheet of lightly floured wax paper; don't worry about ragged edges. Transfer the pastry to one of the sheets, then spoon 1 cup of the tomato sauce down the length of the pastry, spreading it to within 1 1/4 inches of all sides. Cover the surface with half of the quartered tomatoes and half of the wilted onion and pepper. Carefully fold the 4 edges up over the filling, using a wide spatula or dough scraper to slide under the dough if needed.

Immediately put the first pizza in the oven, then assemble the second pizza and bake that one. Bake the pizzas for 40 minutes, sprinkle the cheese over them, and bake for 5 to 7 minutes longer, until the cheese just begins to bubble. Let the pizzas cool on the sheets for 5 minutes, then slice each one into 6 pieces using a sharp knife. Sprinkle the pieces with the parsley and serve, the sooner the better.

White Pizza

MAKES 2 LARGE PIZZAS,
ABOUT 24 SERVINGS

Here is a different kind of pizza. The topping is an uncomplicated mixture of sour cream and cottage cheese — no extras like green peppers or onions or sausage. You end up with a smooth, soft surface, broken only by small pieces of onion. The dough is rolled and placed in 2 large baking sheets — this is a large recipe, perfect for entertaining — topped, and baked to a turn. (If you don't need this much, you can halve the topping ingredients and turn the other half of the dough into a French-style loaf; see the instructions in the dough recipe.) Keep in mind that this is a creamy pizza, so if you are using it as an appetizer, follow it with something sharp and clean — like a salad.

 1 recipe Mixed Grain Cuban Bread (page 174)
TOPPING
 3 tablespoons unsalted butter
 2 cups finely chopped onions
 1 pound small-curd cottage cheese
 1 cup sour cream
 1/2 teaspoon salt
 freshly ground black pepper to taste
 a little good-quality olive oil to brush on the crust
 hot red pepper flakes to sprinkle on top
 1/2 cup chopped fresh parsley

While the prepared dough rises, make the topping: Melt the butter in a large heavy skillet over medium heat. Add the onions and sauté them, stirring often, for about 8 minutes, until they turn a light golden brown. Scrape the onions into a mixing bowl and stir in the cottage cheese, sour cream, salt, and a generous amount of black pepper. Cover and refrigerate. Lightly butter 2 large baking sheets.

When the dough has doubled, preheat the oven to 450°. Punch the dough down and turn it out onto a floured surface. Divide the dough in half and knead each half into a ball. Roll each half into an oblong about 12 inches long and lay them on the sheets. Wait 2

196

minutes, then use your fingers to pat and push the dough into a larger, thin oblong; this dough can be stretched quite thin. Let the dough rest for 5 minutes.

Divide the topping evenly between the 2 crusts and spread it to within 1 inch of the perimeter. Brush the exposed border of each pizza with a little olive oil, then give each one a light dusting of red pepper flakes. Bake for 25 minutes, until the bottom crust is dark and crisp. These pizzas can be sliced and served right away or allowed to cool on racks and served at room temperature. Either way, sprinkle them with the parsley just before serving. Wrap leftovers in foil and refrigerate.

Savory Baking
for
Holiday
Entertaining

French Onion Tart in a Cornmeal Basil Crust

MAKES 6 TO 8 SERVINGS

This tart is good winter food — rich and smooth, served piping hot — and its simplicity makes it a wise choice for holiday entertaining. It's a free-form tart, assembled directly on a baking sheet. The sides are simply turned up to contain the filling, so the tart has a rustic personality that seems right at home at an intimate, informal dinner party. To bring out the best in this tart, it's important to cook the onions slowly, so they don't burn and take on a bitter taste; slow cooking accentuates their sweetness. The onions are mellowed with a little cream poured over the filling — though that can be eliminated if you want to reduce the richness of the dish — and finished with Gruyère cheese.

1 recipe Cornmeal Basil Pastry (page 239)

ONION FILLING

3 tablespoons unsalted butter
5 cups halved (lengthwise) and thinly sliced onions
1/2 teaspoon salt
freshly ground black pepper to taste
1/4 cup heavy cream
1 cup grated Gruyère cheese

Chill the prepared pastry. Meanwhile, make the filling: Melt the butter over low heat in a large, heavy skillet; cast iron works nicely. Add the onions and salt and sauté over low heat for 15 to 20 minutes, stirring often; you want the onions to turn a light golden color, but they shouldn't start to get mushy. Remove the onions from the heat and scrape them onto a plate to cool. Preheat the oven to 400°.

On a sheet of lightly floured wax paper, roll the pastry into an oblong almost as wide as the paper and about 13 1/2 inches long. Invert the pastry onto a large, heavy baking sheet. Distribute the onions over the surface of the tart, leaving a 2-inch border all around. Fold the sides up over the filling; as you do so it will most likely crack in places and form natural pleats; that's fine. Give the surface of the tart a dusting of pepper.

Bake the tart for 15 minutes, then pull it out and spoon 2 tablespoons of the cream over the tart. Bake for 15 minutes more, then spoon on the remaining 2 tablespoons cream and sprinkle the cheese on top. Bake for 20 minutes more, until the tart is bubbly and

brown. Let the tart cool on the pan for 5 minutes, then slice and serve. Wrap leftovers in foil and refrigerate.

N O T E : This tart can be served warm instead of piping hot; you can cool it directly on the pan on a rack.

An Easy Eggnog

Eggnog is a rich, spirited drink that I think goes best at a holiday party where there aren't a lot of other rich foods being served (to go with a bounty of rich foods, try the Hot Spiced Cider on page 223). You can also use bourbon or rum for the spirits, but I quite like this version, given to me by my friend Pat Mitchamore, who develops recipes for the Jack Daniel's folks. Be sure to start this eggnog the day before, so it has plenty of time to chill and mellow.

> **12 large eggs, separated**
> **1 cup sugar**
> **1 cup milk or half-and-half**
> **2 cups Jack Daniel's sour mash whiskey**
> **1/2 teaspoon salt**
> **6 cups heavy cream**
> **ground nutmeg, preferably freshly grated**

Using a whisk or an electric mixer, beat the egg yolks with the sugar until the mixture is fluffy and lemon-colored. Stir in the milk or half-and-half, Jack Daniel's, salt, and cream. Stir well, then pour into a large serving bowl and cover. Refrigerate the egg whites overnight.

Remove the egg whites from the refrigerator about 30 minutes before you plan to serve and pour them into a large mixing bowl. When you are ready to serve, beat the egg whites until they hold soft peaks, then whisk them into the chilled eggnog. Dust the top of the bowl with lots of nutmeg. Makes 2 1/2 quarts, enough for a good-size gathering.

N O T E : Please be aware that there is a small, though serious, risk of salmonella poisoning when consuming raw eggs. If you're unsure of the safety of your egg source, serve hot spiced cider instead.

Brussels Sprout Tart

MAKES 8 SERVINGS

Brussels sprouts are usually in good supply during the winter months, and we eat a fair amount of them at the holiday season. On special occasions I like to serve this rather unusual brussels sprout tart; even people who find the flavor of brussels sprouts too assertive will appreciate the way the flavor is mellowed and complemented by the Parmesan and custard base. This tart would be excellent for a sit-down holiday dinner or family meal; serve it warm — it just isn't the same at room temperature. When you select your brussels sprouts, choose firm heads, the brighter green the better; yellowing is an indication of age. If possible, hand-select ones of approximately the same size.

> 1 9-inch tart shell made with Whole Wheat Tart Pastry (page 240)
> 1 pound medium-size brussels sprouts
> salt to taste
> 1 tablespoon unsalted butter
> 1/2 cup finely chopped onions
> 2 large eggs
> 1 large egg yolk
> 3/4 cup heavy cream
> 1/2 teaspoon salt
> 1/4 teaspoon freshly ground black pepper
> pinch of ground nutmeg, preferably freshly grated
> 3/4 cup (about 3 ounces) finely grated Parmesan cheese

Partially bake the tart shell as directed in the pastry recipe and set aside to cool. Meanwhile, trim the base of each sprout even with the bottom of the head and remove any loose or tired-looking outer leaves. Cut each sprout in half lengthwise, then steam them in a covered saucepan for about 6 or 7 minutes, until barely tender. Transfer the sprouts to a plate, salt them lightly, and set aside to cool. Preheat the oven to 375°.

Melt the butter in a small saucepan and stir in the onions. Sauté over medium heat for 5 minutes, stirring occasionally. Remove from the heat.

In a medium-size mixing bowl, lightly beat the eggs, egg yolk, cream, salt, pepper, and nutmeg. Ladle about one third of this custard into the tart shell and bake for approximately 12 to 15 minutes, just until the custard is set.

Starting at the edge, arrange the brussels sprouts in concentric circles, with the base of each pointing toward the center. Take any leftover halves and cut them in half lengthwise and then crosswise, and fill in here and there with the pieces. Sprinkle the brussels sprouts with the cheese and the sautéed onions, then ladle the rest of the custard into the tart; try to dampen all of the exposed cheese. Bake for another 30 minutes, just until the custard is set and the top begins to brown. Cool the tart in the pan on a rack for 10 minutes, then unmold and serve. Wrap leftovers in aluminum foil and refrigerate.

A Very Big Broccoli, Olive, and Cheddar Quiche

MAKES UP TO 28 APPETIZER SERVINGS

Broccoli and Cheddar has always been the one kind of quiche you can count on to have universal appeal; it's the one all my kids will eat. I present this to you here in the extra-large size, big enough to feed a whole houseful of company as an appetizer and half that many as part of the main course. The only tricky part here is getting the pastry into the pan, but this is actually no more difficult than getting a pie pastry into the pan. Only the shapes are different; you roll out rectangles instead of circles. The prep work is minimal—just grating cheese and steaming some broccoli— and in the end you'll feel like a professional chef, pulling this big sheet pan of quiche out of the oven. This quiche can be made earlier in the day you plan to serve it, or the day before, and warmed in the pan. To break the recipe into manageable chunks, you can prepare the crust one day and bake the quiche the next, if you like.

> **2 recipes dough for Basic Tart Pastry (page 234) or Whole Wheat Tart Pastry (page 240), shaped into squares about 3/4 inch thick and chilled**
> **1 1/2 cups (1/4 pound) grated sharp Cheddar cheese**
> **2 teaspoons Dijon mustard**

FILLING

> **1 large head of broccoli, washed**
> **3 tablespoons unsalted butter**
> **2 cups (about 3 medium) chopped onions**
> **8 large eggs**
> **2 1/3 cups light cream**
> **1 teaspoon salt**
> **freshly ground black pepper to taste**
> **1/8 teaspoon ground nutmeg, preferably freshly grated**
> **1 teaspoon dried dill or oregano**
> **1 cup good-quality pitted green olives, chopped (optional)**
> **1 1/2 cups (1/4 pound) grated sharp Cheddar cheese *or* half Cheddar and half feta cheese**

Lightly butter a 12- by 18-inch jelly roll pan.

Working with one piece of pastry at a time, roll the dough into a rectangle measuring 10 by 14 inches. Lay it over half of the pan, gently tucking it into the creases. The long edge of the pastry should run slightly beyond the center of the pan so you can overlap it with the other piece of pastry. Roll the other piece of pastry the same size.

Lightly moisten 1/2 inch of the long edge of the first sheet of pastry, then lay the second sheet over the other half of the pan. Let the 2 sheets overlap by about 1/2 inch. Press down firmly and repeatedly on the seam to seal it. Brush the overhang lightly with water, then fold it over and press it into the sides to beef them up. The sides should be flush with the top of the pan or slightly higher. Freeze the dough for 30 minutes.

Preheat the oven to 400°. Line the chilled pastry with 2 sheets of foil placed side by side, overlapping slightly; tuck it into the creases as you did the pastry. Fill the foil with dried beans or rice to weight it. Bake the pastry for 15 minutes. Remove the pan from the oven and carefully remove the foil with the beans or rice still in it; do half at a time. Pierce the bottom of the pastry 4 or 5 times, at well-spaced intervals, with the tines of a fork. Bake for another 12 minutes. Open the oven door, slide the shelf out, and sprinkle the cheese over the bottom of the shell. Be certain to cover the fork holes to seal them, or the custard will run out and make the crust soggy. Bake the crust for 2 more minutes to melt the cheese, then remove it from the oven. Cool the pastry on a rack. When the crust is cooled, dot the surface with the mustard and paint it over the surface with a pastry brush.

To make the filling, cut the broccoli into small flowerets, reserving the stalks for another use. Steam the flowerets for about 5 to 7 minutes, until not quite tender. Remove from the heat. Melt the butter in a large skillet over medium heat. Add the onions and sauté them for about 7 minutes, stirring often, until golden. Remove from the heat. Whisk the eggs in a mixing bowl until blended, then whisk in the cream, salt, pepper, nutmeg, and dill or oregano.

When you're ready to bake the quiche, preheat the oven to 350°. Slowly pour the custard into the shell, then scatter the onions, broccoli, and olives evenly in it. Sprinkle the cheese over everything and bake for 35 to 40 minutes, until the top is very lightly browned. Cool the quiche in the pan on a rack. To serve, slice into 4 rows lengthwise, 7 rows across. Or cut larger pieces, as you please. To store, wrap 3 or 4 pieces in individual sheets of aluminum foil and refrigerate. Reheat in a 400° oven for about 15 minutes.

V A R I A T I O N : With this recipe as your blueprint, there are any number of big quiches you can make up: feta, provolone, and olive; sautéed peppers, Parmesan, and Fontina; cooked scallops or shrimp with smoked cheddar.

Wild Mushroom and Madeira Pizzas

MAKES 4 OR 8 INDIVIDUAL PIZZAS

This is one of my wife's favorites, the re-creation of a great little pizza we once enjoyed at a restaurant on the Massachusetts North Shore. It makes a terrific appetizer for a larger group of up to 8 or an entrée portion for a smaller gathering of 4. I have used all sorts of exotic fresh mushrooms — including shiitake and oyster — as well as the usual cultivated kind, and each is good; use whatever your budget allows. Since the stems of wild mushrooms tend to be rubbery, be sure to remove them before sautéing. The pizzas should be eaten right away, so plan accordingly. It's fun to prepare these pizzas in the company of your friends — if you have a bit of the showman in you — as long as you have all of your ingredients ready to go.

> 1 recipe Mixed Grain Cuban Bread (page 174)
> 1/4 cup unsalted butter
> 1/3 cup minced onions
> 2 pounds fresh mushrooms, stems removed
> salt to taste
> 2/3 cup Madeira
> 1 cup (1/4 pound) freshly grated Parmesan cheese
> 1/2 cup heavy cream
> freshly ground pepper to taste
> 2 cups (5 to 6 ounces) grated provolone cheese
> 1/2 cup chopped fresh parsley

While the prepared bread dough is rising (it will take under an hour to double), prepare the mushrooms: Melt the butter over medium heat in a large nonreactive skillet. Stir in the onions and sauté for 2 to 3 minutes, stirring often. Stir in the mushrooms, salt them lightly, then cover the skillet and cook for 2 or 3 minutes, until the mushrooms have put off a good deal of liquid. Add the Madeira, raise the heat to high, and continue to cook, stirring occasionally, until most but not all of the liquid has cooked off; there should be a thick, heavy coat of liquid left in the bottom of the pan. Remove from the heat.

Once the dough has doubled, punch it down and turn it out onto a lightly floured surface. Knead for 30 seconds, then divide the dough into 4 equal pieces and knead the pieces into balls. Lightly oil 2 large cookie sheets, preferably dark, heavy ones. Place 2 balls of dough, well spaced, on each of the cookie sheets. Dust the tops of the balls lightly with flour, then let them sit for 5 minutes. After 5 minutes, use your fingertips to pat them into circles about 8 inches in diameter; if the dough sticks to your fingers, use a little more flour. Let the dough sit for 10 minutes while you preheat the oven to 450°.

After 10 minutes, divide the Parmesan cheese among the 4 circles of dough, sprinkling it evenly over each one. Spoon one quarter of the mushrooms — and some of the mushroom juice — over each, then drizzle 2 tablespoons of cream over each. Salt and pepper them, then bake for 18 minutes. Pull the sheets out and sprinkle about 1/2 cup of the provolone cheese over each one. Bake for about 4 minutes longer, just until the cheese has melted. Sprinkle some of the fresh parsley over each pizza before serving. Cut each one into quarters and serve. Wrap leftovers in aluminum foil. Reheat in a 400° oven, right in the foil, for 10 to 15 minutes.

N O T E : To make 8 smaller pizzas, divide the dough into 8 pieces and proceed as directed, using proportionately less topping on each one. Also, if you can find good fresh herbs at this time of year, feel free to mix a modest quantity in with the parsley before chopping it.

Parmesan and Basil Focaccia

MAKES 1 LARGE FOCACCIA,
10 TO 12 SERVINGS

This big flat peasant bread is a great party finger food because it has no messy topping and it tastes just as good at room temperature as it does warm. We make many different focacce throughout the year, most of them simply drizzled with olive oil and sprinkled with herbs — fresh garden herbs in the summer. They're one step easier than pizza, since there is no red sauce to make. This winter version derives its flavor from dried basil and Parmesan cheese, though of course you can use fresh basil — up to 2 tablespoons chopped — in the dough if you can find it. Serve the focaccia with almost any soup or stew or at any potluck, but it goes especially well when there are a number of antipasti on the table — like marinated vegetables, roasted peppers in oil, and marinated bean salad.

1 recipe Mixed Grain Cuban Bread (page 174), modified as outlined
1 cup (1/4 pound) finely grated Parmesan cheese
2 teaspoons dried basil *or* up to 2 tablespoons chopped fresh
3 tablespoons good-quality olive oil
salt to sprinkle on top

Prepare the Cuban bread as directed, omitting the rye flour. After adding the first cup of unbleached flour, stir in the Parmesan cheese and basil. Add the remaining flour as directed. In the kneading the dough may absorb a little extra unbleached flour because the rye has been omitted. Rub a little olive oil into a ceramic bowl and place the dough in it, turning to coat the entire surface. Cover the bowl with plastic wrap and set the dough aside in a warm, draft-free spot until doubled in bulk; it will take a little less than an hour. Meanwhile, oil a large, heavy baking sheet, preferably a dark one. I like my 14-inch square one for this, to make a big round focaccia.

Once the dough has doubled, punch it down and place it in the center of the baking sheet. Let it rest for 10 minutes, then drizzle 1 tablespoon of the olive oil over the dough. Dip your fingers in the oil, then press and pat the dough into a large circle (or an oval if you are using a rectangular baking sheet; it should measure 12 by 18 inches). Cover the dough with lightly oiled plastic wrap and let it rest in a warm, draft-free spot for 20 minutes.

After 20 minutes, dip your fingers in a little more olive oil and dimple the entire surface of the dough by dancing your fingers over it. Re-cover the dough and set aside for 15 minutes while you preheat the oven to 425°.

After 15 minutes, drizzle the remaining 2 tablespoons oil over the dough. Sprinkle the surface of the focaccia with 2 or 3 pinches of salt and bake for 25 minutes, until the top is golden brown. Slide it onto a cutting board and slice into wedges or, if you aren't serving it right away, transfer it to a rack to cool. Store leftovers wrapped in foil.

Olive Whole Wheat Flat Bread

MAKES 8 TO 12 SERVINGS

Some of the simplest breads are surely some of the best, like this round wheaten loaf studded with imported green olives. It's perfect for a holiday party; this picturesque, olive oil–drenched bread can be served as a main course, perhaps with a light pasta dish, or as an appetizer with wine and a selection of mild cheeses. To cut down on last-minute chaos, you can make this early in the day and reheat it right on the baking sheet — about 8 minutes at 400°.

> 1 1/2 cups lukewarm water
> 1 1/4-ounce package (about 1 tablespoon) active dry yeast
> 1 teaspoon sugar
> 2 cups whole wheat flour
> 1 1/2 teaspoons salt
> 1 to 1 1/4 cups unbleached flour
> 1 1/2 cups pitted imported green olives, cut into quarters
> 1/4 cup good-quality olive oil
> 1 teaspoon dried rosemary *or* 2 teaspoons fresh, chopped
> hot red pepper flakes
> salt

Pour the lukewarm water into a large mixing bowl. Sprinkle on the yeast, add the sugar, and stir. Set aside for 5 minutes. When the yeast is dissolved, use a wooden spoon to beat in the whole wheat flour 1 cup at a time, beating for 1 minute after each addition. Stir in the salt. Gradually add enough of the unbleached flour to make a soft, kneadable dough. Turn the dough out onto a floured surface and knead for 7 minutes, using only enough of the remaining flour to keep the dough from sticking. Place the dough in an oiled bowl, turning to coat the entire surface. Cover with plastic wrap and set the dough aside in a warm, draft-free spot until doubled in bulk, 45 minutes to 1 hour. In the meantime, lightly butter a large, heavy baking sheet, preferably a dark one.

Once the dough has doubled, *do not punch it down.* Instead, dump the dough directly onto the center of the baking sheet. Using floured hands, pat and press the dough out into a large circle or oval 1/2 inch thick or just slightly less; the dough may tend to pull back as you do this. If so, just let it rest for a few minutes before proceeding. Scatter

the olives evenly over the dough and cover the top with lightly oiled plastic wrap. Let the dough rest for 15 minutes.

After 15 minutes, use your fingers to push all the olive pieces down into the dough. They don't have to hit bottom, but you should embed them into the surface. Cover the dough again for 15 minutes and preheat the oven to 450°.

Drizzle the olive oil evenly over the surface of the dough. Sprinkle on the rosemary and dust the surface with a few shakes of red pepper flakes and 2 pinches of salt. Bake the bread for 20 minutes, until well browned and crusty on top. Transfer to a board, cut into wedges, and serve hot or warm. If you're not serving right away, transfer the bread to a rack to cool. Wrap leftovers in aluminum foil. Reheat in a 400° oven for about 15 minutes.

Savory Baking
for
Holiday
Entertaining

A Variety of Bruschette

MAKES 12 APPETIZER SERVINGS

*Think of these as New Year's toasts — toasted or grilled slices of crusty
bread eaten with a simple brushing of olive oil or various other toppings.
The basis for these bruschette is the Mixed Grain Cuban Bread (page
174). If you're planning a large party, you'll want to double or even triple
the bread recipe; figure about 12 slices of bread per loaf, and also figure
that unless there is a lot of other food, one hungry hombre can easily eat 3
of these. The plain bruschetta is an excellent accompaniment to robust
stews, soups, and Italian meals. The topped bruschette are meant to be
served as appetizers, a dish unto themselves. Traditionally, bruschetta is
grilled over an open fire, but since that's impractical for this time of
year — unless you have one of those specially made grills that slide into
your fireplace — the method described here uses the broiler.*

    *Ideally, these should be made not too long before serving so the bread
is still warm, though they're fine — if somewhat chewier — once the bread
has cooled off some.*

> 1 loaf Mixed Grain Cuban Bread (page 174 or good-quality
>   Italian bread
> 3 garlic cloves, peeled
> 1/3 cup good-quality olive oil

Preheat the broiler. Cut the bread into slices about 3/4 inch thick;
don't use the rounded ends. Arrange the slices on a baking sheet that
will fit under your broiler. Broil them on each side, about 5 to 6
inches from the heat, just long enough to get a nicely browned
surface. Transfer the slices to a rack; when they're cool enough to
handle, rub one side of each slice with the garlic, which will rub off
into the dry surface. Brush or drizzle some of the olive oil over the
garlic side of the bread and serve right away. To make any of the
following variations, proceed from this point.

BRUSCHETTE WITH OLIVE PUREE: In a food
processor, combine 1 cup good-quality pitted green or black olives
with 1/3 cup olive oil. Process until you have a puree of very fine
olive chunks; you will have to stop the machine occasionally to
scrape down the sides. Divide the puree among the slices of bread,
spreading it evenly on top of the oiled surface.

BRUSCHETTE OF MADEIRA MUSHROOMS:
Prepare the Madeira mushrooms as for the Wild Mushroom and
Madeira Pizzas (page 204). Spread a large spoonful over each slice
of bread and dust with freshly grated Parmesan cheese.

BRUSCHETTE OF ONIONS AND GRUYÈRE:
Slowly sauté 4 cups halved sliced onions in 3 tablespoons unsalted
butter — about 15 minutes over medium-low heat — until golden
brown. Cover each bruschetta with a spoonful of the onions and top
with a little grated Gruyère cheese. Broil just until the cheese melts.

BRUSCHETTE OF CREAM CHEESE AND
CHERRY TOMATOES: Spread each slice with a light
coating of cream cheese. Top with halved cherry tomatoes, salt,
pepper, and chopped parsley.

Everyone likes presents, but one of the nicest holiday gifts is given when old friends, family, or an out-of-town buddy drops by unexpectedly, on short notice or no notice at all. Such occasions demand a bit of an impromptu feast, something a little more impressive than a round of Oreos and tall glasses of milk. But what's a home baker to do?

Well, plenty. With a little forethought and planning, you can appear to possess almost superhuman baking abilities when you want to throw something together in a flash. Naturally these tactics aren't limited to coping with surprise visits; think of them as timesaving tricks to use throughout the holiday season.

• Keep a prebaked tart shell in the freezer; freeze it right in the pan. This way you can throw together a simple free-form quiche — featuring cheese, olives, and chopped ham, for instance — and have it on the table in under an hour. The tart can go in the oven while the shell is still frozen.

• A frozen loaf of Mixed Grain Cuban Bread (page 174) can be thawed quickly in the oven (400° for about 15 minutes, unwrapped). Use it for a warm hero sandwich or bruschetta (page 210) or pile on some steamed broccoli, olives, and cheese and broil just until the cheese melts. Use it for sloppy joes. The mixed grain Cuban bread is a good dough to master because it's so fast and versatile — much faster to make and let rise, in fact, than to freeze and thaw.

• Keep a jar of good olives on hand to make Olive Whole Wheat Flat Bread (page 208).

• Keep some Whole Wheat Cheese Wafers (page 232) in the freezer, warm them on a baking sheet (5 minutes at 400°), to freshen and serve with cheese and wine. This dough will also keep in the fridge for several days, so you can slice and bake the crackers on demand.

• As for sweets, almost all cookies freeze well; keep some in the freezer in a tin and bring them to room temperature on a plate in a warm area — takes only a few minutes. For a freshly baked cookie, keep a log of Oatmeal Date Pinwheel Cookies (page 78) in the fridge, slice, and bake.

• Another trick is to mix up the dry ingredients for a quick bread or cookie recipe, then throw the mix in the freezer (be sure to mark it). This foresight can cut preparation time for some recipes in half. Try it with any muffin, scone, soda bread, or biscuit recipe.

• If you have a soup in the fridge and Cornmeal Sage Breadsticks (page 166) on hand — they're excellent keepers — you have a meal. Warm in a 400° oven for 5 to 10 minutes to crisp them.

• Of course, pie pastry can be made ahead and frozen, but you'll save valuable time by getting the crusts rolled and into the pans before you freeze them. I'm not crazy about disposable aluminum pie pans, because they reflect too much heat and don't brown the crust nicely, but they'll do if you want to freeze several and your pie pan stock is limited.

Shrimp, Bacon, and Jarlsberg Tart

MAKES 8 TO 10 SERVINGS

A well-made tart is one of the best party dishes going, and I particularly adore a good seafood tart like this one. At our own New Year's Eve parties I have seen seafood tarts disappear like lightning, and I always wish I had made extras. Shrimp makes an especially good tart, and it really shines here with the saltiness of the bacon and mellow flavor of the Jarlsberg cheese. If you happen to have any ham on hand, you can substitute an equal amount for the bacon. I have also used smoked Cheddar in place of the Jarlsberg.

1 9-inch tart shell made with Whole Wheat Tart Pastry (page 240) or Basic Tart Pastry (page 234)

FILLING

6 slices bacon
3/4 pound medium-size shrimp
2 large eggs
1 large egg yolk
1 1/8 cups light cream
1 teaspoon Dijon mustard
pinch of cayenne pepper
3/4 teaspoon salt
1 1/2 cups (1/4 pound) grated Jarlsberg cheese

Partially bake the tart shell as directed in the pastry recipe; cool. Meanwhile, fry the bacon until crisp and blot it dry on paper towels; chop it coarsely and set it aside. Bring a pot of water to a boil and drop in the unshelled shrimp. By the time the water comes back to a boil the shrimp should be done. Drain. Shell, devein, and set aside.

When you're ready to bake the tart, preheat the oven to 375°. Whisk together the eggs, egg yolk, light cream, mustard, cayenne pepper, and salt. Chop the shrimp coarsely, so none of the pieces is larger than bite-size, and scatter them evenly in the partially baked shell. Spread the bacon over the top of the shrimp and spread the cheese over that. Pour the custard over the cheese and bake the tart for approximately 40 minutes, until the top is slightly puffy and the edge has begun to brown. Cool the tart in the pan on a rack for at least 10 minutes before slicing and serving. This tart is also good warm or at room temperature. Cover the tart with plastic wrap and store in the fridge.

Pantry Items and a Few Ideas for Leftover Breads

Just like a good home pantry, here is the place to look for some of the basics: the little stockpile of crusts, curds, crackers, sauces, and other preparations called for elsewhere in the book.

I've also stocked this section with some of my favorite ways of using up leftover breads. I hate to waste bread, especially homemade bread, so I take this business of leftovers seriously; I'm sure our local bird population wishes it were otherwise. So you will find several bread puddings here, both sweet and savory. One is an interesting twist on the brown Betty theme; another is called Crumb Croûte of Pears, a delicious rendition of sliced pears on leftover brioche.

This may be the last section in the book, but it certainly isn't the least useful. I've always thought one of the most accurate measures of a good cook is how he or she uses up leftovers. Giving not-so-fresh bread a second chance is a noble act indeed.

Lemon Curd

MAKES ABOUT 1 1/2 CUPS

*Lemon curd is an intensely lemon-flavored concoction, with a consistency
like thick fruit butter, that can be used in all sorts of baked goods, from
tarts (page 135) to bars (page 92). Even if you aren't using this in a
baking recipe, it makes an excellent spread for biscuits, muffins, toast —
wherever you might use preserves. It's not difficult to make, though it
does require about 15 minutes of nearly constant whisking to keep it lump-
free — a pleasant 15 minutes, I should add, because the lemon vapors
rising from the stove have a way of making one almost giddy with the
holiday spirit. At least that's the way it works for me. Sometimes lemon
curd recipes instruct you to strain the finished curd to remove the grated
zest, but I skip that step — I love the zest. Stored in a tightly sealed jar,
this curd will keep for several weeks in the refrigerator. Needless to say,
it's a wonderful Christmas gift.*

1 large egg
4 large egg yolks
1 cup sugar
1/2 cup fresh lemon juice (about 2 large *or* 3 medium-size lemons)
1 teaspoon lightly packed finely grated lemon zest
1/2 cup (1/4 pound) cold unsalted butter, cut into 1/2-inch pieces

Put enough water in the bottom of a double boiler to reach almost to
the bottom of the insert and bring to a simmer. Add the egg and egg
yolks to the top of the double boiler and immediately start to whisk
them, gradually adding the sugar, lemon juice, and lemon zest. With
the water still at an active simmer, gently whisk the curd for about
12 minutes, until noticeably thicker — thick enough that when you
stick a teaspoon in it, then take it out and blow on it for 5 seconds, it
pretty much stays on the spoon if you turn it upside down. At that
point, whisk in the butter a piece at a time, adding another only after
each one melts.

   After the last piece of butter has been added, cook for about
2 minutes more, still whisking, then scrape the curd into a small
bowl. Press a piece of plastic wrap directly onto the surface so it
doesn't form a skin. Cool to room temperature, then spoon the curd
into a jar with a tight-fitting lid. Store in the refrigerator.

Pearsauce

MAKES ABOUT 2 CUPS

This recipe is so simple and so good. It makes 2 cups, but both of the recipes in the book that use it — Pearsauce Walnut Bread (page 158) and Pearsauce Squash Tart (page 154) — require only 1 1/2 cups, because that's how much I usually have left by the time I finish snitching from the batch I've just made. What you don't snitch makes a good topping for biscuits and muffins. I've played around with both pearsauce and applesauce in my baked goods, and I think the pearsauce gives a better fruit flavor, whereas applesauce sometimes just gets lost. If you plan to bake with this, you can make it well ahead because it will keep in a sealed jar for at least 10 days, perhaps longer.

> **4 cups (4 to 5 large) chopped peeled pears**
> **1/4 cup water, pear juice, or apple cider**
> **1/4 cup sugar**
> **juice of 1 lemon**

Combine all of the ingredients in a large nonreactive saucepan. Bring to a boil over medium heat and cook, covered, for 10 minutes at an active simmer, stirring occasionally. As the pears become soft, mash them right in the pan using a potato masher. Remove the cover and cook for another 5 to 10 minutes, until the sauce becomes the consistency of applesauce. Scrape into a bowl and cool to room temperature. Transfer the pearsauce to a jar and seal tightly. Store in the refrigerator.

Almond Paste

MAKES ABOUT 1 POUND

Almond paste is a dense but pliable concentration of blanched ground almonds and sugar. It is available in some supermarkets and specialty stores, for a price, but is cheaper and quite easy to make at home. Almond paste is traditionally used to make macaroons, in Danish pastry filling, and sometimes in tarts or bars. Ideally, the paste should be made a week before you use it so the flavor has time to develop. But don't feel bad if that isn't possible; it'll still taste good.

> 2 cups (about 1/2 pound) whole blanched almonds (see note)
> 1/2 cup water
> 1 cup sugar
> 1/2 teaspoon almond extract
> 2 teaspoons orange juice concentrate, thawed

Put the almonds in a food processor and process until they make a very fine meal. In a small saucepan, bring the water and sugar to a boil over high heat. Boil, without stirring, until the mixture reaches 235° on a candy thermometer. Pour this sugar syrup into a measuring cup and stir in the almond extract and orange juice concentrate.

Turn the food processor back on and start adding the sugar syrup in a thin stream; the mixture will become very thick and dense. After all the syrup is added, scrape the almond paste out of the processor bowl and shape it into a ball. Store in a sealed plastic bag in the refrigerator. It will keep for at least 1 month.

N O T E : I think it's a hassle to blanch almonds, and doing it yourself rather than buying them already blanched probably makes little difference unless you have a source for terrific, hard-to-find almonds. Deborah Madison, author of *The Greens Cookbook* and *The Savory Way* (Bantam), says that the California-grown Mission almond is worth blanching if you can get your hands on some.

In any case, to blanch almonds, simply put them in a big bowl and pour boiling water over them. Let them stand for about 1 1/2 minutes, then drain. Slip the skins off by pinching the almonds between your thumb and forefinger. If some are stubborn, repeat the boiling water bath for them. Before making the almond paste, spread the almonds on a baking sheet and dry them in a preheated 250° oven for 8 minutes.

Mincemeat

MAKES ABOUT 1 QUART

Real mincemeat — the kind made with real meat — has never appealed to me, but I like to bake with this mock version made with apple chunks, dried fruit, bourbon, and spices; it makes an especially fine coffee cake filling (see page 44). There is a measure of leeway here for improvisation. For instance, I have added a cup of fresh cranberries to the basic mixture, which gives a little tartness and body. You can skip the candied pineapple and add chopped prunes. And you can play around with the spices, though I find too much spice can easily spoil the flavor, so I don't recommend using a greater quantity than I have here; nutmeg and ginger are also good. I also sometimes include chopped walnuts. If you plan to use this mincemeat in your baking, you can make it ahead and store it in the fridge for up to a week in a sealed jar.

> 4 large Granny Smith apples, peeled, cored, and coarsely chopped
> 1 cup chopped pitted dates
> 1 cup raisins
> 1/2 cup dried currants
> 1/2 cup finely chopped candied pineapple
> 1/2 cup apple cider or water
> 1/2 cup packed light brown sugar
> finely grated zest of 1 lemon
> finely grated zest of 1 orange
> juice of 1 lemon
> 1 tablespoon red wine vinegar or apple cider vinegar
> 1 teaspoon ground cinnamon
> 1/4 teaspoon ground cloves
> 1/4 teaspoon ground cardamom
> 2 tablespoons bourbon

Put all the ingredients except the bourbon into a large nonaluminum pot, preferably one with a heavy bottom. Bring to a boil over medium heat, then cover and cook at a low boil for 5 minutes, stirring occasionally. Uncover and cook about 7 more minutes, stirring occasionally, until most of the liquid has boiled off, leaving a thickish glaze. Stir in the bourbon, cook for another 30 seconds, then remove from the heat. Cool slightly in the pot, then transfer to a bowl to cool. Refrigerate in a sealed jar if you aren't using it right away.

Poached Calimyrna Figs

MAKES 1 1/2 POUNDS POACHED FIGS

Dried figs prepared like this become soft, fragrant, and juicy — excellent alone as a breakfast compote, but I use them mainly in baking. This method also works for dried Black Mission figs, but I am not partial to the Turkish figs; the skins tend to be so tough that they are less than ideal for baking.

> 1 1/2 pounds Calimyrna figs
> 1 1/2 cups zinfandel or other full-bodied red wine
> 3/4 cup water
> 1/3 cup mild honey, such as orange blossom
> 4 or 5 fresh or dried lavender leaves (optional)

Put all the ingredients in a heavy nonreactive saucepan. Bring to a boil, reduce the heat to a simmer, and cover. Cook the figs over low heat for about 40 minutes, stirring them several times, until the skins feel very tender when pierced with the point of a sharp knife. Remove the figs from the heat and transfer them to a ceramic or glass bowl. Cool to room temperature, then cover and refrigerate. They will keep at least 1 week.

Cranberry Apple Brown Betty

MAKES 6 TO 8 SERVINGS

Those of us who bake a lot of holiday breads often find ourselves with odd ends of loaves a bit past their prime. This super-easy and fast dessert — or breakfast — is a great way to recycle them. Use whatever plain or sweet bread you have on hand, but no savory breads. One of the little steps you must observe here is letting the fruit mixture stand for 30 minutes to draw the juices out of the fruit; skip that step and this will come out on the dry side. Baking this dessert in a shallow casserole, as opposed to a deep one, gives you a large surface area of baked-on glaze underneath where the juices accumulate, a glaze something like the top of an upside-down cake. This is one of the few desserts I like without ice cream or pouring cream; either one can quickly turn the crisp crumbs soggy. If anything, a little whipped cream on the side is fine.

> 4 large apples (any kind), peeled, cored, and coarsely chopped
> 2 cups fresh cranberries, coarsely chopped
> 2/3 cup packed light brown sugar
> 1/3 cup plus 2 tablespoons sugar
> 1/2 cup raisins
> 1/2 cup (2 ounces) chopped walnuts
> juice of 1 lemon
> finely grated zest of 1 lemon
> 1 1/2 teaspoons ground cinnamon
> 1/2 cup (1/4 pound) unsalted butter
> 5 cups bread crumbs in about 1/2-inch cubes

In a large mixing bowl, combine the apples, cranberries, brown sugar, 1/3 cup of the sugar, raisins, walnuts, lemon juice, lemon zest, and cinnamon. Mix well, cover, and set aside for 30 minutes. Meanwhile, butter a shallow 8- by 12-inch casserole with 1 tablespoon of the butter and melt the remaining 7 tablespoons. Put the bread crumbs in a large bowl and pour the melted butter over them, tossing to coat them evenly.

After 30 minutes, spread half of the fruit mixture over the bottom of the casserole. Spread half of the buttered bread crumbs over the fruit and sprinkle it with 1 tablespoon of the remaining sugar. Cover the bread crumbs with the rest of the fruit and juice, then cover that with the rest of the crumbs. Sprinkle the last tablespoon of sugar on top. Using your palm, press down on top of the crumbs to compact everything. Set the casserole aside for 15 minutes while you preheat the oven to 375°.

After 15 minutes, bake for approximately 45 minutes, until the top is nicely browned. Cool for at least 10 minutes before serving. Cover leftovers with plastic wrap and store in a cool location.

Hot Spiced Cider

There are few things as inviting as a big pot of hot spiced (sometimes called *mulled*) cider sitting on the stove. The fragrance of apples mingling with cinnamon, cloves, orange, and lemon is utterly intoxicating. From Halloween through Thanksgiving and New Year's, we always make a big pot when friends stop by, to chase down cookies, slices of quick bread, and other holiday baked treats.

First, to make good mulled cider you need a good cider, made without preservatives. A good cider is sometimes difficult to find. The more interesting ciders come directly from the cider mill through smaller suppliers or right to the consumer. Some of these mills press on an ongoing basis, so the flavor is good and fresh, not insipid. And smaller orchards generally try to use a variety of apples to get just the right flavor and sweetness.

I think it's important to strain the spiced cider before serving it; I don't like to see spice bags and cinnamon dust floating on the surface.

To make half a gallon of hot spiced cider — enough for a small gathering — put that much cider in a large nonreactive pot with 5 cinnamon sticks, 10 whole cloves, and a big pinch of ground cardamom. Using a sharp paring knife or a zester, cut the zest from 1/2 lemon, lengthwise, and add that too. Bring the mixture to a boil, then lower the heat and simmer gently for 15 minutes. Strain through cheesecloth or a double thickness of paper toweling. Put the cider back on very low heat and add a few thin orange slices to the pot. Serve hot, giving each serving a light dusting of nutmeg.

To make a pretty red *cranberry mulled cider*, add 1 1/2 cups rinsed fresh cranberries to the pot. Bring to a boil and simmer as directed. Just before straining, mash the cranberries against the bottom of the pot with a potato masher. Strain, pushing the cranberries against the strainer with the back of a big spoon to squeeze out as much juice as possible. Put it back on the heat and serve as described; the cranberry and orange flavors are great together.

And for those who like theirs fortified with something a little stronger, my friend Sam Johnson suggests his *mulled cider special:* a shot of bourbon — he likes Ezra Brooks — mixed with his hot spiced cider. Makes those 20-below nights — when the car won't start and the woodstove's burning logs like matchsticks — a little easier to face.

Cheddar and Bacon Breakfast Pudding

MAKES 6 SERVINGS

Here's a simple way to serve bacon and eggs to a crowd, combined in a savory breakfast pudding. You will need one leftover loaf of Mixed Grain Cuban Bread (page 174) or a good boughten loaf. If the crust is quite hard, don't worry, because it softens as the pudding bakes. The bread absorbs some of the custard, and what it doesn't absorb settles around the edges to form a soft pudding. The Cheddar cheese gives the top a gratin sort of crustiness, with the mustard and onions adding a savory jolt. A simple steamed vegetable or salad would turn this into the perfect brunch dish.

12 slices bacon
1 medium-size onion, finely chopped
3 tablespoons unsalted butter, softened
1 short loaf (about 12 inches long) leftover Mixed Grain Cuban Bread (page 174) or French bread
2 teaspoons Dijon mustard
4 large eggs
2 large egg yolks
2 1/2 cups light cream
1/2 teaspoon salt
1/8 teaspoon freshly ground black pepper
1 1/2 cups (1/4 pound) grated sharp Cheddar cheese

Fry the bacon, pouring off some of the fat as it builds up. When the bacon is crisp, remove it, blot it dry, and set aside. Pour off all but about 2 tablespoons of the fat and add the chopped onion to the skillet. Sauté over medium heat for about 7 minutes, stirring often. Remove from the heat.

Preheat the oven to 350° and bring a kettle of water, for the water bath, to a boil. Butter a 10-inch casserole or another 2-quart shallow casserole or gratin dish; it should be ceramic or glass, not metal. Select a second shallow casserole large enough to hold the first one.

Butter the smaller casserole with 1 tablespoon of the soft butter. Cut the bread into 1-inch-thick slices and butter one side of each slice with the remaining butter. Slather mustard over the butter on each piece, then arrange the slices in the buttered casserole, fitting snugly against one another. Sprinkle the sautéed onion over the bread. Crumble up the bacon and strew that on top.

In a bowl, beat the eggs and egg yolks with a whisk, then blend in the cream, salt, and pepper. Pour the custard over the bread and let it sit for 5 minutes. Sprinkle the cheese over the top. Place the smaller casserole in the larger one, then pour enough of the boiling water into the larger casserole to come halfway up the sides of the smaller one.

Bake the pudding for 40 minutes. Remove the casserole from the oven and carefully lift the pudding out of the water bath. Cool on a rack for about 5 minutes before serving. Leftovers should be covered with foil and stored in the fridge, though this is best the first time around.

Pantry Items
and a Few
Ideas for
Leftover Breads

Brioche Cinnamon Bread Custard

MAKES 8 SERVINGS

This is classic comfort food, a sweet, rich breakfast for a happy holiday morning. Warm, it even makes a soothing late-evening dessert. Thick slices of brioche are baked in a vanilla-scented custard. Toward the end of the baking, the custard is sprinkled with a mixture of brown sugar and cinnamon, which gives the surface a sweet, crisp texture. You can — and I have — made this with other types of bread with varying results. A light-textured cinnamon bread is good; dense breads don't work nearly as well because the custard and bread tend to remain separate rather than fuse into one soft entity. The brioche is by far the best choice. Serve squares of this custard on individual plates with sliced fruit on the side.

> 1/2 loaf (approximately) Whole Wheat Brioche (page 168)
> 1 1/2 cups light cream
> 1 cup heavy cream
> 1/2 cup sugar
> 1 teaspoon vanilla extract
> 1 large egg
> 4 large egg yolks
> 1/4 cup packed light brown sugar
> 2 teaspoons ground cinnamon

Preheat the oven to 400°. Pour about 1/2 inch of hot water into a 9- by 13-inch shallow casserole dish and place it in the oven. Generously butter a 7- by 11-inch shallow casserole.

Cut the brioche into 3/4-inch slices and line the buttered casserole with it. Trim the rounded part off each slice so you get a tight-fitting arrangement with no gaps. In a medium-size saucepan, bring the light cream, heavy cream, and sugar to a near boil, stirring occasionally. Remove from the heat and stir in the vanilla.

In a bowl, gently whisk the egg and egg yolks. Stir about 1/2 cup of the hot cream mixture into the egg yolks. Whisk in the rest of the hot cream, then ladle the custard over the brioche slices. Slide the larger casserole out of the oven and place the smaller one in it. Add enough additional hot water to come about halfway up the sides of the smaller casserole. Bake for 30 minutes.

While the custard bakes, mix the brown sugar and cinnamon in a small bowl. After 30 minutes, pull out the casserole and sprinkle the brown sugar mixture evenly over the custard. Lower the oven temperature to 350° and bake for another 10 minutes. Remove the smaller casserole from the hot water bath and cool on a rack until serving time. This custard is good at almost any temperature, including cold. Once it has reached room temperature, however, it should be refrigerated.

*Pantry Items
and a Few
Ideas for
Leftover Breads*

Crumb Croûte of Pears

MAKES 4 SERVINGS

*A fast dessert like this is just what you need when friends drop by during
the holidays on short notice. All you do, basically, is arrange fruit on slices
of pound cake, brioche, quick bread, or sweet yeasted bread. Then you cover
that with streusel crumbs and bake or broil until browned. It makes an
excellent fast breakfast or dessert, even elegant enough for company if you
add a little ice cream on the side. Pears are my fruit of choice around the
holidays, but I have used strawberries, blueberries, and peaches, depending
on the time of year and availability. Sweetened whipped cream is also
perfect with this, and you can tinker with flavorings according to the fruit
you use. If you're using pound cake for the base, and the slices are on the
small side, use 2 pieces per serving, placed so the bottoms face one another.
This recipe is adapted from one in* Everyday Cooking with Jacques
Pépin *(Harper & Row).*

CRUMB TOPPING
> **6 tablespoons unbleached flour**
> **1/4 cup packed light brown sugar**
> **2 tablespoons cold unsalted butter, cut into 1/4-inch pieces**
> **1/2 teaspoon ground cinnamon**
> **pinch of salt**

THE BOTTOM LAYERS
> **4 large slices Whole Wheat Brioche (page 168), sweet yeasted
> bread, pound cake, or quick bread**
> **2 tablespoons unsalted butter, softened**
> **2 large pears, peeled, cored, and thinly sliced**

Prepare the crumb topping by rubbing those ingredients together
with your fingertips until you have fine, uniform crumbs; refrigerate.

Get out a large baking sheet, preferably a dark heavy one.
Spread each slice of bread or cake with 1/2 tablespoon of the butter.
Place the bread slices on the baking sheet and arrange the pear slices
neatly on the buttered side of the bread, working from the perimeter
in toward the center, covering the bread or cake completely; your
arrangement should somewhat resemble the petals of a flower.
(Strawberries should be sliced in half, but most berries can go on
whole.) Divide the crumb topping among the 4 servings, spreading
it over the fruit evenly.

To cook, either broil them — about 6 inches from the heat — until the crumbs are golden brown, about 5 to 8 minutes, or bake on the top rack of a preheated 500° oven for about 10 minutes, until the crumbs are golden brown. If you're using the latter method with pound cake, put a second baking sheet under the first one so the bottom of the cake doesn't burn. When done, the fruit will have softened and the juices may be starting to seep below. Cool on the sheet for 5 minutes before serving.

Chocolate Raisin Bread Pudding

MAKES 8 SERVINGS

Bread pudding is the best sort of old-fashioned dessert, at once frugal, simple, and delicious. This recipe is all of those but with an edge of chocolate decadence, which along with the cinnamon and raisins makes it just right for the holidays. Almost any kind of sweet or nonsavory bread can be used here; I like the light-textured sweet breads, but plain whole wheat bread crumbs are just as inviting. Frankly, any differences are largely obscured by the chocolate. Whipped cream or ice cream is a good accompaniment, but since the pudding is rather rich, a puddle of plain cold milk is really all it needs.

> 3 cups bread crumbs in 1/2-inch cubes
> 1/4 cup unsalted butter, melted
> 1 1/4 cups packed light brown sugar
> 1 teaspoon ground cinnamon
> 2 cups milk
> 6 ounces unsweetened chocolate
> 2 teaspoons vanilla extract
> 3 large eggs at room temperature, lightly beaten
> 1/2 cup raisins

Preheat the oven to 350° and butter a 10-inch deep-dish pie pan or casserole. Put the bread crumbs in a bowl and pour the melted butter over them. Add 1/4 cup of the brown sugar and the cinnamon, and toss to coat.

In a medium-size saucepan, heat the milk and chocolate over low heat. When the chocolate is almost melted, stir in the remaining cup of brown sugar. Whisk until smooth and the chocolate is fully melted. Whisk in the vanilla. Pour into a medium-size bowl and cool for 10 to 15 minutes, until lukewarm. Stir the beaten eggs into the chocolate mixture. Fold in the bread crumbs and raisins, then turn the mixture into the buttered pan.

Pour about 1 inch of very hot water into a shallow casserole large enough to hold the baking dish. Place the baking dish in the water bath and bake for 45 minutes. Remove the baking dish from the water and cool the pudding for at least 10 minutes before serving. This dessert is good served at any temperature, though the texture becomes denser as it cools. Store leftovers in a cool location, covered with plastic wrap.

Romano Cheese and Basil Crackers

MAKES 24 CRACKERS

I like packaged crackers, but like anything else baked, they can't match your own. At the holidays, homemade crackers really stand out on a cheese and cracker board. I like to serve these with a sharp blue cheese ball (see page 238) on a large platter with an assortment of grapes, small Seckel pears, and quartered apples. You can cut these any way you like, but I like the wedges you get when you roll circles and cut them pizza style, using a ravioli cutter for a pretty, crinkled edge.

- 1 cup whole wheat flour
- 1 cup unbleached flour
- 1 tablespoon yellow cornmeal, preferably stone-ground
- 1 teaspoon dried basil
- 1/2 teaspoon baking powder
- 1/4 teaspoon salt
- 3/4 cup finely grated Romano cheese
- 1/4 cup cold unsalted butter, cut into 1/4-inch pieces
- 1/2 cup milk
- 1/2 cup heavy cream

In a large bowl, mix the flours, cornmeal, basil, baking powder, salt, and Romano cheese. Add the butter and cut it in until the mixture resembles fine crumbs. Make a well in the dry mixture, add the milk and cream, and stir until the dough coheres. Divide the dough in half, flour each half lightly, then flatten them into disks on individual sheets of wax paper, about 3/4 inch thick. Wrap up the disks and refrigerate for 15 minutes. Meanwhile, preheat the oven to 400° and lightly butter a large baking sheet.

After the dough has chilled for 15 minutes, lightly dust your work surface with flour. Roll the dough, one disk at a time, into a thin circle about 14 inches in diameter and about 1/16 inch thick. Cut the dough into wedges with a sharp knife, pizza cutter, or ravioli cutter and transfer the wedges to the baking sheet. Prick each wedge 2 or 3 times with a fork. Bake the crackers for 12 to 14 minutes, until golden brown and crisp. Transfer them to a rack to cool, then roll and bake the other portion of dough. Store the cooled crackers in a sealed plastic bag.

Whole Wheat Cheese Wafers

MAKES ABOUT 60 SMALL WAFERS

Crackers are fun to make, but if rolling them out makes you nervous, these are for you. They're like crackers, but perhaps more like what you might call a savory shortbread; the texture is not really brittle, but short and somewhat crumbly. The dough is shaped into a log, refrigerated, then cut into thin slices. The wafers look like little whole wheat silver dollars, and their cheesy bite makes them a natural accompaniment for cheese and wine. They're also good nibbles for a beer and chili bash. The recipe is easy to double or triple, so you might want to make extra and pack them into small tins, between layers of tissue paper, for your friends.

> 1/2 cup (1/4 pound) unsalted butter at room temperature
> 3 ounces cream cheese at room temperature
> 1 1/2 teaspoons Dijon mustard
> 1 teaspoon hot red pepper flakes
> 1/2 teaspoon salt
> 1 garlic clove, finely minced
> 1 1/2 cups (1/4 pound) grated sharp Cheddar cheese
> 1 cup whole wheat flour
> 1 tablespoon cornstarch

In a mixing bowl, cream the butter, cream cheese, and mustard with an electric mixer. Stir in the pepper flakes, salt, and garlic. Add half the cheese, stir it in with a wooden spoon, then stir in the remaining cheese.

Into a separate bowl, sift the whole wheat flour and cornstarch. Add the flour mixture to the creamed mixture in 3 stages, stirring just enough to blend the mixture evenly. Tear off a sheet of wax paper about 18 inches long. Scrape the dough out of the bowl, flour it lightly, and shape it into a log, on the paper, about 12 inches long. Place the log right up to the long edge closest to you and begin to roll it up; roll it tightly to make a round tube of dough about 16 inches long. It will lengthen as you roll it. Pinch the ends of the paper off to seal and place the dough in the fridge for at least 1 hour and up to 24 hours. (You can also freeze the dough for up to 2 months, but overwrap in foil first. Transfer it to the refrigerator the day before you plan to bake.)

When you're ready to bake, preheat the oven to 350° and lightly butter a large, heavy baking sheet, preferably a dark one. Unwrap the dough and cut the log into slices 1/4 inch thick or perhaps a hair thicker. Lay the slices on the sheet, leaving only about 1 inch between them. Bake for approximately 22 minutes, just until they show a slight browning around the edge. Cool the wafers on the sheet for 1 minute, then transfer them to a rack to cool. Store in an airtight container.

Basic Tart Pastry

MAKES ENOUGH PASTRY FOR
1 9-INCH TART SHELL

*There are times, for one reason or another, when I prefer this basic tart
pastry — which appeared in my earlier* Ken Haedrich's Country
Baking *— to a whole wheat pastry, so I repeat it here if you missed it
there. As with any other pastry, make sure you chill it for about 30 to 45
minutes before you attempt to roll it, a brief interlude that relaxes the
dough and gives the butter a chance to firm up. It's fine to chill the dough
longer than that, but you must remove it from the fridge about 10 or 15
minutes before you plan to roll it; otherwise it will be too hard.*

> 1 1/2 cups unbleached flour
> 1 tablespoon sugar (omit if you're making a savory tart or quiche)
> 1/2 teaspoon salt
> 10 tablespoons (5 ounces) cool unsalted butter, cut into 1/4-inch
>   pieces
> 1 to 2 tablespoons cold water

In a large bowl, mix the flour, sugar (if you're using it), and salt. Add
the butter and cut it in until the mixture resembles very small
crumbs, with all the flour having been dampened by the fat; it
should actually be starting to clump together without the water. At
that point, add the cold water a teaspoon at a time, tossing and
compacting the mixture with a fork until the dough coheres.

When the dough coheres, knead it once in the bowl to distribute the butter, then flatten it on a sheet of plastic wrap into a disk
about 1/2 inch thick. Wrap and refrigerate for about 30 minutes
before rolling it. It can be refrigerated for up to 2 days, but take it out
of the refrigerator about 10 minutes before you plan to roll it.

To roll the dough, place it in the center of a lightly floured sheet
of wax paper. Dust the top of the dough with flour and roll it into a
12-inch circle. Invert the pastry over a 9-inch (by 1-inch-high) tart
pan with a removable bottom, peel off the paper, and gently tuck the
pastry into the bottom seam without stretching the dough. Wherever the dough sticks up over the sides, either just push it down flush
with the top of the pan or fold it over and press, both of which will
beef up the side. Cover and freeze the pastry for at least 15 minutes
or until baking time.

To bake the shell, preheat the oven to 400°. Line the shell with foil and weight it with beans, rice, or pie weights. Bake for 15 minutes, remove the foil with the weights still in it, and bake for another 7 minutes — for a partially baked shell — or about 12 minutes for a fully baked shell. (Save the weights for future tart shells.) If the shell starts to puff during the second part of the baking, pierce it once or twice with the tines of a fork to let the steam escape. (If you're putting a loose filling in the shell and baking it further, which is often the case, fill the little fork holes with a tiny bit of flour and water "paste" before you add the filling, so it doesn't leak out.) Cool the shell on a rack.

*Pantry Items
and a Few
Ideas for
Leftover Breads*

Buckwheat Cocoa Tart Pastry

MAKES ENOUGH PASTRY FOR
1 9-INCH TART SHELL

*A buckwheat pastry has only so many uses, since the buckwheat flavor is
strong and not particularly easy to match to a filling. But it's different,
delicious, and nearly perfect with the Chocolate Buckwheat Tart (page
145). The cocoa, I have found, is a good way to tone down the buckwheat,
smooth out its rough edges. But if you don't take to this sort of cocoa
infringement, feel free to omit it. This pastry also works with most
chocolate fillings and vanilla custards; you could even use it for banana
cream pie. I've done that, and it's excellent.*

> 3/4 cup buckwheat flour
> 1/2 cup unbleached flour
> 2 1/2 tablespoons sugar
> 1 tablespoon unsweetened cocoa powder, sifted
> 1/4 teaspoon salt
> 1/2 cup (1/4 pound) cold unsalted butter, cut into 1/4-inch pieces
> 1 1/2 to 2 tablespoons (approximately) ice-cold water

In a large bowl, combine the flours with the sugar, cocoa powder,
and salt. Stir well. Add the butter and cut it in quite thoroughly,
until the mixture resembles fine crumbs. Sprinkle on 1 tablespoon of
the water, tossing and compacting the mixture with a fork as you go.
Sprinkle on another 1/2 tablespoon of water and continue to toss and
compact, adding the remaining 1/2 tablespoon water if needed to
allow the dough to be gathered into a ball. Knead the dough several
times, right in the bowl, to distribute the fat.

Put the dough on a sheet of plastic wrap and flatten it with your
palm into a disk about 1/2 inch thick. Wrap the dough in the plastic
wrap, then refrigerate for about 30 minutes before rolling. If you
wait much longer than that, it will be too cold to roll out easily. If this
is the case, simply let the pastry sit at room temperature for about 10
minutes before rolling.

To roll out the crust, lightly flour a sheet of wax paper and roll
the dough into an 11-inch circle. Leave the pastry on the paper and
invert it over a 9-inch tart pan. Center the pastry, peel off the paper,
then *gently* tuck the pastry into the crease of the pan. This pastry is a
little fragile and sometimes develops cracks at this point, but this is
easily remedied by pushing the dough back together. Take any

overhanging dough and push it down the side so it is even with the top of the pan, to beef the side up. Refrigerate or freeze the pastry for 30 minutes to firm it up.

To bake the shell, line it with foil and weights as for the Basic Tart Pastry (page 234). Preheat the oven to 400°. Bake the shell for 20 minutes, remove the foil and weights, and bake another 10 to 12 minutes. It will turn a shade or two darker when done and will feel crisp — not soft — to the touch. Cool the shell in the pan before filling.

*Pantry Items
and a Few
Ideas for
Leftover Breads*

A Great Blue Cheese Ball

MAKES 1 VERY LARGE CHEESE
BALL OR 2 LOGS

*We love to eat, give, and serve homemade crackers during the holidays.
When we do, this is often what goes with it: the cheese ball we've been
making for years. We're well past the tinkering stage with this recipe, and
we think you'll agree this couldn't be much better.*

> 2 1/2 cups walnut pieces
> 1/2 pound cream cheese, softened
> 3 cups (about 1/2 pound) grated sharp Cheddar cheese
> 1 1/4 cups (about 1/4 pound) crumbled blue cheese
> 1/2 cup chopped fresh parsley
> 2 tablespoons finely minced onions
> 1 or 2 minced garlic cloves (optional)
> 1/4 cup minced pickled jalapeño pepper
> 1 tablespoon fresh lemon juice

Toast the walnuts according to the instructions on page 111. When
they're done, transfer them to a large plate or dump them onto your
work counter and let them cool.

Put the cream cheese, Cheddar cheese, and the blue cheese in a
large mixing bowl and work them with the back of a wooden spoon
until they're blended. Add the remaining ingredients — except the
nuts — and mix them with a spoon or your hands until everything is
evenly blended. Chop 1 cup of the nuts by hand, then work the nuts
into the mixture. Cover and refrigerate for 15 minutes.

While the mixture chills, chop the rest of the nuts into small
pieces by hand (a processor will make some of the pieces too fine).
Put a 14-inch piece of wax paper on your work counter. Spread the
nuts in the center of the sheet. Using your hands, shape the cheese
mixture into a giant ball in the nuts. Wrap and refrigerate for at least
30 minutes before serving.

If you'd prefer to have two logs instead of a giant ball, shape the
cheese mixture into a log 10 inches long. Roll the log in the nuts,
simultaneously pressing and sculpting it into a longer cylinder about
13 inches long. The whole log should be generously covered with
nuts. Cut it in half and press the ends in the remaining nuts. Wrap
the logs separately and refrigerate them for at least 30 minutes
before serving. Serves 10 to 12 as an appetizer.

Cornmeal Basil Pastry

MAKES ENOUGH PASTRY FOR
1 POT PIE OR TART

This is the pastry I use for the French Onion Tart on page 198 and when I want something pretty and grainy for topping a pot pie. It should not be refrigerated quite as long as other pastry doughs before rolling it — 20 to 25 minutes is good — because the cornmeal sometimes makes it a bit crumbly if it gets too cold. It can, however, be refrigerated for up to 48 hours; just take it out of the refrigerator about 15 minutes before you plan to roll it.

- 1 1/3 cups unbleached flour
- 1/4 cup yellow cornmeal, preferably stone-ground
- 1 teaspoon dried basil
- 1/4 teaspoon salt
- 10 tablespoons (5 ounces) unsalted butter, at room temperature, cut into 1/4-inch pieces
- 2 to 3 teaspoons cold water

In a medium-size mixing bowl, mix the unbleached flour, cornmeal, basil, and salt. Add the butter and cut it in quite thoroughly, until the mixture resembles fine, clumpy crumbs. Sprinkle the water over the dough a teaspoon at a time, tossing and compacting it with a fork; it should cohere easily. If not, add another drop or two of water. Knead the pastry once in the bowl, then flour it lightly and place it on a sheet of plastic wrap. Using your palm, flatten the dough into a disk about 3/4 inch thick. Wrap and refrigerate until using.

Whole Wheat Tart Pastry

MAKES ENOUGH PASTRY FOR
1 9-INCH TART SHELL

One of my best discoveries in the past few years has been finding out what a good tart pastry you can make with whole wheat pastry — *not bread — flour. Because whole wheat pastry flour is low in gluten, it makes a wonderfully tender crust, excellent for both sweet and savory tarts. I have added just a small amount of unbleached flour, as well as an egg yolk, to make this pastry easier to handle; without it the dough will just barely hold together. However, if you're already an adept pastry roller, you could use all whole wheat pastry flour and do just fine. (One exception to these proportions is when I'm using this pastry to make a free-form tart or* crostata, *in which case I like to use 1 cup whole wheat pastry flour and 1/2 cup unbleached flour, a combination that reduces the cracking you sometimes get at the edge of the tart.)*

It seems much easier to roll this dough if you don't give it too much chilling time; 15 to 25 minutes is good. Much more than that, and it tends to crack. If that starts to happen, just give the pastry a few minutes to rest at room temperature before proceeding.

> 1 1/4 cups whole wheat pastry flour
> 1/4 cup unbleached flour
> 1 tablespoon sugar (omit if you're making a savory tart)
> 1/2 teaspoon salt
> 7 tablespoons cool unsalted butter, cut into 1/4-inch pieces
> 1 large egg yolk
> 1 to 1 1/2 tablespoons cold water

Mix the flours, sugar (if you're using it), and salt in a large bowl. Add the butter and cut it in until the mixture resembles very small crumbs; the butter should become almost invisible — no big pieces — and the mixture should be quite clumpy. Beat the egg yolk and 1 tablespoon of the water together in a small bowl and drizzle it over the flour, at the same time stirring with a fork; the fork should be both compressing the dough and lifting up the drier particles that fall to the bottom of the bowl. Add the rest of the water in drops, if needed, until the dough pulls together, then pack it like a snowball and knead it once or twice right in the bowl. With a floured palm, flatten the dough right onto a sheet of plastic wrap; wrap and refrigerate for 15 to 25 minutes, until it feels semifirm.

To roll the dough, place it in the center of a lightly floured sheet of wax paper. Dust the top of the dough with flour and roll it into a 12-inch circle. Invert the pastry over a 9-inch (by 1-inch-high) tart pan with a removable bottom, peel off the paper, and gently tuck the pastry into the bottom seam without stretching the dough. Wherever the dough sticks up over the sides, either just push it down flush with the top of the pan or fold it over and press, both of which will beef up the side nicely. Cover and freeze the pastry until baking.

To bake the shell, preheat the oven to 400°. Line the shell with foil and weight it with beans, rice, or pie weights. Bake for 15 minutes, remove the foil with the weights still in it, and bake for another 7 minutes — for a partially baked shell — or about 12 minutes for a fully baked shell. (Save the weights for future tart shells.) If the shell starts to puff during the second part of the baking, pierce it once or twice with the tines of a fork to let steam escape. (If you're putting a loose filling in the shell and baking it further, fill those holes with a tiny bit of flour and water "paste" before you add the filling so it doesn't leak out.) Cool the shell on a rack.

Pantry Items
and a Few
Ideas for
Leftover Breads

Three-Grain Butter Pastry

MAKES ENOUGH PASTRY FOR 1
9-INCH DOUBLE-CRUST PIE OR 2
9-INCH SINGLE-CRUST PIES

If this pastry looks familiar to readers of my first book, Ken Haedrich's
Country Baking, *it should. I have fiddled around with a lot of grainy pie
doughs in the time since I wrote that, and some of them have been quite
good. But I can't hide the fact that this one is still the best. So here it is
again — an excellent crust for any of your holiday pies.*

> 1/2 cup yellow cornmeal, preferably stone-ground
> 1/2 cup rolled oats (*not* instant) or oat flour
> 1 1/2 cups unbleached flour
> 1 tablespoon sugar (omit if you're making a savory pie)
> 1/2 teaspoon salt
> 14 tablespoons (7 ounces) cold unsalted butter, cut into 1/4-inch
>   pieces
> 1 large egg yolk
> 3 1/2 to 4 1/2 tablespoons ice-cold water

Put the cornmeal and rolled oats into a blender and pulse the
machine on and off until the oat flakes are reduced to small flecks; a
few remaining larger pieces are fine (if you're using oat flour, skip
this step). Transfer to a large mixing bowl and stir in the unbleached
flour, sugar, and salt. Add the butter and cut it into the dry ingredients until the mixture resembles a coarse, damp meal, with the
largest pieces about the size of split peas.

Beat the egg yolk with 3 tablespoons of the cold water. Sprinkle
this liquid over the dry mixture, working the mixture with a fork;
push on it with the tines to help pack it. If the mixture is still dry, add
another tablespoon of water, this time packing the dough with your
hands. Pack it with some authority — you'll be surprised at how it
coheres when you do. If the dough still seems dry, add more cold
water in dribbles. Stop adding cold water when the dough pulls
together in a dampish but not tacky-wet ball.

Divide the dough in half, then flatten each half into a disk about
1/2 inch thick; flatten it with your palm right onto a piece of plastic
wrap. Wrap the dough in the plastic wrap and refrigerate for at least
30 minutes before rolling. You can also freeze the dough, over-
wrapped in foil, for up to 1 month. Thaw it in the fridge and let it sit
briefly at room temperature before rolling it.

To roll the dough, lightly flour a piece of wax paper and roll it into a 12-inch circle; dust the top of the pastry if the pin seems prone to stick to it. Invert the wax paper and pastry over the pan. Peel off the paper and gently tuck the pastry into the bottom crease without stretching it. If you're making a double-crust pie, leave the overhang. If you're making a pie shell for a single-crust pie, tuck the overhang back and under, at the same time sculpting it into an upstanding ridge.

To partially bake the pie shell, freeze the unbaked pie shell for 15 minutes and preheat the oven to 400°. Line the pastry with foil, tucking it into the bottom crease of the pastry. Weight the pastry with enough rice or beans to almost fill the pan. Bake for 20 minutes. Carefully remove the foil and weights from the pan. (Save the weights for future piecrusts.) Pierce the bottom of the shell several times with the tines of a fork and put the shell back in the oven for about 7 or 8 more minutes. To make a fully baked crust, bake about 12 more minutes. If you are baking the tart further, and you'd like to prevent the filling from leaking through the fork holes, make a small amount of flour paste (a tiny bit each of flour and water, mixed) and dab it into the holes.

Stuffing for Success

Stuffing, around here at least, is no small hill on that vast landscape of food we pile on our Thanksgiving Day plates. It's a virtual *mountain*, a comforting amalgam of herbaceous flavors floating on a cloud of soft bread. We eat it hot, cold, mixed into soups, and even on top of salads.

Most homemade breads will make fine stuffing, so long as they are not sweet, taste of molasses, or have any other strong or unusual flavor. Plain whole grain breads, French and French-type breads (like the Mixed Grain Cuban Bread, page 174), and herb breads are all good choices. Ideally the bread should be a few days old, not fresh, so the bread can soak up the stock you moisten it with.

To make a terrific basic stuffing, enough to stuff a 12-pound turkey, you'll need about 8 to 10 slices of sandwich bread; more if you're using a smaller French loaf. If the bread is fresh, dry the slices a little by leaving them out on a rack overnight or for several hours.

Cut the bread into 3/4-inch cubes and measure out 8 cups. Set aside. Meanwhile, melt 1/2 cup (1/4 pound) unsalted butter over medium heat in a large skillet. Add 1 cup minced celery and 1 cup chopped onion or scallion and sauté gently for about 7 minutes. If you like, add 1 small minced garlic clove and sauté for another few seconds.

Turn off the heat and stir the bread cubes into the skillet, stirring and pushing them all around to soak up the butter. Scrape the mixture into a large bowl and stir in 1/4 cup minced fresh parsley, 1 teaspoon crushed dried sage, 1/2 teaspoon crushed dried rosemary, and 1/2 teaspoon dried thyme; use double or triple the amount of fresh herbs, if they're available.

Some folks like their stuffing on the dry side; others like it moister. We're in the latter category. We moisten ours, stirring gently, with about 1 to 1 1/4 cups vegetable broth, which we make with a vegetable bouillon cube and salt to taste. Chicken stock is traditional, but if you're using canned broth, dilute it with water, because it's too salty as is.

Of course, you can dress up your stuffing with bits of this and that. Some cooks like to add a cup of chopped mushrooms to the sauté. Others add oysters. And some cook up the giblets and add them. They're all wonderful.

Wheaten Yeasted Pastry

MAKES ENOUGH PASTRY FOR
1 LARGE TART

Yeasted pastry might sound like some people's two greatest baking phobias wrapped into one, but this is nothing to be afraid of: Sturdier than a conventional pastry (and therefore easier to handle), with no lengthy rising involved, it makes a wonderful crust for a variety of our favorite holiday tarts and coffee cakes. As you might expect, its baked texture is bready, but still short, like piecrust — a nice change of pace. We use the same dough to make Yeasted Pastry Candy Canes (page 162).

1/4 cup lukewarm water
1 1/2 teaspoons active dry yeast (half of a 1/4-ounce package)
1 1/2 cups unbleached flour
1/2 cup whole wheat flour
2 tablespoons sugar (omit if you're making a savory tart)
1/2 teaspoon salt
6 tablespoons cold unsalted butter, cut into 1/4-inch pieces
1 large egg, lightly beaten
1 teaspoon vanilla extract (omit for savory tarts)

Pour the lukewarm water into a small bowl and stir in the yeast. Set aside for 5 minutes. Mix the flours, sugar (if you're using it), and salt in a large bowl. Add the butter and cut it in with a pastry blender until the mixture resembles coarse meal; the pieces of butter should be virtually invisible.

Make a well in the center of this mixture and pour in the dissolved yeast, egg, and vanilla. Stir until the dough coheres in a dampish ball; cover with plastic wrap and let sit for 2 or 3 minutes. Lightly flour your hands and a work surface, then turn the dough out and knead gently for 30 seconds, using little sprinkles of flour, if necessary, to keep the dough from sticking.

Flour the dough lightly, then flatten it into a circle about 3/4 inch thick on a large sheet of plastic wrap. Wrap the dough, then slip it into a plastic bag. Secure with a twist tie and refrigerate for at least 30 minutes before rolling.

NOTE: This dough may be refrigerated overnight or frozen, wrapped as described, for up to 1 month. Thaw in the fridge before proceeding.

The Gift of Time

Joyful as they are, the holidays always seem to bring with them a corresponding sense of the doldrums: Despite our best intentions, the holidays leave us feeling drained, emotionally, physically, and — quite often — financially. When this happens, we think we have failed, that the spirit and joy of the holidays have passed us by unawares. Instead of feeling blessed, we feel blitzed.

What can we do, then, to experience the real joy the season has to offer?

I don't have all the answers, but I do think we can begin by giving the gift of time, especially to our children. M. Scott Peck, writing in *The Road Less Traveled* (Simon & Schuster), has something nice to say about time, and children, that's worth reflecting on during this time of year. He says, "When we love something it is of value to us, and when something is of value to us we spend time with it, time enjoying it and taking care of it. . . . So it is when we love children; we spend time admiring them and caring for them. We give them our time."

I don't think we should banish toys and such from the holidays, but I do think we should acknowledge the fact that nothing we give our kids is so valuable as the time we spend with them. Whether we're baking, creating a homemade manger scene, making Christmas cards, or cutting paper snowflakes for the windows, our kids love to work with us and make their own contributions to the work of the holidays. Working as a family gives each of the kids a sense of belonging, one of our strongest human needs. Sure, it takes time to track down supplies, work alongside your kids, and clean up the mess in the end. And it takes patience to give instructions, several times over perhaps. But the payoff is that you are building a relationship and bond with your kids that will last long after the thrill of a new toy is gone.

Of course, your gift of time doesn't have to be spent strictly on holiday business. It can be as simple as sharing more meals together; family breakfasts are big fun. Or snuggling up on the couch together and reading favorite books. Or — one of our favorite family pastimes — taking family walks. Again, it takes time to find six pairs of mittens, six hats, put on snowsuits, take them off to pee, put them back on, and finally actually get out the door. But try to remember that having a goal — taking a family walk or baking two dozen cookies — is far less important than going about it in a way that generates excitement, brings happiness, and creates warmth with your children. Those are gifts they'll carry with them the rest of their lives.

Menus

Designing a holiday or any other menu is such a personal affair that the following suggestions should be taken as just that: suggestions. What might sound like a nice balance of flavors, textures, and colors to me might not appeal to you, or only partially appeal to you, in which case you should of course make the changes you see fit. Naturally, since this is exclusively a baking book, there are only so many recipes you can incorporate into a single menu; you should refer to other cookbooks for the specifics of the recipe idea presented here.

NOTE: An asterisk (*) indicates the recipe is included here; please consult the index.

Holiday Breakfast Menus

Apple Cider
Jam Muffins with Crumb Topping°
Grapefruit Halves Drizzled with Maple Syrup

Tomato Juice
Three-Grain Biscuits°
Cheddar Cheese Omelets
Home Fries

Fresh Orange Juice
Lemon Poppy Seed Muffins° Served with
Lemon Curd°
Plain Yogurt Topped with Sliced Bananas

Hot Chocolate
Cranberry Scones°
Vanilla Cup Custard

Fresh Coffee and Tea
Wheaten Popovers°
Hot Breakfast Ham or Canadian Bacon
Scrambled Eggs with Sautéed Mushrooms

Hearty Holiday Brunch Menus

Lemon Herb Tea
Cardamom Pear Butter Cake°
Winter Fruit Salad of Grapefruit, Oranges, and Bananas
Assorted Cheeses

Coffee and Herb Teas
Brioche Cinnamon Bread Custard°
Bacon or Sausage
Melon Slices and Grapes

Tomato Juice Spiked with Cayenne Pepper
Herb Shortcakes with Creamed Turkey and Corn°
Cranberry Sauce

Fresh Orange Juice
Cheddar and Bacon Breakfast Pudding°
Buttered Corn or Steamed Broccoli
Baked Apples or Sautéed Apple Slices

Grapefruit Juice
Poached Eggs Served over Leftover Turkey Hash
Three-Grain Biscuits° or
Toasted Slices of Mashed Potato Bread°
Poached Pears Served with Whipped Cream
or Mascarpone

Cozy Family-Style Menus

Deep-Dish Lamb Pie with Mint Gremolada°
Mixed Grain Cuban Bread° or Crusty French Bread
Tossed Green Salad with Vinaigrette
Quartered Ripe Pears and Sliced Dried Figs

Salad of Spinach, Halved Cherry Tomatoes, Feta Cheese,
and Olives Drizzled with Vinaigrette
Shrimp, Bacon, and Jarlsberg Tart°
Lemon Lime Pudding Cake

Assorted Marinated Vegetables
Wild Mushroom and Madeira Pizzas°
Chocolate Chip Pecan Brownies° with Coffee Ice Cream

Caesar Salad
French Onion Tart in a Cornmeal Basil Crust°
Raisin Date Bars with Mascarpone Topping°

Assorted Raw Vegetables with Dips
Tortellini or Other Cold Pasta Salad
Olive Whole Wheat Flat Bread°
Provençal Fig Tart° with Mascarpone

Salad of Mixed Greens with Vinaigrette
Pastry Pizza with a Whole Wheat Crust°
Fresh Mussels Steamed in White Wine Served with
Melted Garlic Butter
Chocolate Almond Kahlúa Tart°

A Variety of Bruschette°
Assorted Marinated Vegetables
Eggplant Parmesan
Coffee Hazelnut Cookies with Coffee Icing°
and Coffee Ice Cream

Whole Wheat Cheese Wafers° Served with
Pâté and Cornichons
A Very Big Broccoli, Olive, and Cheddar Quiche°
Spinach Salad with a Creamy Garlic or
Blue Cheese Dressing
Whole Wheat Chocolate Chunk Fantasy Cookies°

The
Baker's Guide to
Gift Giving

Everybody loves something baked for the holidays. But you can add a personal touch, another dimension to your holiday gift baking, by giving a baked gift that touches the heart and soul of the individual recipient. That said, here is a handy little baker's guide for matching your baked goods to the people on your gift list.

For the *sophisticated:*

Pear Pie with Sour Cherries in Port
Cranberry Apricot Tart with Sour Cream Topping
Bourbon Pecan Cake
Pear and Port Fruitcake
Cardamom Shortbread Cookies

For the *adventurous:*

Cranberry Cornmeal Soda Bread
Brussels Sprout Tart
Chocolate Almond Kahlúa Tart
Wheaten Savarin with Rum Maple Syrup

For the *hard-core chocoholic:*

Ben's Best Whole Wheat Chocolate Cookies
Chocolate Almond Torte
Chocolate Chip Pecan Brownies
Chocolate Buckwheat Tart

For the *traditionalist:*

Steamed Winter Squash and Date Nut Bread
Foolproof Spiced Apple Pie
Whole Wheat Parker House Rolls
Boiled Cider Pie
Maple Cutout Cookies

For the *romantic:*

Rose Water Almond Nuggets
Rose Water Lemon Curd Cookies
Light Lemon Tart

Index

255

Index

256

Index

Index

Index

Index

Index

266

Index

267

Index